A winter in Tibet

A winter in **Tibet**

Charles and Jill Hadfield

Impact Books

First published in Great Britain 1988
by Impact Books, 112 Bolingbroke Grove, London SW11 1DA

© Charles and Jill Hadfield 1988

British Library Cataloguing in Publication Data

Hadfield, Charles, *1952–*
    A winter in Tibet : letters from Tibet.
    1. Tibet. Description & travel
    I. Title   II. Hadfield, Jill, *1952–*
    915.1'50458

ISBN 0–245–54773–8

Typeset by Photoprint, 9–11 Alexandra Lane, Torquay, Devon
Printed and bound in Guernsey by The Guernsey Press

*For the people in Lhasa
who made us so welcome.*

Acknowledgements

We would like to express our gratitude:

to Jean-Luc and Philippa for their patient help, encouragement and trust that we would eventually finish our typescript;

to the people who read various versions of the script and made invaluable comments: Catriona, Jerome, Stephen, Martine, Penny, Jean and Norman, Sharin Akiner;

to Malcolm for his help and support;

and, most importantly, to those without whom there would have been no book: our family and friends, who kept writing to us in Lhasa and who were in return the recipients of the original letters.

It is bizarre and disquieting that after two thousand years the basic ethical question is the same, only more urgent; and the man who now says, 'Love one another!' knows there isn't much time left for it.

Elias Canetti, *The Human Province*, 1944

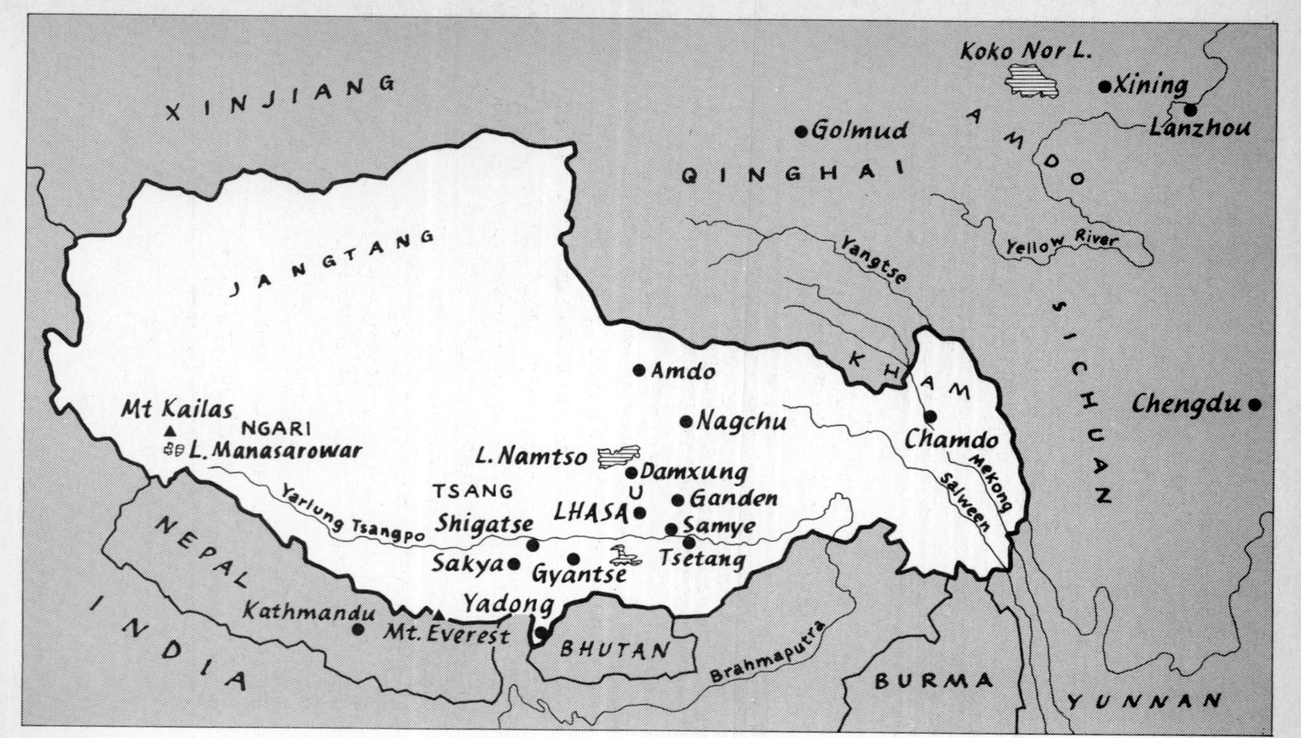

XINJIANG
Koko Nor L.
Xining
Lanzhou
Golmud
QINGHAI
AMDO
Yellow River
Yangtse
JANGTANG
KHAM
Chengdu
SICHUAN
Amdo
Nagchu
Chamdo
Mekong
Salween
Mt Kailas
NGARI
L. Manasarowar
L. Namtso
Damxung
U
Ganden
TSANG
LHASA
Samye
Yarlung Tsangpo
Shigatse
Sakya
Gyantse
Tsetang
Yadong
Kathmandu
Mt. Everest
BHUTAN
NEPAL
Brahmaputra
BURMA
INDIA
YUNNAN

Contents

Introduction

We are in a very fortunate position of being able to combine our work as teachers with travel. We first went to Tibet in 1985, after two years' working in central China when the 'autonomous region' had just been opened officially to individual foreign visitors. We immediately fell in love with Tibet during this first six-week visit, and determined to return if we could. Little did we know that within a year we would see an advertisement asking for a teaching couple to work in the new university of Tibet. While overjoyed to have this opportunity, we undertook the work fully aware of the country's recent history and of the underlying tensions there. We decided to go hoping that, in a small way, we might be able to contribute to the building of a better education system. It is too early to say what, if any, effect our work has had; but it had a profound effect on us personally. In this book, we hope to be able to convey some of the experiences we had of that beautiful land and its people, by re-editing some of the letters we sent home during our stay in Lhasa.

Since the time we lived and worked in Lhasa, the situation there has changed for the worse and the borders are once more closed to the outside world. As we write this introduction the world is beginning to learn in more detail of the scale and horror of the recent violence. Tibet is once more isolated behind its high mountains and the little news that trickles out is overwhelmingly bad.

In this book, we describe a different, rather happier time. It seemed to us then, and to many of our friends there, that the situation was improving, though tensions and difficulties were never far below the surface. We hesitated for months before deciding to publish this account of our time in Lhasa, and we do so now in the hope that our readers may gain some understanding of Tibet and its people, and why they mean so much to anyone who visits that sad and beautiful country. We have edited the letters hoping to make people conscious of the complexities of a situation that could, through the simplicities of rhetoric and violence, degenerate into yet more bloodshed, sadness and repression.

Most books about Tibet since 1950 have been written from a political standpoint, either pro-Chinese, or pro-Tibetan independence. This book does not take a political stance. Given our position there at the time of writing, we felt it essential not to get involved politically; we tried not to 'take sides' but to understand the situation and the people involved in it. Our book is simply a portrait of the details of daily life in Tibet as we experienced it, of people, places and encounters at a particular point in time. We cannot claim that it gives a complete picture: it is just one small piece of a very complicated mosaic. But more importantly, we feel that taking a political standpoint necessarily entails the selection and distortion of facts, interpretations and re-interpretations of history and statistics. It seems that each political view of Tibet comes as a 'package' whereby any subscriber to one opinion must take on all the opinions in the package. Thus any criticism of Chinese policies or of human rights violations in Tibet is interpreted by the authorities as 'propaganda for independence'; any praise for anything the Chinese have done is interpreted by Tibetan exiles and the pro-independence movement as 'collaboration with the illegal occupation of Tibet'. There seems to be no middle ground between these two entrenched positions, but if constructive dialogue is to take place, a middle ground must surely be found.

Since this book is concerned with the particular and incidental, we will try here to put the letters into some kind of broader historical context, particularly as the situation there has changed so greatly since we left.

Before 1950 essentially the same political and social systems had been in operation for several centuries. Tibet was ruled by the Dalai Lama and his *Kashag* or Cabinet, which consisted of

2

monk and lay officials, drawn from the aristocracy, who gave their services as a form of tax. The Dalai Lama was chosen by the reincarnation principle. (The present Dalai Lama is the fourteenth incarnation.) When the old Dalai Lama dies, a search begins for his successor, to be found in a young child who must possess a number of identifiable physical features and pass a number of tests before he is recognized as the new Dalai Lama. Tibet was ruled by a Regent until the Dalai Lama reached his majority, when he assumed the role of both temporal and spiritual leader. The importance of religion to the Tibetans cannot be overestimated. It has always permeated life on every level. Practically all Tibetan literature and art is religious, and from one quarter to one third of the male population were monks.

Outside the monkhood, secular Tibetan society was highly stratified. The main divisions were the aristocratic landowners, who owned houses in Lhasa or Shigatse, and had estates in the country; the peasants, who owed service to the landowners in return for land; nomads; and traders. But religion was the focal point of everyone's life. The mental and social organization of early twentieth century Tibet must have been very like that of medieval Europe, in the way that society was structured, the unquestioned hierarchy, the stable and unified world view, and the enormous part played by religion.

China had had a long-standing though ill-defined relationship with Tibet; a relationship which has been called suzerainty or 'patron-priest', with China giving backing to the rulers of Tibet, and occasionally sending in troops to dispel invading forces, in return for spiritual guidance from Tibetan lamas. When the Chinese troops entered Tibet in 1950 after the Communist Revolution in China, a Seventeen Point Agreement was signed. This provided, among other things, for the integration of Tibet into China, and for the integration of the Tibetan army into the People's Liberation Army, but it maintained traditional relationships by promising that existing political structures would be allowed to stand and by guaranteeing freedom of religion. The status quo prevailed until 1959, when, following an uprising in Kham, in eastern Tibet, the Tibetans in Lhasa rioted and the Dalai Lama fled into exile in India, followed over the years by some 100,000 fellow Tibetans.

The next twenty years were a nightmare for Tibet. Mao Zedong's command to grow wheat was interpreted literally, and Chinese cadres forced the Tibetan farmers to grow wheat instead of barley, the traditional crop. Wheat will hardly grow at such high altitudes, and the result was widespread famine. This was coupled with famine in China, which meant that no supplies could be sent into Tibet, and Tibet's scarce food supplies had to feed new Chinese settlers and troops as well as the indigenous Tibetans. Many Tibetans starved.

Destruction of the monasteries started in 1959, following the uprising, and a few years later the onset of the 'Great Proletarian Cultural Revolution' brought a twin attack on Tibetan religion and culture. Of Tibet's 6,500 monasteries, only a handful remain standing in any recognizable form today; the rest have been razed to the ground. Religious objects and works of art were mutilated, destroyed or taken for sale in China. Monks and nuns were forced to renounce their vows and join the laity, or were sent to prison or labour camp. Ordinary people were forbidden to practise their religion. Houses were ransacked by the Red Guards, religious objects were confiscated, and family altars destroyed.

Alongside this attack on religion, there was an attack on the Tibetans' cultural identity and sense of themselves as a people. They were forbidden to wear Tibetan clothes, for example, and traditional art forms such as the Tibetan dance-drama were banned, to be replaced by Jiang Qing's 'Eight Model Revolutionary Operas'. An attempt was made to suppress the Tibetan language. Many schools were closed down and education came to a standstill. Many thousands of people were forced to confess to imaginary crimes in 'Criticism-Struggle' sessions with the Red Guards and thousands were imprisoned, killed, tortured or sent to do forced labour.

The Cultural Revolution happened in China too, so it is not a *simple* question of one nation persecuting another: in

China too you can see the ruins of smashed temples, and talk to people who spent long years in labour camps. But in Tibet, the Cultural Revolution was different in nature: it was an attack on the very core of Tibetan belief, on their whole identity. This was not the case in China; the Chinese sense of identity, as a race, was never under threat. The Cultural Revolution in Tibet involved the denouncing and banning of everything that made Tibetans Tibetan, the attempt to erase one cultural identity and to replace it with another. So although one cannot view the Cultural Revolution in Tibet simply as one nation persecuting another, it is also too simplistic to view it as part of and on the same level as the Cultural Revolution in China proper: the psychological legacy, in the deep divisions it has created between Tibetans and Chinese, is different.

After 1979 the situation for Tibetans improved. There was for a while some rapprochement with the Dalai Lama's 'administration in exile'. Delegations from Dharamsala visited Tibet, and were horrified at what they saw. Hu Yaobang also visited Tibet, and was also horrified at what he found. He apologized publicly to the Tibetan people and promised reforms. Since then, there has indeed been some liberalization in all spheres: political, cultural and religious, as well as economic. The opening of Tibet to travellers and the agreement under which we went to Tibet to teach were part of this liberalization.

Han–Tibetan relations are not easy, as even the most casual visitor can observe, and as the world has seen since the recent violence. Tibetans cannot forget the misery of the terrible years between 1959 and 79. Even though things were in some ways better during our stay, there was still a terrible legacy of fear and mistrust. 'Things are better now, but why?' said someone to us once, 'What are they going to do to us next?' The Chinese for their part did not help with their all too often superior and intolerant attitudes towards the Tibetans, whom too many regard as dirty, backward and superstitious.

Despite this, we felt sympathy for the Chinese in Lhasa, many of whom are plainly miserable; lonely, ill, bored, missing their family and their hometown, they find the climate and altitude difficult, and life uncomfortable. Some have volunteered to go to Tibet, for a variety of reasons ranging from the mercenary to the altruistic, but many have been sent there. Although a few we met were making a real attempt to understand the place they were living in, most seemed to wall themselves up in their work units, taking no interest in Tibetan society or culture. Tibetans go on living in their own way, avoiding contact with the Chinese if they can. This situation is obviously very unhealthy, and leads to a vicious cycle of racial tension, of resentment, fear, and ever-widening social divisions, ultimately leading to the recent explosions of violence. The Chinese authorities have chosen to use force to deal with this state of affairs, but unless they attempt to enquire sympathetically into the causes and deal with them carefully, rather than just suppress the symptoms, this problem will not go away. Indeed it may well, all too predictably, be exacerbated.

We did find instances of harmony, but generally relations were not very happy and the atmosphere was uneasy. In this situation, we did the only thing we sensibly could, which was to ignore nationality, see people as individuals, and try as far as possible to make friends.

Other aspects of life in Tibet seemed more positive, and we felt a qualified optimism that things were getting better, albeit slowly. It was an optimism tinged, as always in China, with fear that the central government policies would change. It *did* seem to us that Tibetans were gradually assuming more and more responsibility. The ultimate power, though, is of course still Chinese: we always asked why the Governor of Tibet himself was not a Tibetan. Much of the power is still held by Chinese officials who cannot speak Tibetan, have no understanding of the culture and fail to perceive, let alone understand, Tibetan needs and wants. Things are changing, slowly; there is a new generation of university educated Tibetans who are just beginning to take up jobs, and the first Tibetans have now been sent to study abroad, so if government policy continues, matters may yet improve in this respect.

However, if change was beginning at the top of the social scale, we were more disturbed by what we observed lower down the social ladder. Particularly at the bottom. Tibet has its fair share of unemployed youth, as does China, but there doesn't seem to be much provision for training or occupying the young unemployed and morale is very low.

Many Tibetans and many Chinese immigrants have, of course, found work, official and unofficial, in the tourist industry, which while we were there was changing the face of Lhasa in countless ways. On the whole we thought it was good that Tibet, through contact with foreigners, had begun to feel connected to the outside world (perhaps for the first time in its history). But we had many reservations about the other effects of tourism on Lhasa.

Prosperity was undoubtedly increasing through the introduction of the Responsibility System, in the Lhasa valley and countryside as well as in the cities, though the general standard of living is still far below that of China generally. Many people are desperately poor, in particular the nomads, and people in small towns and villages outside Lhasa. There are still many beggars in Lhasa. The Chinese have established education and health care systems, neither of which existed in Tibet before 1950, so things have obviously improved in this respect, but both are still basic and standards are below those in China.

The policy of 'religious freedom' meant that ordinary people were once again allowed to practise Buddhism and to worship in their own way, and that many monasteries were being rebuilt. Some teaching of Buddhism was permitted inside the monasteries, but the 'propagation' of religion was forbidden and the monasteries were subject to State control. Other freedoms remain restricted. It is still an imprisonable offence to advocate 'Tibetan Independence' and the death penalty is in force for a range of crimes including theft, rape and embezzlement, as well as murder.

Restrictions on freedom to travel had, however, been eased a little. While we were there, Tibetans-in-exile were allowed to return to visit their families in Tibet, provided they described themselves on their visa applications as 'overseas Chinese', which not all were willing to do. Tibetans from Tibet were allowed to visit relatives in Nepal, India and other countries, but a whole family were not permitted to travel together in case they were tempted to abscond.

Since we left, however, the situation has changed drastically. The reaction by the authorities to the violent unrest has meant that Tibet is once again closed to the outside world, while reports filter out of hundreds of arrests and of police armed with bayonets and machine guns patrolling Lhasa streets. Our letters give a picture of an earlier, happier time, but one where the seeds of the discontent that erupted into rioting were undoubtedly present.

Living in Tibet was an experience which was both exhilarating and saddening: the indescribably beautiful landscape, the fascinating and complex culture, and above all the infectious good nature of the Tibetans all made the experience a deeply rewarding one for us. We still dream about Tibet and miss it greatly. But life there was not easy: we could not talk to Tibetans without anguish and horror at all they had suffered, but also admiration for their resilience and courage. It was impossible to be in Tibet without being affected by the goodwill, kindness and often gaiety of its people, but it was also impossible to be unaware of the tensions just below the surface, and any optimism we felt about new developments was always tempered by fear of a return to repression.

We have both fears and hopes for the future. Our fears are that there could be a clampdown on these small first steps to Tibetan self expression and a return to the earlier days of forced conformity to a Chinese norm. But even more threatening in the long term is the thought of the influx of Chinese settlers in large numbers. China is a densely populated country with a rapidly expanding population and her people need *Lebensraum*. If this happens, the Tibetan population will be reduced to a small minority within Tibet like the Indians in the USA or the aborigines in Australia. The Chinese authorities deny that there is any massive immigration programme planned for Tibet. Time alone will tell if this is true; if it isn't, it will be too late to do anything about it and our world will be the poorer for it.

Our hopes for the future centre on the furthering of recent positive developments, a genuine attempt to understand Tibetan needs and wants, and progress to further real autonomy together with restriction of Chinese settlement. Finally our greatest hopes must include some reconciliation between Peking and Dharamsala. The Tibetans both in and outside Tibet can never be happy when such a large refugee population continues to exist outside their homeland. The Dalai Lama himself is exiled. His return and reintegration would of course require a really creative leap of the imagination, but in an age where scientific discoveries are almost daily wrenching apart our preconceived notions of what things are, and transforming our idea of reality, is it too much to hope that politicians too can come up with some new concepts, some category-shattering ideas? Our era has seen some truly creative compromises on the political scene, and we dare to hope, even in the face of the recent violence in Tibet, that the Chinese leadership may yet initiate an open discussion with the Dalai Lama. The problem is not one of history, it is one of tomorrow, next year, and the decades to come.

May 1988

Letter one: **Arriving in Tibet**

We landed at Peking in a thunderstorm, hoping that this was a
good omen. A drenched PLA soldier stopped a dripping queue
of cyclists and pedestrians from crossing the runways as we taxied
in. Greens, blues, greys, rain, armed sentries around the perimeter
in the downpour. Lightning flashed, thunder rolled, we suddenly
felt very jetlagged and very confused. After an hour of queuing,
pushing and shoving in the baggage reclaim hall, we finally cleared
customs with its myriad forms to fill in and were met by three
smiling, bowing, handshaking figures. One, young, with very
good English, was in charge of our stay in Peking; another was
actually from Lhasa. Had he come all this way just to meet us
off the plane? It turned out he had been on six months' leave in
Peking and would accompany us back to Lhasa. The third figure,
the driver, looked in dismay at our luggage and tried to cram it
into the boots of the two cars. (There always seem to be a huge
galvanized iron bucket and a heavy wooden crate of tools taking
up half the boot space in a Chinese car.) Under the downpour,
in the puddles, we just about managed to get it all in, and we
sloshed our way into Peking, to a hotel near the zoo. Mule carts.
Bicycles. Lines of plane trees. The continual *Honk! Honk!* of buses
and trucks, the creaking suspension and rattling bodywork of the
older vehicles, always seemingly overloaded.

We swirled into the entrance of the hotel. It looked very
modern. 'Is this a new hotel?' 'Yes, but you are staying in
the old part.' Built in 1950s Stalinesque style, it was cavernous
and dreary. Bored floor attendants lolled around, chatting and
smoking. Out-of-date and unread copies of *China Daily, China*

Reconstructs and *Beijing Review* littered the service counter. The dining room was vast, capable of seating 400 people at a banquet in cold, echoing splendour. Three or four tables were occupied. It took an age to get a menu, but the food, when it came, was delicious. At an adjacent table sat a solitary bored diplomat from some African country, billeted in the hotel. We told him we were en route for Tibet. 'Tibet, man?' he said, 'You be careful,' and chuckled hugely. 'Why?' 'Oh, man, the ladies there,' he said, 'they EAT men,' and slapped his thigh, chuckling delightedly, at the thought of treats in store, while we mentally added this new myth to the jumble of weird rituals, magic happenings and barbaric punishments that form the popular image of Tibetan culture. Feeling disorientated, but well-fed, we went off in search of bed and much-needed sleep.

There are many ways of getting to Tibet, none of them easy. Last summer a 45-hour bus journey from Golmud had, after a thousand miles of cramped discomfort and countless breakdowns, deposited us at midnight under the looming shadow of the Potala. This year we were to travel in more style and in far greater comfort by plane, but even that was not without its hitches, as we were to discover. The next day found us at the airport again for the evening flight to Chengdu. Mr Wu, who had met us on arrival, a gentle but flappable man in his fifties, was at the end of six months' leave home in Peking. He said goodbye to his wife at the airport entrance and came over to join us. 'Isn't your wife coming too?' we asked. 'Oh, no,' he said, 'she teaches in Peking.' He had been working in Lhasa for ten years, seeing his wife perhaps twice a year, at Spring Festival and in the summer. These long-distance marriages seem to be a feature of Chinese academic life, since the State assigns jobs to individual teachers and lecturers, and couples may find themselves miles apart.

Our other travelling companion was Mr Ding, a smiling philosophy professor, who at 58 was going to Lhasa for the first time and was obviously very nervous and unhappy, like a child about to go off to a new school. He and Wu followed each other round in circles, anxiously checking and rechecking tickets and luggage

tags. We had far too much luggage – mostly teaching materials
– and this evidently presented a problem to Wu. However, after
meticulous searches by the Security Check, we eventually boarded
the plane, with tons of cabin baggage 'in order to save weight'.
The 2½-hour flight was uneventful: sticky cakes, spicy dried
meat and chrysanthemum tea were handed out, an odd change
from the champagne and cordon bleu food of the flight from
London. But then Cathay Pacific don't give you a free fan covered
with pictures of cuddly pandas as a souvenir!

We landed at Chengdu in the darkness. We left the plane
and entered a sauna bath of Sichuan steam. 'Very hot, very hot,'
muttered Mr Ding, fanning himself with his cuddly panda fan and
mopping his brow. 'Very hot,' we echoed. The midsummer night
was full of the loud buzzing and ticking of insects and the whine
of mosquitoes. Slap, slap, slap. Damn, where could we get away
from the mosquitoes? We followed the other passengers into a sort
of neon-lit cage, where eventually, after much fussing, pushing
and pulling, we managed to retrieve our luggage. We staggered
out into the carpark and were met by pitch black night – and
nobody. 'In Peking you are in my hands. In Chengdu you will
be in the charge of the Tibet Office.' Our minder's last words on
seeing us off now sounded like a warning. The night buzzed and
rattled around us, a truck and then a bus snorted off down the
lane. Mr Ding, Mr Wu and we two were marooned in the middle
of nowhere, at 9.45 on a Sunday night.

A hot group of airport staff sat with their trousers rolled up to
their knees, slurping tea, shirts unbuttoned, fanning themselves
and watching a dubbed *Dallas* on TV. They were unconcerned
at our plight. We had answered an advertisement asking for a
'hardy married teaching couple', so we tried to look as if we felt
hardy, but in fact we were just confused and very jetlagged. Mr
Ding circled the dark carpark, moaning 'very hot, very hot'. Mr
Wu had vanished. Of course his worries were greater, because
he had *volunteered* to see us safely to Lhasa. 'Well,' I said to
Jill, three quarters of an hour later, 'it's only nine hours
till the plane leaves.' 'And,' she said, 'we'll probably not

even get on it.' Nothing like optimism, I thought. But what farsightedness!

Finally, Mr Wu came back. And a while later, a bus was heard grinding its way up the lane and into the carpark. We were piled in, and the bus lurched off. Chinese drivers seem to like driving blind, and any drive in the countryside at night is a dangerous game of guesswork. Headlights are only switched on when you think there might be something in the way. Our journey along a winding bumpy track around the outskirts of Chengdu was not made any easier by the crowds and crowds of late-night shadows. It was as crowded as a Saturday morning market, and in fact it turned out to be a late-night market. Thousands of people were out enjoying themselves in the relative cool of the evening, singing, chatting, drinking, shopping, at hundreds of little candlelit stalls lining the road: a strange and moving sight. In the flickering candlelight, the figures flitted around mysteriously like ghosts or figures in a dream. The driver flashed his lights, blared his horn, and eventually we swung into the courtyard of a hotel.

Since we left again before dawn, our memories of Chengdu are of darkness punctuated by occasional highly illuminated scenes; the neon-lit airport, the glittering chandeliered and mirrored lobby of the incongruously luxurious hotel where we spent the night, random street scenes floodlit by the driver's headlights: a family sitting on low stools outside their doorway, a wayside noodle stall, morning *tai ji* exercises, cyclists wobbling to work.

We got to the airport at 7.15. Hordes of Western tourists were queuing for the Lhasa flight check-in. I had a strange foreboding that we wouldn't get on the 8.15 flight – there were far too many Westerners. The sun was up, and Mr Ding had already started mopping his brow and muttering, 'very hot, very hot,' – which was no less than the truth. Gingerly, I asked Mr Wu, 'Do you have the tickets?' and, equally gingerly, he replied, 'There is some problem.' The tourists had started checking in now, and our pile of luggage was not yet at the back of the queue. We met the Tibet Office in the person of a girl in curlers who had a frantic conversation with Wu, in which I could only make out the words '. . . ticket . . . money . . ..' It turned out we didn't have either.

Once more, we piled all our luggage back into the old bus. Once more, the gears were ground, and we lurched off out of the airport carpark. 'I wonder if we're going back to the hotel,' Jill said. 'Perhaps we'll be here for days.' Neither Ding nor Wu had answers to our questions. They didn't know what to do either. It was hard to tell which of them was the more despondent. It seemed to be up to the girl in curlers. As she had failed to meet us off the flight last night, none of us had much ground for optimism. Curiously, we only drove a couple of hundred yards. The bus stopped outside a building called CAAC HOTEL. It was a sort of dormitory for airport personnel. We humped all our luggage out again, and this time it was locked up in a store room, which seemed a sensible idea, if we were going to be stuck in Chengdu for a few days waiting for planes. Next, we were led down the corridor, to a dusty room with battered furniture and old, unmade beds with dirty sheets. A dead cockroach lived in one of the two rusty teamugs. The thermos flask was empty. 'Wait a minute. Now, please have a rest,' smiled Mr Wu. We tried. The building was at the end of a runway, and every fifteen minutes or so an ancient Illyushin would wind up its engines with a deafening roar of propellors and trundle hopefully off down the runway, taxi back again, and stop. Fifteen minutes later, the experiment would be repeated. In the intervals we dozed, read and tried to be 'hardy', as befitted the job description. But people kept knocking on the door to see how we were or to give us hot water. In the end, we left the door ajar, so as not to be disturbed by the knocking. Airport staff then just poked their heads in and stared. Occasionally, Wu would come back and say, 'Wait a minute.' After two hours' 'rest' he finally came in and asked us to get ready. 'For what?' we asked, 'you mean you have tickets now?' 'Wait a minute,' he said, and went off again. We will never quite know that Mr Wu had been up to that morning, but by the time lunch time came, he was in too much of a fluster to sit down and eat. Mr Ding, on the other hand, looked much more cheerful, had stopped complaining about the heat, and called for a bottle of Green Leaf beer. Things were looking up.

We could hardly believe it when the flight was announced. We boarded the old 707, were issued with our sticky cakes, crystallized fruit and panda fans, and took off while sucking chrysanthemum tea through a straw. I never want to see Chengdu airport again.

At last! Out of China, towards Tibet. Within minutes, we were over high mountain ranges. It is a fantastic flight, as you can see from a glance at a map. It was cloudy much of the way, but we still had good views of the massive deep river valleys, all running southwards, where the Yangtze, Salween and Mekong have cut their way through the mountains. Huge mountains, glaciers like motorways of ice, on and on as far as the eye can see. The flight lasted a couple of hours, and we were glued to the windows most of that time. The stewardesses on the other hand, having issued the panda fans, decided they felt sick, pulled down the tables and dozed on their arms, even while we were coming in to land. As we flew westward, the ground became drier and drier, and then suddenly we were over the wide, brown river valley of the Yarlung Tsangpo (which later becomes the Brahmaputra), and down to starboard we could see the Samye monastery, its white stupas on the surrounding mountains, and the track leading to the river edge and the ferry point, where we had trudged in the hot sun last year. The plane does a terrifying bank, skims the rocky, arid mountain tops, and is suddenly down on the airstrip.

The doors opened and everyone, Chinese, Tibetan, Western, was strangely quiet. Perhaps, like us, they were anxiously waiting to see quite how thin the air would be, how intense the sunlight. Sniffing curiously, we disembarked. A group of Tibetans welcomed another group home with white prayer scarves and smiles. We were in a wide river valley, surrounded by barley fields, where peasants were busy harvesting. A small group of people were waiting for us by the gate, beside a Toyota Landcruiser. Wu was clearly relieved the trip was over. Ding was frowning and feeling his brow, wondering whether or not he had a headache. We were simply glad to have arrived and not to have to touch our luggage again – it would be following the next day.

Our flat is on the second floor of a long three-storey concrete building occupied by university teachers and their families. In comparison to other accommodation on campus, the building is very grand, with running water and inside toilet. By Chinese standards too, this bare four-roomed flat is palatial accommodation for a couple: most families here live in two rooms. The flat is decorated in typical Chinese style with blue paint to halfway up the wall and white paint above that. The floors are cement and the yellow painted window frames have green fly-screens. It could be anywhere in China really. The teaching rooms at the University look just the same, so there is no sense of a real divide between work and home. However, we do have a couple of bright Tibetan rugs and gaudily painted Tibetan cupboards to relieve the gloom. And we have a fridge, connected for some reason to the light bulb in the 'dining room', so that we have to choose between having the light on all night or defrosting the fridge (actually the electricity does not work all that often anyway, so we have taken the bulb out and have meals mostly by candlelight). We have two desks, two bookcases (one of which we use as a wardrobe), a big iron bedstead, a kettle, an electric ring on the floor of the 'kitchen' and a paraffin stove for when the electricity isn't working, except that apparently there is no paraffin available, just petrol. 'It is all right to use petrol because of the altitude,' we were told. We are the proud possessors of that ultimate proof of status, a colour TV. There are Chinese and Tibetan channels. The Chinese channels have a mixture of variety shows, rather sentimentally moralistic films and plays, Chinese opera and various earnest programmes of an improving nature; the Tibetan channel seems more fun – Hindi movies seem to make up the bulk of its diet. The 'kitchen', which is also the bathroom, depending on the time of day, contains, apart from the electric ring and paraffin stove, a concrete sink in the other corner. We have more sophisticated washing facilities, however, in the 'toilet and shower room'. This is a little cubicle with a tiled floor with a hole in it (the toilet) and a metal pipe sticking out of the wall (the shower). There is an erratic supply of cold water (water and electricity rarely coincide, so boiling the kettle requires a combination of advance planning and opportunism), which is fine in the dusty summer heat but we may need to be braver as the weather gets colder!

Our immediate environment, the campus, is a wasteland of dingy apartment buildings and dusty trees. Attached to the lampposts are, unfortunately, loudspeakers: the campus public address system for music and announcements. But, from our windows, we can see towering behind the roofs . . . MOUNTAINS! Bare jagged peaks, with a sprinkling of green grass. Lhasa is just over 12,000 feet, so the surrounding mountains must be about 15,000 or 16,000 feet. We have designs on the nearest mountain, which has a path going up to some prayer flags fluttering at the top.

Just at the end of the dirt track which leads from the city centre, past the University, is the Lhasa river, the Kyichu or 'Waters of Pleasure'. It is lovely to be able to go for an evening stroll down there, the banks crowded with people washing clothes, fishing, having picnics. It is the 'picnic season' in Lhasa now, and most of Lhasa seems to be out eating, drinking and enjoying the sunshine.

Letter two: **Lhasa**

Lhasa itself is now two towns, which live next to and within each other. There is what is left of the old Lhasa: beautiful solid-looking whitewashed Tibetan houses, mostly two-storey with black-painted window frames, flat roofs and bright flower boxes full of painted tin pots of geraniums, marigolds, asters and hollyhocks, which thrive in the sun. Above most windows are curious flapping 'pelmets', white, rimmed with red or blue or yellow. They ripple prettily in the breeze.

The old town is centred on the Jokhang, the main temple. The focus of all the pilgrimages, this is a wonderful building which would need a whole book to describe properly. Around it, a roughly circular street called the Barkor acts as the main thoroughfare. It is a narrow street, always full of people walking round it clockwise, traditionally the correct way to circumambulate a holy place. Pilgrims, monks, nomads, peasants, traders and, of course, Chinese and Western tourists cram this half-mile-long circuit which is both a holy path and the main shopping street. On each side are stalls selling all kinds of goods: yoghurt (best yak) in old fruit jars; turquoise beads and pendants; silver jewellery of unknown age and provenance; amulets encrusted with coral and turquoise; brightly coloured tassels which Tibetan women braid into their long black plaits; daggers and dagger holders; old bayonets, some of which are ex-Indian Army; ancient stirrups of silver, decorated with dragon heads; prayer wheels (of silver, of bone, of wood, of brass, of leather, of all sizes and detailed decorations, but all with *Om Mani Padme Hum* on the outside), twirl one clockwise and the prayers inside are sent spinning up to heaven; long white scarves called *katag*, of fine muslin or silk; prayer flags, woodblock-printed in the bright holy colours of blue, green, yellow, white and red. Clumsily printed woodblock prayers and drawings of Buddhist deities; peacock feathers; garish posters of the Dalai Lama or the Panchen Lama. Pirated cassettes of disco and Indian film music, blaring out from a huge stereo recorder. Tins of snuff, with gaudy designs, also imported from India. Embroidered Tibetan boots, with curly upturned toes. Trinkets. Soap. Shampoo. Warm hand-knitted winter leggings. Brass ladles. Pots and pans. Grey pebble-like chunks of dried yak cheese, strung together and looking like strange edible necklaces. Yak butter in reeking greasy skins of yak, sewn up into 20- or 30-pound lumps. A gruesome yak butchers' alley, with dogs desperately panting in hope of a morsel and flies circling the blackening carcasses. Flat bread. Glucose biscuits from Nepal. Watermelons, raisins and walnuts from Xinjiang. Crab apples, pears, peaches, tomatoes and cucumbers. Bags of *tsampa* or roasted barley flour. Bricks of tea. Jars of mango pickle from Madras. Spices (unidentifiable except for cumin and saffron). Garlic. Big bundles of sweet-smelling juniper branches, to be burned as offerings in the huge bulb-shaped 'kilns' whose smoke rises to the sky. Carpets, with dragons and phoenixes. Skins of wild animals – wild cats, leopards, snow leopards, foxes and others unknown. Sheepskins to line your winter coat. Tibetan shirts made of coarse cloth. Hats. Brightly striped woollen cloth to be sewn into aprons. Indian nail varnish, lipstick and hair oil. Electronic goods, including the world famous SHRAP CALCULATOR (sic!) copied in China. Streetside dentists-cum-watchmenders, working with cigarette in hand on the unfortunate but stoical patients, who spit their blood and teeth into the dust under the tables with their displays of new teeth, gold inset with ruby or turquoise, and old teeth neatly arrayed in rows – presumably you choose the dentist who has pulled the most. Old biscuit tins from the Indian Raj, 'HUNTLEY AND PALMERS BEST BISCUITS' used as cash boxes by stall holders, or 'H.O. WILLS GOLD FLAKE, 500 IN PACKETS OF TEN'. Bales of silk and brocade. Brass butter-lamps . . .. Everywhere we look there is more to see; every time we go round, we notice new details.

It takes about twenty minutes at a reasonable amble to circumambulate the Jokhang, but it can take much longer if you are prostrating as you go. Really pious pilgrims can often be seen doing this. They wear leather protective aprons, and wooden 'sandals' on their hands. Continuously saying prayers, they raise their arms above their head, bring their hands together down to their forehead, throat and then chest, and then dive out full-length face down in the dust. They then rise and pace forward to where their outstretched arms reached. You can prostrate your way lengthways, as most seem to do, or even prostrate sideways, continually crossing and recrossing the road. It must take weeks to get round that way. We asked our neighbour how often she would perform this rite. 'Never,' she said, 'we don't need to, we *live* in Lhasa!' Being born in this holy city is enough to ensure merit and rebirth into a better life. Those stretching themselves out in the dust and scrambling to their feet are pilgrims, who may have made the journey to Lhasa from their village in the same laborious fashion.

In the middle of the road will be monks of all ages, on their own or in small groups, ringing bells and chanting prayers. Tired beggars may be asleep, holding out bowls for offerings of money or food. A child pulls at your coat, pleading 'Dalai Lama picture! Dalai Lama picture!' Chinese faces, Nepali faces, Tibetan faces, all ages and sizes. Motorbikes (Chinese, or Hondas made under licence in Chongqing) rattle through the crowd. Cyclists, although forbidden, make a desperate attempt to weave their way through without falling off. Chinese soldiers walk up the street in a little knot, determinedly going anti-clockwise. Overweight Westerners, bulging out of their shorts, poke telephoto lenses at everything and pay excruciating prices for junk.

It is a fascinating, always novel, experience to wander round the Barkor. Since we were here last year, prices have gone up, there are more phoney 'antiques' and souvenirs (most of them made in Nepal by the Tibetan community there), but there is also more evidence of variety and prosperity: many more vegetables, for instance, and better quality.

Running off from the Barkor are muddy, narrow alleys, with fascinating glimpses into the courtyards of the old Tibetan houses. One road, leading back home for us, passes the mosque, which is surrounded by Muslim traders in skullcaps, and little Halal restaurants where you can drink delicious *longyan* or dragon's eye tea – very sweet – and eat a bowl of spicy noodles and mutton.

When we arrived last year, the area in front of the Jokhang was one vast, muddy, treacherous building site (flying chippings of stone from the masons' chisels, spikes of wire and rusty metal sticking out of the dirt – best not to wear sandals). It is now an open 'plaza' which leads into the modern, Chinese-style town. Opinions vary about this plaza. It is a symbol of the 'new' Lhasa, and a wide concrete boulevard, which could be anywhere else in China, leads into it. Before, the Jokhang was surrounded, probably rather like a medieval European cathedral, by the stalls and houses and alleys of the Tibetan town. Now a big open space with kitschy standard lamps, flower beds, fountains and railings, and with shops and restaurants on each side, has been created. You can now see the whole front of the Jokhang with its golden roofs, golden wheel and antelopes, in its full glory. The space is used, rather like the area in front of Covent Garden in London or the Pompidou Centre in Paris, by a variety of street entertainers: a man dancing solo, spinning round and round in a slow tap dance to a melancholy tune played on a two-stringed fiddle; two slapstick comedians chanting a story, covering each other in white *tsampa* flour and hitting each other over the head; a monk prescribing treatment for illnesses, mumbling prayers and charms, revealing and hiding again in the folds of his robe precious images of Buddha and other deities. Standing in small groups around these figures is an amazing variety of people: proud-looking, tall Khampas from eastern Tibet with big boots, red braided hair and long knives or bayonets; girls dressed up in their finery, their silver, turquoise and coral jewellery all for sale; beggars in huddles with their few possessions beside them in the dust; toothless old ladies, leathery skin deeply wrinkled by decades of sun and wind, spinning their prayer wheels, looking like grotesque elderly babies with rattles; 'Change Money?' men, approaching you quietly and talking from the side of their mouth as they try to steer you into a corner to do a black market deal; young men in Western clothes – jeans, T-shirts, leather jackets – slouch around looking bored; snot-nosed kids grab you by the hand and frantically ask, 'Pen! Pen!', while writing on one palm with a finger; monks prowl around in their curly-toed boots, deep red robes flapping, or sit in dusty rows, chanting.

Beyond this fascinating confusion of colour, smell and sound, stretches the new Chinese town. Obviously Tibetans feel at home in a Tibetan environment and Chinese in a Chinese. This part of town could really be anywhere in China, with its wide roads and undistinguished grey concrete buildings. Stallholders sell melon seeds and sweet bottles of lurid coloured pop. Bicycle menders lay their bits and pieces all over the pavement. Fat cadres waddle along, plastic briefcases in hand. Soldiers, weedy-looking in their canvas shoes, shuffle past arm in arm. Trucks and jeeps *honk! honk!* and creak by. Slow-motion cyclists wobble along, always looking about to topple over. Police, looking like South American generals in green uniforms and reflector sunglasses, stand on traffic islands or rattle past on ancient motorbikes. A water lorry rolls past, spraying water to lay the dust, playing an ice-cream van version of Beethoven's 'Ode to Joy'. The department stores are dark and dusty, the attendants look bored out of their wits, and there's not really much to buy, although Lhasa does have a far greater variety of tinned and bottled foods than cities in 'inland' China.

However, towering over all this, to the west, is the Potala! It is the most magnificent sight, like some huge white cliff. Its top pinnacles and roofs of gold glint in the sun, the massive bulk of whitewashed and dark maroon stone is pitted with line upon line of windows; giant staircases zigzag in great sweeps across the front, and at each end are enormous round turrets. The Potala completely dominates Lhasa, dwarfing every other building in the valley, but is itself tiny against the mountains behind. It seems, with its powerful asymmetry, to be a product of some geological process rather than of man's imagination, as if it has arisen naturally from the savage rocky landscape. Windows, walls, doors, roofs, all echo the vaster shapes of the slopes and peaks behind. It looks like a jumble of mountain features: pinnacles, cliff faces, rock walls, which have all somehow been arranged by a giant hand to form an extraordinary, unimaginably beautiful building. Formerly, the Potala sat isolated on its rock, with the village of Shölat at its feet. Here were the prison and various government offices. Opposite was the Chakpori Medical College. Now all the ruins from the Chinese shelling in 1959 have been cleared away and an enormous TV mast stands in their place. At the foot of Chakpori, however, is one of the most delightful temples – a little cave temple, with a lovely view across to the Potala – called Palhalupuk. It is dark and buttery, and a few monks work there printing woodblock prayers and making butter sculptures for the altars.

In the old days, stretching right round the outskirts of the city, running along the shores of the river, turning past Chakpori, leaving the Potala to the east and then running round the north of Lhasa, ran the holy Lingkor, a sort of ring-road version of the Barkor. It was a track, a holy path, encircling the Holy City. Unfortunately the Lingkor is now all but obliterated by new roads, factories, municipal buildings and other work units. Both Perceval Landon (1904) and Spencer Chapman (1938) have detailed descriptions of the Lingkor in their books, and it is quite interesting, if depressing, to compare the two walks, old and new.

The northern part is now entirely along paved roads: it starts a few hundred yards west of what used to be the great West Gate, between the Chakpori and Marpori hills. By the road bridge, near a large green department store, a track leads north onto the main road which runs behind the Potala. You cross another bridge, just before the Bank of China, then dip down to pass the Public Security Bureau. Somewhere out there to the west, among the fields and willow groves, is the great house where Younghusband was quartered in 1904, all those years ago. The road then turns eastwards, just north of the Lukhang, which is a fenced-in, rather dusty park, with a ring of trees round the small lake in its centre. To your left are work units, government offices, walled-in enclosures with guards on duty at the locked gates.

This could be anywhere in China, except for the backdrop of the Potala to your right and, all around, the bare mountains, dry brown against the dazzling deep blue sky. You are walking along a hot, dusty city road, with green trucks, jeeps, motorbikes rattling past, with an incessant honking of horns and ringing of bicycle bells. Only a few people are walking round, probably pilgrims from far away from Lhasa. You leave the pale blue 'People's Hospital' to your right, the Potala drops behind, until you reach a huge ornamental traffic circle – Chinese Civic Kitsch at its finest. Here you turn due south, past the Telecommunications Building, and walk down a road lined with small shops and noodle stalls, until the whitewashed stone of Old Lhasa appears to your right. You now turn west, past the boot factory and the Sunday bike market, past the green minaret of the mosque, and you enter an alley. As you pass Ani Sankhung, a little nunnery, you may perhaps begin to feel you are, at last, on the route of the 'old' Lingkor . . . but soon you come out again onto a busy main road. On both sides are walls, but these are set far back behind the avenue of trees leading westwards along the south side of Lhasa. You can see the Potala, ahead of you to the right, as you pass the Culture Palace, mainly used as a dance hall, its style a strange blend of neo-Tibetan and Stalinesque pomposity. Two crossroads later, just past a PLA barracks on the right, you finally see the Lhasa river sweeping in from the south.

Robbers' Island, a popular picnic spot and a good site for photographs of the Potala (its trees hide the new buildings!) is just across a few metres of swift, snow-cold water and can be reached by paying a few *fen* and crossing the little suspension bridge bedecked with prayer flags. At this point, most pilgrims cross the road to walk along the embankment, following the line of small stone cairns and smouldering juniper fires. People are washing clothes, or fishing, or just sitting and gazing at the river and the mountains on the other side.

To the north, the Potala seems to grow longer and longer behind the blank walls of yet more military and government units. Here and there a bored-looking sentry with fixed bayonet stands in a giant gateway, guarding a chained driveway. The mast on top of Chakpori looms higher and higher, and now you can see the steep rock wall of 'Iron Hill', all but obliterating the Potala. Suddenly, you spot a pile of *mani* stones, just beside the entrance to a petrol station. The Lingkor here seems to dive into a tunnel, a narrow alley squeezing between the high walls of a military unit on one side and the petrol station on the other. If there are no pilgrims in sight, you fear you have made a mistake; but the alley makes a dog's leg, and suddenly you are right at the foot of 'Iron Hill', behind the petrol station, and the path here becomes a steep notch in the limestone cliff, which climbs for a hundred yards along the base of the hill. The rock wall beside you is carved with images and prayers, hung with flags, with piles of *mani* stones and yak horns. You feel that this is as it always used to be . . . but to your left, below you, instead of the swirling waters of the river described by Landon, are yet more walls, more petrol dumps, and the rusting debris and weeds of the forgotten corners of any modern city. The Kyichu is now contained behind the high embankments some hundred yards to the south.

At last, you reach the most impressive part of the whole walk, and are amazed to find that it still exists: below the towering rock faces of Chakpori there is a huge rock-carving of hundreds of Buddhas, exactly as in a photograph taken by Heinrich Harrer in the 1940s. Some pilgrims are burning juniper and prostrating in front of the rows and rows of painted carvings, red, yellow, green, blue, gold, which sit on their huge rock screen, perhaps forty feet in height and twenty in width, but this is the only part of the old Lingkor remaining. The rest of the walk, back to the main road 300 yards north, runs between a ditch and another high, blank wall. To the right, you can see a huge web of prayer flags slung from the rocks of Chakpori, across to the lower slopes of Marpori and the Potala. Here used to stand the great West Gate, which they are now planning to rebuild. Presumably the design will have to be changed somewhat, to permit the continued passage of ever more lorries, jeeps and buses.

So, apart from the occasional prostrating pilgrim, the old Lingkor, the outer circuit of the Holy City, which used to run through meadows and parkland, is now mainly indistinguishable from any other network of roads round the outskirts of any Chinese city.

Fortunately though, modernization can do little to change the natural scenery: the huge backdrop of brown mountains, the deep blue sky and, from a distance, the Potala which dominates the valley. The Lhasa river, or Kyichu, is a wide, fast-flowing, grey, cold current which in the Lhasa valley becomes a network of different streams running around little islands. The edges are lined with willow groves, where people go to bathe, wash, fish and, at this season, to picnic. Gipsy camps of nomads, travellers, truck and tractor drivers are established along the banks. The river runs only a few hundred years from our door, so we can go for very pleasant strolls along it (but with a wary eye on the look-out for roaming packs of dogs). The mountains around are beautifully varied. Hints of snow on the farther, higher peaks, which must be up to 17,000–18,000 feet, and after a rainstorm there are definite splashes of white on the lower slopes, which must be about 15,000 feet. It looks rather like the Scottish Highlands, but much more arid.

The rocky slopes are a dry brown most of the time, but at 8 a.m., as the Chinese national anthem blares out from the loudspeakers, and the first sunlight touches them, they become a golden olive colour, and if it has rained at all there is a definite green tinge to them. In the evenings, with late sun on the other peaks, there are spectacular cloudscapes, with shafts of sun onto distant peaks. Black thunder-clouds develop. (This is the 'wet' season – a decent downpour for an hour or so every three or four days. Last week, a phenomenal thunder-and-lightning display kept us awake for three hours.) Most of the time, though, the sky is an intense hot blue – it is easy to get burnt at this altitude. In the shade, it is surprisingly cool.

Along the river, in the trees, there are quite a lot of birds – the most usual are, of course, sparrows. The next most common are hoopoes, cheerful-looking with bright golden brown and white striped plumage, long curved beaks and their gorgeous black and white crests. They fly in little spurts, and can be seen all over the place. Over the river are gulls and terns. Circling above the city and outskirts, looking for food, are kites. And further out, especially towards Sera, where the sky burials take place, are the vultures, which make all the other birds look tiny and insignificant. There are lots of ravens, surprisingly tame, which hop up and down along the walls near the river or croak in the trees. There are many smaller, less easily identifiable birds too – one like a rock pipit, with a white eye-stripe and another like a very bright red and black redstart.

Letter three: **Yoghurt Festival**

Yesterday our 'leader', a very nice Chinese teacher, came round and said: 'The school leaders want to inform you to visit their welcome party tomorrow afternoon, and to be very merry.' We looked at each other, as we had planned to go out this afternoon with some friends, but it wouldn't have been politic or polite to say so, so we nodded and he went on: 'And I should tell you the exact time for the welcome party tomorrow.' 'Can you tell us now? Have they made the arrangements?' 'Up till now, they haven't informed me. But you should be ready for the party in the afternoon. I hope you will have a very merry time.' And with that he left. And we have been waiting all day. I expected someone would have told us this morning, if the party was going to be in the afternoon. We have been waiting, and waiting, and no one else that we could speak to knew anything about it. Perhaps it's all supposed to be a surprise. Anyway, it's now 4.30, and our 'leader' has just popped in again to say we should be ready at 6.30 for the 'welcome banquet'. (We have been here three and a half weeks now!) We hoped he would be coming too, as we appreciate all the trouble he takes on our behalf. But no: 'The banquet is for the school leaders.' 'But you are our leader and anyway you could help us out with our bad Chinese.' 'No, sorry, I am not invited. Have a very merry evening.' As he is our main contact for personal affairs and teaching matters, and rushes from meeting to meeting trying to get things moving on our behalf, we were surprised that he was not coming. But that's life in China. . . .

A few days after arrival, we were taken on a trip, in an 'official' black Shanghai saloon, complete with net curtains over the windows and a Chinese 'minder'. We went to see a festival in the Norbulingka, which is all of forty minutes' walk away along the river. I think we know more about the Dalai Lama's Summer Palace than our Chinese guide did. Mr Ding, the philosophy professor who travelled from Beijing with us, was also brought along on this new arrivals' treat. Since then, I really don't believe he has been off campus. He is a very gentle, scholarly old man, whom we like very much, and with whom we have leisurely and courteous games of chess in the evening, but I don't think he wants to be here at all, and he is in fact going back home before Christmas, having cut short his term here.

Well, we swished through Lhasa in our Shanghai saloon and went into the Summer Palace gardens. It is a very beautiful walled park, full of flowers and trees; not surprisingly, the present Dalai Lama much preferred its light and air to the rather gloomy atmosphere of the Potala. In the fifties, a new Summer Palace was built, an elegant two-storey country house in mixed modern and Tibetan style. You can see all over the house, including the bathroom, which, we were proud to see, boasts Shanks plumbing! The basin and bathtub were full of money, thrown in as offerings by pilgrims. A Russian *Mir* radio set, a Philips radiogram, rather like the one I remember in our living room as a child, and an Anglepoise lamp all looked very incongruous next to the *tangka*, murals, prayer scarves and thrones. The Dalai Lama used the house only a few times before his flight in 1959.

We were then taken to a clearing in the woods, covered by a large awning, overlooked by an ornamental gateway, for a performance of Tibetan dancing and singing – it was 'Yoghurt Festival' or *Sho Dun*. The name comes from a ceremony observed at Drepung monastery where the chief proctors handed over authority to their successors. The whole congregation was traditionally treated to a gift of sour milk. The name has been transferred to the 'opera season' in the seventh month of the Tibetan calendar. These operas were held in the Norbulingka, performed by the best opera troupes from all over the country, and the grounds were thrown open to the public only at this time of year. In the old days, this must have been a splendid occasion for picnics and days of merrymaking, and the Dalai Lama used to sit in a room at the top of the ornamental pavilion and gateway, looking down on the performances from behind a curtain of yellow gauze. In 1986, what we saw was a very artificial, and rather sad, resurrection of this old custom.

One could see very clearly just what has happened to the old arts and dances and music. The life has been taken out of them; far from being a spontaneous, joyful expression of the culture, it was a rather lifeless, state-directed and choreographed 'going through the motions': expertly drilled but joyless dancers twirled and swirled and smiled in that ever-so-sweet sentimental and insincere way. It was very well done, but it wasn't real! What a difference, to see the dances taking place in front of the Jokhang, or the work-songs that gangs of women sing, making roofs, singing and dancing while they work, all day long. That is real culture, folk culture. What the State provided for us was very interesting for all that. A huge party of cadres, Tibetan and Chinese, sat behind rows of tables, slurping tea. A West German TV crew were frantically dodging in and out of the performers, trying to get the best camera angles, obstructing the view of the ordinary Tibetans who *were* enjoying themselves, sitting cross-legged in a great circle around the dusty bit of ground that served as a stage, drinking *chang*. At one moment, they all threw handfuls of *tsampa* flour into the air with a great cry, and of course the TV crew and equipment got covered ('serve 'em right!' we thought smugly).

'Traditional' songs from Tibet (all sung in Chinese!) alternated with Hong Kong style pop songs, TV crooners in Engelbert Humperdink style alternated with instrumentalists on *erhu* and flute. Some of the latter were very good indeed, most of the former excruciatingly bad. Throughout, bored-looking Chinese cadres chainsmoked and slurped tea, and one wondered what thoughts were going through the minds and behind the public smiles of the older Tibetan officials, who are all caught up in the present day government, but who must remember the old days. The younger Tibetan cadres are often people who, at an early age, are 'selected' by the Chinese and sent off to school in China, perhaps later to the National Minorities Institute in Beijing.

Last night, we were 'treated' to a similar display of modern Chinese-Tibetan culture, in the big concert hall, here on campus. As it was much less pompous than the Yoghurt Festival, and its intentions not propagandist, it was actually much more fun. But it is strange that Tibetan music seems to have survived the Cultural Revolution only to be threatened by the invasion of Western pop! There was very little traditional Tibetan music or dance in the 2½ -hour performance. Again we had Tibetan songs in Chinese, and the plastic-looking masks of the highly made-up and highly stylized dancers. These alternated with a quartet of male singers, backed by two Tibetans in traditional costume with electric guitars, a drummer and electric organ, singing sentimental songs. There was one brilliant Tibetan solo dance and some excellent instrumental music, but the climax of the evening was when an electric organ soloist played on and on, with flashing coloured lights blinking completely out of time with the music, and wouldn't leave the stage (he kept being called back for encores, which we could not understand at all!)

After we had been here two weeks, we met our students for the first time: well, we met some of them, the Second-Year group, because the First Years haven't arrived yet. We are teaching the grand total of one hour each per day, but this will increase to a more reasonable amount soon.

They are a friendly, very young-looking group of sixteen students, most of them in their early twenties. There are three boys and thirteen girls – twelve are Han Chinese, two are pure Tibetan, and two half-Han, half-Tibetan – but almost all of them 'come from' Tibet. That is, they were born in Tibet or have lived here for a very long time, but if you ask them, 'Where do you come from?' they will always reply 'Shanghai' or 'Chengdu' or 'Chongqing' – a province or a city 'inland' which is where their family originates. They may actually have been there only once or twice in their entire life!

They are all very shy. On our first day of teaching, we decided to give them short interviews in order to try to find out their English language level – a scheme doomed to failure, as they were so scared they would hardly open their mouths, and we had to resort to an interpreter in most cases to extract basic information such as age, background, aspirations, etc. Mostly they would reply in hesitant whispers – a sign of extreme politeness, or of fear? The Tibetans seemed particularly timid – the two girls came in very slowly and kept their tongues out (a sign of respect in Tibet), heads down, not daring to look at us, all through their interviews. Even now, after we have been teaching the class for some days, the Tibetan students are extraordinarily (to our eyes) shy, reply in whispers and stick their tongues out humbly, lowering their heads, whenever asked a question!

One girl, the 'class monitor', is less shy, and she caused us some alarm the other day when she arrived unannounced at our front door and, on being offered a seat on our (very uncomfortable but impressive looking) sofa, started her conversation with an abrupt, 'Do you believe in God?' We weren't sure whether this was (a) the Thought Police coming round to inspect our morals, (b) an appeal from a covert believer or (c) a mistaken belief that this was how Westerners usually opened light conversation. Since then, however, she has been round twice more and on both occasions her opening gambits have been no less startling. 'I think I have problems with my mind' was one, and 'What is the meaning of life?' the other. We have concluded that her problems are a combination of an adolescent identity crisis and a lack of small talk. We entertain her with tea and melon seeds and try to convince her of our inability to provide neat answers to her metaphysical problems.

Our new First Year will be all Tibetans – twenty-five of them from all over Tibet, and they will have virtually no English. This is part of a new policy to extend educational opportunities more widely to Tibetans, and to try to redress the balance, which is unfairly weighted in favour of the Chinese. Since most middle school (secondary school) teachers are Chinese, teaching is done through Chinese, and the Tibetan children are disadvantaged.

Most Tibetans do not get the chance to learn English at school, since they all have to learn Chinese.

We are at present negotiating the timetable. At the moment, out of eighteen hours a week, only two are spent on 'listening and speaking', the rest on grammar (taught in Chinese) and a peculiar Chinese invention called 'Intensive Reading', which involves spending about ten hours a week on one page of text, minutely analyzing every sentence. A bit like the French system of *explication de texte* maybe, except that the texts are all about such topics as Norman Bethune and the Eighth Route Army, or (our favourite) 'Lenin's Visit to London' – 'Although the weather was bad, Vladimir Ilyich brightened up at once and began to look at this stronghold of capitalism with curiosity . . .'. There are also sentences to translate like: 'I will never forget the day I was first admitted to the Party.' 'Our Party is great, glorious, and correct.' 'Day is just breaking, but most of the comrades are up and working already.' 'Chairman Mao worked throughout the night to bring the day of Liberation closer to the Chinese people.' We are bargaining for more time for oral English and more modern materials. We are also supposed to be teaching Methodology to the university English teachers – this should be getting off the ground next week. And since many of the teachers seem to be on leave in China, we have suggested that the course be extended to include middle school teachers of English. To our surprise, this suggestion has been adopted, so we should have a mixed group of university and middle school teachers from next week.

Last week, we were given a tour of the university campus by the President's wife, a cheerful lady in her mid-forties. (The President, a Tibetan, is at 40 the youngest university President in all of the People's Republic.) Our strongest impression of the campus was one of emptiness! Seventeen Art and Music students rattling around in a big new Tibetan Arts Department. A huge four-storey science building, most of the labs locked and unused. Piles of dusty books and periodicals awaiting classification in the library, which had prominently and proudly displayed a complete set of Buddhist scriptures in their Tibetan wood and cloth bindings. A

Tibetan library looks very different from a library anywhere else in the world. Tibetan books consist of a pile of long narrow loose-leaf sheets, woodblock printed, held between two wooden covers and wrapped up in a yellow cloth. The books in the library were stacked in piles, each with an embroidered brocade title marker hanging down: decorative, but also practical – they gave the catalogue number for easy identification.

The University opened only last year and is obviously in the initial stages of development. Part of our job is to liven up the Languages Department. The arrival of our brightly coloured new English textbooks has made quite an impression already on the students and teachers, who are all keen to borrow books to take home and read. There are about 700 students altogether in the University – and about 500 teaching staff! About sixty per cent of the students are Tibetan; most of the teaching staff are Chinese, although the administration, President and numerous vice-presidents are nearly all Tibetan. There are some general departments: Science, Social Science, Languages; and some specifically Tibetan subjects: Tibetan Language and Literature, Tibetan History, Tibetan Medicine, Tibetan Art and Music.

Tibetan students are concentrated in the Tibetan subjects; Chinese students in the more general courses. Four hundred of these students are doing Tibetan language, literature and history, forty are studying English, seventeen Art and Music, so there are presumably about two hundred Science and Social Science students. All students have to do Tibetan Language and Chinese, and the whole University has Political Study on Thursday afternoons and Manual Labour on Saturday afternoons: cleaning up the classrooms, sweeping the campus, etc. There are a few days at the beginning of each term too when everyone goes off to plant trees or put in a spell of work at the university farm.

Our students live in long low barrack-like huts, cement-walled with tin roofs, seven or eight of them to a room. The furnishings are meagre: there is no room for anything but four sets of bunk beds and a table in the centre. Their possessions are confined to an enamel washing bowl, thermos, rice bowl, a few books and a change of clothes. Water must be fetched from the standpipe and the communal pit toilets are a short walk away.

We were very impressed by the Tibetan Arts Department, where lots of *tangka* depicting gods and goddesses were hung in various stages of completion. Tibetan art is, with few exceptions, religious in nature. The Tibetan pantheon is enormous and very complex and Tibetan Buddhism has a bewildering variety of deities, inherited both from Indian tantrism and from the old animistic *Bön* religion, which it incorporated and transformed. The aspiring Tibetan painter must learn to paint Buddhas, bodhisattvas, tantric and protector deities in wrathful and compassionate aspects as well as representations of historical figures and great lamas, mandalas and narrative paintings showing scenes from the life of Buddha or of the great yogis. We watched a class learning to paint Drölma, the green goddess of compassion who is the patron saint of Tibet. They were copying very precisely from a diagram which laid down not only all the elements of the painting, but their exact proportions and position on the canvas. Tibetan art is highly stylized, with a very complex symbolism, and Tibetan artists traditionally painted from visual or very detailed verbal models, which laid down exactly how the deity should be portrayed. Green Drölma, for example, is always portrayed sitting on a lotus flower, her right foot extended and resting on a small lotus. In her hands she must hold two blue lotus blossoms, symbols of compassion. Nothing like creativity in the Western sense of fusing different elements to form new and previously unthought-of combinations. But even working within these precisely defined limits, the artists infuse the paintings with their own feeling and imagination: the students' paintings, though identical in form, were all subtly different. The department also teaches Chinese and Western Art and we were excited by the creative fusion between Western styles and techniques and Tibetan themes and images in many paintings we saw hanging there.

The University does feel a little like a hillbilly cousin of universities in China though; one problem being that the really bright students are creamed off and go to university in China. Another problem is that most of the teachers come from China on short contracts, and this high turnover of staff spells a disastrous lack of continuity and commitment. However, the people at the top seem caring and committed to making it work. It is good to be in on it at this stage, we feel there is an exciting sense of a new venture. However, as soon as something is built in China, it immediately begins to look old. For instance, the main entrance building (where we teach) has an ornamental fountain which is already, after less than a year, rusty and full of junk, the stairways are filthy and chipped, the walls are streaked with grime, the windows are dirty, and rubbish collects in the corners.

It is now 9.15, and we have just rolled back, very merry and very full, after an excellent banquet with all the college top brass, hosted by the President, for Mr Ding and us, the newly-arrived teachers, and for a very ill-looking Chinese official, who is retiring after ten years here and returning to his family in Peking. We had, if I can remember after too much beer, seventeen courses: an array of cold plates to start with, including crystallized pork crackling, spiced duck, egg and meat roll, spiced dried beef with chillies and sesame seeds, cold chicken laid out in the shape of a chicken, with yellow-dyed turnip legs, a fungus neck and a red-dyed head and crest, sugared tomatoes, yak slices, sugared orange slices fried in pork fat, sweet and sour black beef with onions. Then came a delicious fish with shallots, spices and tomatoes, from the Lhasa river; another spicy pork dish; a delicious stew of local fungus in a white sauce; a spicy duck; a chicken in arrowroot; all winding up with a symbolic (for we were too full) bowl of rice, and *momos* which are meat-stuffed dumplings, with a tomato and egg soup. Bloated? This was all washed down with innumerable toasts of beer, which comes all the way from Lanzhou on the backs of trucks and survives the journey admirably. The President is a charming man with twinkling eyes, and it was a very pleasant meal. The Tibetans seem to have a very natural sense of informal fun. While there were plenty of speeches, they were not full of platitudes, but real attempts at communication and friendship — more like a family gathering than a business occasion.

Letter four: **Pillars of the State**

A couple of weeks ago we acquired sturdy Chinese bicycles, a 'Magpie' and a 'Flying Flower', after much haggling in the bike market, since purchase through official channels seemed to be a creakingly slow affair. Since then we have been much more mobile and have ventured further afield to visit some of the temples and monasteries around Lhasa, though strenuous activity is hard at this altitude and at first a ride of any distance would reduce us to gasping and puffing wrecks.

Many of the travellers' tales of old Tibet make the same comment: 'All Tibetan temples are alike,' or 'One Tibetan temple looks very much like another.' Our first impressions were that this was true – all Tibetan temples blended together in our minds into a sort of proto-temple, whose carved pillars and butter-lamps and murals and hangings stood for the pillars and lamps, murals and hangings of all the temples we had visited. I suppose a Tibetan visitor to English churches would find them all alike at first: everywhere the same confusing tangle of saints he could not recognize and symbols whose meaning he could not understand; the motifs of stained glass and stonework, vaulted ceilings, wooden pews, pulpits and altars repeated in church after church.

After a while, with more familiarity, the temples began to come apart from one another in our minds, each distinguished by a particular atmosphere or some oddity or idiosyncrasy peculiar to it alone – a striking statue or a fine mural, a row of painted prayer wheels or a courtyard full of flowers. Nevertheless, there is an archetypal temple standing behind its various manifestations: a massive stone structure, trapezoid in shape, with inward-leaning walls, the lower walls whitewashed, the upper parts made of tightly packed brushwood, claret in colour and decorated with gold ornaments like huge medallions. The building is crowned with curving gold roofs, ornamented with lions' heads and dragons, antelopes and dharma wheel, and curious structures that look like gold chimney pots.

Passing through the gateway, you come into a large square courtyard paved with flagstones. A few dogs lie sprawled asleep in the sunlight, and bright marigolds, hollyhocks, dahlias grow in old tin cans, lining the steps that lead up to the temple entrance. Wooden pillars, painted red and branching at the top into elaborate tendrils and flowers, support a porch over the entrance. On either side of the door into the temple are the temple guardians: sometimes statues, more often murals, always four of them, one for each compass point. Flapping above the porch is a white canvas canopy decorated with blue *appliqué* designs of the eight auspicious symbols. These have become popular symbols of protection and good luck, but their original meaning is the representation of offerings made to Buddha after he gained enlightenment, and each has a symbolic meaning: the parasol symbolizes protection from evil, the conch shell announces enlightenment, the banner is a banner of victory over ignorance, the golden fish stand for spiritual liberation, the vase contains spiritual jewels, the dharma wheel symbolizes the Buddha's teachings, the lotus means purity and compassion, and the endless knot is a symbol of eternal love and harmony.

At either end of the porch is a huge gaily painted prayer wheel, with gaudy patterns of flowers. It requires quite an effort to turn one and set the prayers spinning, but you are rewarded by the ring of a bell as it turns. Behind the prayer wheel, painted on the wall, is another wheel, held by a demon-like god who peers over the top, grasping the wheel in his teeth and claws. This is Yama, the lord of death, and the wheel is the Wheel of Life, the Tibetan vision of the endless round of existence. At the top of the wheel are the gods in a paradisiacal realm of fruit and flowers. Below them, to the left, are the demi-gods. They cultivate a tree which branches upwards into the gods' segment of the wheel where it bears fruit. Opposite the demi-gods is the human world. This looks very busy, peopled with tiny figures going about their daily business of ploughing, sowing and reaping. Below these are two more worlds: the animal world with a population of deer, leopards, lions, horses and mangy discontented dog-like creatures; and the world of the hungry ghosts: strange beings with huge distended bellies and tiny thin necks. They can never eat enough food to fill their stomachs. At the bottom of the wheel is a Bosch-like vision of hell, or rather a variety of hells, cold and hot. One man is being boiled alive in a huge cauldron. Demons with whips pursue a group of terrified naked people. Four or five men are wandering naked in snowy mountains, another is wound up in a tangle of writhing snakes. In the bottom left-hand corner someone is being flayed alive, spread-eagled with all his innards revealed like a frog on the dissecting table. At the centre of the wheel a pig, a snake and a cock chase each other in a circle, symbolizing the greed, hatred and delusion which trap us in the meaningless round of existence.

You enter the temple through a pair of great red doors with elaborate gold hinges and lion's-head door handles worn smooth by rubbing and greasy with butter. Inside is a strange combination of gloom and bright colours. Dazzled by the glare of the afternoon sunshine, your first impression is of total darkness coupled with an overpoweringly cloying, rancid, suffocating smell. That is the smell of yak butter, which has permeated every corner of the temple: silken hangings impregnated with it, a thin patina of grime and grease on walls and statues, the flagstones on the floor smooth as a skating rink.

As your eyes grow accustomed to the gloom, images seem to leap out at you from the darkness, some serene, some horrific. A forest of pillars, branching upwards into the twilight, blossoms into brightly painted curlicues and florets. Between the trunks, as if in some enchanted wood, you catch glimpses of dreamlike or nightmare images. A pot-bellied blue-black god, with sharp fangs and a crown of skulls, leaps and dances against a background of swirling clouds, his hair rising like flames from his face. A dark-blue goddess materializes out of a sea of blood, riding a white horse. The reins are snakes. She is chewing a corpse, whose arms and legs dangle limply from her mouth. Two animal-headed gods dance attendance on her, proffering skulls filled with plucked-out eyes. Dragons swirl in and out of cloudscapes. Further on a multi-headed deity tramples on a pile of bodies which writhe beneath his feet. Flames dance above oceans of blood. A wall full of serene blue-faced Buddhas seem unperturbed by all this activity and look on benignly. Two deities are locked in an embrace: he has three heads and six arms, she has one head and two arms. The arms not involved in the embrace hold snakes; the feet crush the heads of two sprawled out corpses. Next to these scenes of passion and violence, a delicate white goddess with a tranquil smiling expression is seated cross-legged in the centre of a flowering lotus which rises out of a milky lake. Monks drift through the heavens on clouds, reading or meditating. Paradisiacal visions of lush green mountains, waterfalls and rivers, flowering gardens, fantastically coloured trees laden with fruit, domed and turreted cities floating among the clouds alternate with the frenzied oceans of fire and blood. Oddly domestic and homely details from the life of Buddha or various bodhisattvas float between these visions of heaven and hell: two men sleep in a courtyard under a tree, a woman welcomes a visitor at the door of her house, a group of horsemen ride towards a village, a house with one side removed, like a room in a stage set, contains two women cooking and one sewing. In another house a banquet is going on. Further on, a boat sails out of a calm lake into a maelstrom of clouds and the nightmare begins again: two birds of prey hold human organs in their beaks, others peck at living bodies as they writhe in torment on the ground, skeletons dance in and out of licking flames.

Wandering around a Tibetan temple is a combination of hallucinatory dream, a ride on a fairground ghost train and Dante's tour of hell. Nothing like our peaceful, composed and harmonious English churches. I wonder if a Tibetan visitor would find these too composed, too complacent? Tibetan temples seem designed to knock you out of your complacency, to question the basis for it. I find them a deeply disturbing experience. An English church is an intellectual experience compared with the assault on your subconscious delivered by a Tibetan temple. As we learn more about temple art and Tibetan Buddhism, we can recognize more of the images and statues and understand their significance and symbolism. But I feel my first visits, when I was totally disorientated, bombarded by images and cut adrift from the familiar, were more profound than what I now experience: an intellectual understanding, the vaguely comforting feeling of recognition, of being able to put a label on things.

Since last writing, we have been to three great monasteries outside Lhasa: Sera, Drepung and Ganden. The first two of these are within cycling distance, located to the north and west of Lhasa: Drepung scattered over a sunny hillside, approached through an almost Italian landscape of scorched earth, shrubs and small twisted pale green thorn trees; Sera more gloomily located in the north of the valley, at the foot of a barren mountain, and reached along an arrow-straight road lined on either side by a wasteland of tin-roofed houses, concrete low-rise blocks, army barracks and rubbish dumps.

Both monasteries were established in the early fifteenth century by disciples of the great reformer Tsongkhapa, who founded the Geluk or 'Yellow Hat' sect of Tibetan Buddhism: a new order offering a strict monastic discipline with an emphasis on austerity and simplicity. Successors of Tsongkhapa became recognized retrospectively as the first and second Dalai Lamas, and by the time of the Great Fifth Dalai Lama, who built the Potala in the seventeenth century, spiritual and temporal power had become united and the Gelukpas were the politically dominant sect, responsible for the training and education of each new young Dalai Lama. The regents who ruled Tibet during the interregnum between the death of the old Dalai Lama and the coming of age of his reincarnation were always Gelukpa and so too were the monk-officials who formed the government together with the aristocracy. Special power was consolidated in Sera, Drepung and Ganden, the three 'Pillars of the State', who dominated the administration of the government, claiming special privileges for themselves.

These monasteries were great centres of learning, like huge universities, though we were surprised to learn that not all the monks became scholars. There was a division between scholar monks and lay monks. The lay monks did the more menial tasks, such as cooking and farming as well as attending services; the scholars would spend up to fifteen or twenty years studying before taking their *geshe*, or doctoral examinations, in the form of oral debates. Sera and Drepung also had 'warrior monks' known as *dobdobs*. These sound almost like modern gangs or semi-tribal youth groups like skinheads or Hell's Angels. These young monks adopted a particular hairstyle, shaven on top with long hair at the sides, like reverse punks. They were known for their reckless and wild behaviour. Feuds, fights and vendettas would often develop between rival groups and at the Great Prayer ceremony at New Year they were let loose to rule the city with whips and clubs.

In the days when every family sent at least one son to the monkhood, these great monasteries were like small towns, with between 5,000 and 8,000 monks apiece. The total number of monks was estimated at around a quarter of the male population. Nowadays there are about 400 monks in each of the great monasteries, and as you wander around the deserted streets, cross empty sunlit courtyards where a few dogs sprawl out asleep on the flagstones, and enter the dark temples where pilgrims are praying in the shadows or fuelling butter-lamps, you can only imagine what it must have been like when the place was filled with a bustle of activity and humming with intrigue.

Drepung always seems sleepy and deserted; it reminds me of an Italian or Spanish village at siesta time – sun beating down from a blank blue sky, whitewashed walls reflecting the glare, narrow streets winding upwards between high walls. In one temple an old monk is chanting solitary prayers, rapidly turning the leaves of his prayerbook. Bees hum outside; their sound is mixed with the low drone of prayers and it is difficult to tell which is which.

Sera seems livelier – a higher proportion of young monks, who have noisy and spirited debates out in a courtyard under the trees in the afternoons. This is a traditional method of philosophical enquiry: trying out what has been learnt in the classes. It is wonderful to watch: the younger monks will take it in turns to sit cross-legged on the ground and reply, or to stand and deliver the questions, physically launching them through the air by stamping and clapping their hands, twisting their rosaries as they do so.

In both places, however, the ghosts far outnumber the living. And further up behind Drepung there are other more sinister ghosts, where ruins of temples scar the hillside – evidence of destruction not yet tidied up for posterity or the tourist: crumbling walls of courtyards and the blind stare of gutted buildings.

Further down the hill another temple, Nechung, is still in the state of desecration it was left in by the Cultural Revolution, though repair work is going on in an inner courtyard. Outside are mutilated and blackened murals, eyes and faces gouged out, 1966 copies of *Tibet Daily* pasted up over the pictures, blackened and blistered paintwork. This temple was famous for the State Oracle, who was consulted on all important matters of government. His prophecies were given in a trance-like state, with bulging eyes and swollen face, his tongue lolling out: the mumbled and disjointed words would be noted down and interpreted by monks.

But the most shocking sight is Ganden. We went there last week with two visiting American geographers. We had been there last year on the back of a truck together with about fifty Tibetan pilgrims, but this second visit was a lot more comfortable – and quicker too. Ganden is about fifty miles east of Lhasa, a huge monastery in a spectacular position on the top of a steep ridge, which curves round, forming a bowl, facing away from the main river valley. There are wonderful views, scenic and strategic, stretching for scores of miles in each direction. Range after range of bare brown peaks flow like waves into the distance, a broad valley lies below, bright with the blue of the river, lined with pastel green willows, and the gold of the barley fields stretching on either side.

During the fighting in 1959 the monastery was bombarded and the destruction was completed during the 1960s. Not a roof beam nor a wall was left intact, and our first horrified reaction to the ruins was that the monastery must have been bombed from the air, so total was the devastation. We later learnt that after the buildings had been dynamited, pickaxes and sledge hammers were used and most of the wooden beams, planks and pillars were taken down into the valley to be used for building elsewhere. It now looks like Warsaw at the end of the Second World War, really a most terrible, saddening sight. But monasteries can be rebuilt; cut-off heads, as Chairman Mao himself observed, do not grow back again. The most terrible thing is not the ruins themselves, but the violence and the hatred that must have accompanied the destruction.

Rebuilding of the monastery apparently began in 1982 on the initiative of the Tibetans, who claim that the truck the local people bought to transport materials up the mountainside was the 'first privately owned vehicle in Tibet'. When we last came here, seven or eight buildings had been reconstructed, now about ten are complete. At this rate history will have been rebuilt in another twenty years.

Ganden today is a blend of past nightmares and future dreams. Here, as elsewhere, the pride of the teenage Tibetans, who are carving wood, moulding clay, painting murals and rebuilding walls and roofs using all the traditional materials and techniques, is wonderful to see. They seize you by the hand and pull you along to see their work. They are learning the old crafts and performing an act of worship at the same time. One of the nicest things about our recent visit was our reception by the monks. We were received very kindly, given butter tea and shown round with great pride. There was a lovely feeling of optimism amid the dust and the banging and the hammering, and we felt a hint that despite the years of past misery something of the old Tibet had survived and was pushing up new shoots.

Our strongest memory, apart from the magnificent views and the birds of prey swooping over the valley, is of the three peasant boys who came to look at us while we were having a picnic above the ruins. I showed them our guidebook, full of beautiful colour photographs from all over Tibet. The boys clawed and pawed their way through the pages with a look of wonder on their faces. I would point north or south or say 'Sakya' or 'Gyantse' – places they had heard of but never seen. When I came to the photo of Ganden, they shook their heads and tut-tutted. Then I suddenly remembered that in my rucksack I had brought a copy of an old black and white photograph of an intact Ganden, taken in the late 1940s. When they saw that they just looked dumbfounded and very sad. They took the photo and pointed out to each other what had been rebuilt and what was still in ruins, then pointed to the real buildings and the real ruins on the hillside below us. It was an amazing moment: the forty-year-old photograph, the ruins, the reconstructions, all in the same positions as on the photograph, and these three young Tibetans, too young ever to have seen the real Ganden, making contact with their past through a photograph.

The trip to Ganden was our own planning and we went with a charming Tibetan driver who had brought along his three children on a pilgrimage round all the temples, bearing jars of butter to pour into the lamps as offerings. We asked our 'leader', who has lived in Tibet for ten years, if he had ever been to Ganden. No! It's only fifty miles away, but none of the Chinese we have met so far have ever been. Most of them stay in their secure work units in an almost entirely Chinese atmosphere. I don't know whether they are just not interested or whether they are officially discouraged.

It is difficult for us to gauge what 'religious freedom' means in China today, let alone in Tibet. The Chinese constitution prom- ises freedom to hold and to practise, although not to 'propagate', religious faith. In practice this seems to mean that personal belief is permitted, as is the study of Buddhism within monasteries and special colleges. Religion may not, however, be taught in schools, and missionary activity is not permitted. Party members are not supposed to hold a religious belief either, but it seems that this rule is not strictly applied in the case of Tibet, where, like the Panchen Lama, people often describe themselves as Marxist-Buddhists. We are always very impressed and moved by the people's devotion. Religion seems to play a vital part in everyone's life, whether they be young or old. Things are surely much better than they were five years ago and incomparably better than ten or fifteen years ago when, at the height of the Cultural Revolution (or should one say the depths?), Tibetans were forbidden to practise their religion, monks forced to renounce their faith, and all the holy sites desecrated, if not destroyed completely.

On the personal level, religious activity seems strong. People can once again feel free to practise their religion without fear. Crowds of pilgrims, once restricted from travelling freely, now flock into Lhasa to circumambulate the Lingkor, the Barkor and to visit all the holy places. All the temples we have seen have been busy with monks and ordinary people praying, making offerings or engaged in building work, and families are again allowed to have altars or small chapels in their homes.

However, one of the most important features of Tibetan Buddhism is the monastic tradition, which ensures that teaching and learning take place, so that fundamental knowledge of the scriptures can be passed down through the generations. The practice of families giving one son to the monkhood was stamped out during the Cultural Revolution but now young monks are once more being 'donated' in this way, albeit on a far more limited scale. The monasteries are again functioning even in their half-built state. But many of the great teachers have died, were killed in the Cultural Revolution, have fled into exile, or were forced to return to the laity. So obviously the quality and extent of current teaching has suffered. Looking around the monasteries today, you can see plenty of young monks and a scattering of very old ones – the middle generation is missing. Learning has had to jump a generation, like a spark across a gap. But an attempt is being made to re-establish the distinctive teaching and learning traditions in the various monasteries, though whether this is encouraged by or in spite of the authorities we don't know. A Tibetan Buddhist College has been set up near Nechung, where a hundred or so monks from all over Tibet will spend up to ten years in study of

Buddhist texts and philosophy, though, as this is a State college, the content of their studies will be subject to State control. The learning is still there – just, but there is not much time left for it to be transmitted. The most sensible thing of course would be for monks to return from exile, where the traditions have been kept alive, but unless relations improve between the Chinese and the Tibetan exiles, this is not likely to happen to any great extent.

At least all these three monasteries have a sense of life, of a working community: the Potala in contrast seems empty, lifeless. We have visited it a number of times and of course see its bulk looming over the town every day. I can never get used to it; I always feel a shock of surprise when I look up while walking along the street or cycling home from shopping and see it there above me. A visit always leaves us gasping, overwhelmed by impressions, and it is hard to make sense of all the countless different tiny details which seem to jostle each other for attention. At times, the details seem to merge and fade into a rich blur of impressions, and you are left with a sense of the building as a whole, a rhythm of movement backwards and forwards, from inner to outer, from room to courtyard, from chapel to rooftop terrace: a constant interplay of simplicity and complication, of dark and light, as you move from gloomy rooms to the dazzle of afternoon sun on white walls in a courtyard, or from the clear outlines and pure colours of gold roofs against a bright blue sky, to the clutter and jumble of brocade hangings, gold statuettes, swirling murals, carved wood, thrones, butter-lamps, pelmets, tassels, portraits, cupboards, carpets, porcelain vases, curtains, painted tables, butter-sculptures, mandalas, books . . . an inner profusion, then outside again to space and silence, from the simple geometry of courtyard walls, doors and windows, back again to an interior which is all whorls and swirls and curlicues.

At other times, your sense of wholeness is drowned in a welter of small perceptions and you find your mind flickering on and off between a thousand bewildering unrelated details, as you move through the maze of interlocking rooms, like a castle in a dream. Corridors, courtyards, galleries, rooms leading out of rooms, staircases going nowhere or ending in a locked door. Objects seem to leap out of the gloom to claim your attention then fade back again as another detail comes forward to take their place. A glass case full of gilded and dressed-up statues. A row of butter-lamps, giving off a fierce heat and a strong rich smell. A vase of plastic flowers. Offerings of tea bricks, *katag*, money, bowls of water, sweets, fruit, *tsampa* cakes. A mandala like a huge doll's house. A many-armed statue of Chenrezi with a pyramid of heads. Patchwork hangings. A huge gold prayer wheel. Beside it, a shelf with a small alarm clock, an electric fan and a kettle. The *hmm hmm hmm* of hummed prayers. A waft of old sheepskin and unwashed bodies as a group of pilgrims shuffles past. A strip of material where people have pinned safety pins and needles, as offerings to sharpen their wits. A gold lion's head with the beard rubbed smooth where people have stroked it. Carved and painted pillars. A mural of the religious landscape of Tibet showing all the main monasteries, with Samye and its 108 temples at the centre. Couches. Beds. Thrones. A monk dispensing holy water, saffron-coloured, from a battered kettle: the pilgrims receive it in cupped hands, drink a little and sprinkle the remaining drops on their heads. A lion with a mouthful of coins and a bell to ring, hanging from his beard. A wallful of Buddhas, the same image repeated over and over again. Stones bearing the impression of the Dalai Lama's footprints. Yellow-hatted statues.

Your companion brings more details to your attention: 'This is Atisha.' 'This is Padmasambhava.' 'Here is the sixth Dalai Lama's room.' 'This is the Dalai Lama's handprint.' Downstairs now, to a vast silent hall, acres of stone floor, wooden pillars like a gloomy forest, and on into a long gallery of enormous pagoda-tombs, elaborate gold and silver work studded with jewels; their pinnacles stretch up into the darkness over our heads. The gloom, the cold and the powerful atmosphere make me shiver. Despite the confusion, the plethora of objects, the Potala is a strangely empty place: it has no heart, the life has gone out of it. It is an eerie silent museum.

I emerge into the bright sunlight, like a diver coming up for air. My student is waiting for me, sitting on a low wall. I join him and we look up above us to where the sun bounces off the golden roofs. A smile lights up his face, and he seems to wriggle with pleasure. 'What are you thinking?' I ask him, amused. 'I am proud of it,' he says simply.

Letter five: **Lhasa Today**

Lhasa society is very complex and not really representative of the rest of Tibet. Or rather it is representative in a way that makes it totally unlike anywhere else in the country. I suppose that all capital cities both stand for and stand apart from the culture they represent.

In the Tibetan countryside there is a sense of timelessness: people go on living according to the rhythms of the day and of the seasons, sowing, ploughing, harvesting in the traditional ways. Despite the enormous changes in the social structure that transformed the Feudal System into the Commune System and then into the Responsibility System, the essential features of life in the Tibetan countryside seem to have survived all the -isms imposed on it and, further out on the remote plateau, the nomads live in a way that eludes systems altogether.

It is in Lhasa that different lifestyles and cultures and periods of history are brought together, sometimes fused, sometimes in conflict. Some anachronisms and relics from the old society are still surprisingly intact, other strange hybrids have grown out of the mix of cultures: Tibetan, Chinese and now, increasingly, Western. Sometimes in Lhasa I feel I am in a medieval marketplace or on a stage set for a Shakespeare play, sometimes in the post-war austerity of the 40s or 50s, sometimes in some grimly Orwellian vision of the future. So, monks and nuns in their flapping red robes, pilgrims from the north in long sheepskins and felt boots, hair richly decorated with coral and turquoise jewellery, Khampas from east Tibet with daggers and red hair tassels, all rub shoulders in the marketplace with Tibetan cadres in Mao jackets and baggy

Chinese trousers or young Tibetans in tight blue jeans and leather jackets. Old ladies in the Barkor can't, or won't, speak Chinese. Many of our young students cannot write their own language, Tibetan. Primary school children coming home from school have slates tied to their backs filled with laboriously copied Tibetan letters. Our new university has a roomful of brand-new computers, scarcely ever used. Shopkeepers in the dingy department stores will tot up your purchases on an abacus, stallholders squatting by the roadside will conduct their side of the bargaining on electronic calculators. Old women shuffle along counting rosaries, young girls teeter past on high heels, mouths daubed with lipstick; old men whirl prayer wheels, young men saunter along carting enormous cassette players. Tibetan music mingles with Hong Kong or Shanghai pop, Madonna and Boney M, and Indian film music from every street corner. Stalls sell Tibetan antiques, tinned goods from China, blue jeans, cheap jewellery, cosmetics and pirated cassettes from India. Restaurants serve *momos*, curry, noodles, sweet and sour pork. One indication of the cultural mix in Lhasa is the variety of tea available: Tibetan butter tea, sweet milky Indian tea, Chinese tea – green leaves floating in a glass of hot water, delicious Muslim tea made in a porcelain bowl with rock sugar and dragon's eye berries.

Lhasa society is so complex because it is divided up in a number of different ways – racially, for a start. The most apparent division is that between the Tibetans and the Chinese. But there are other racial groups living in Lhasa too, who retain their own distinctive lifestyles: the Nepalese and the Muslims. Both have been resident in Lhasa for centuries. The Nepalese are mainly traders and shopkeepers, owning many of the most prosperous shops around the Barkor. The Muslims are mainly butchers and restaurant owners. Tibetans are forbidden by their religion to kill, but because of the barrenness of the land they have found it impossible to survive without eating meat, so the Muslims have traditionally done the job of killing the animals for them. Nowadays many more Moslems are coming into Lhasa from other parts of China, attracted by the new prosperity and the relaxation of restrictions on trade. Their focal point is the mosque and the area around it, in the south-west part of the old town.

There is also the distinction between those resident in Lhasa and those visiting. As a holy city, Lhasa attracts large numbers of pilgrims, those numbers swelling at religious festivals. Nomads from the Chang Tang plateau, peasants from Chamdo or north-east Tibet will camp out in tents along the river and outskirts of the town, moving on after a few days or weeks to be replaced by others making the once-in-a-lifetime pilgrimage to the holy city. Lhasa also attracts other pilgrims of a less religious kind: the sort who drift in from the countryside to the town in any Third World country, in search of the opportunities and attractions offered by big city life. Most of these urban drifters remain on the fringes of society, many of them can be found peddling goods in the marketplace or scraping a living through various underhand trans-actions.

But basically Lhasa society is formed by the collision of two different social systems, the one modifying but not completely replacing the other – like the impact of two massive geological plates, so that the strata are not merely horizontal, but vertical and diagonal as well. Like a geological fault, this social fault also feels profoundly unstable. On the surface, the division of labour is according to the clear-cut Chinese categories of cadre, worker, peasant and intellectual. But cutting across this and jumbled up with it are the old Tibetan categories of noble, monk, peasant, trader, nomad, beggar. There are workers, cooks and shop-keepers, who used to be monks or serfs; cadres and intellectuals who used to be landed gentry, the old nobility; and traders, beggars and peasants, who have always been what they are today.

It amazes me how intact the nobility still is, and what status its members hold, though their ranks must be decimated by those who either died in the Cultural Revolution or who fled to India. Stripped of their estates, their money and most of their possessions after 1959, they are now no longer landed gentry, although there has been some official restoration of depleted assets. Many of them now hold influential positions in government or education, and there is still to some extent the feeling that Lhasa consists of twenty or thirty families who are all interconnected and interrelated. Several times I have been taken aback to find that two people I have known separately for a time are in fact cousins, or, when meeting a family, to observe that every member holds a high position. But on reflection, I suppose it is not all that surprising: education broke down so completely in the Cultural Revolution that in the early 1980s, when some effort was made to replace Chinese government officials with Tibetan ones, the only people left with any education must have been the old nobility, now restored from degradation and dishonour, and in many cases newly released from years in prison.

In addition to these two monolithic systems, both now in process of decay, there is a third source of confusion, a new social class that belongs to Deng's China, not Mao's: the entrepreneurs, the small businessmen, the restaurant and hotel owners, the small shopkeepers and stallholders. With the introduction, more or less simultaneously, of the Responsibility System and the opening of Tibet to tourists, these small private enterprises have been mushrooming. Our photographs taken in 1985 shortly after Tibet was opened to tourists, show a Barkor that is, in comparison to the one today, almost bare of stalls and street peddlars. Three or four new guesthouses have opened up and a cluster of little restaurants, some Chinese-owned, some Tibetan-owned, have sprung up along the main street. Most of these are little one-room shacks with a curtained-off kitchen area, but they boast menus in English and imaginative and entertaining English names such as 'AT THE SKY (FOOD FROM THE HEAVENS: YUMMY AND DELICIOUS)'. My favourite has the vaguely alluring but non-committal title of 'WELCOME YOU, MAYBE FINE'.

The pavements of the main street and the streets around the Barkor are crowded now with people offering their services: watchmenders, dentists, bicycle repairers, cobblers, tailors – all with the tools of their trade laid out on the pavement or arranged on a table in front of them. Dozens of small shops have opened up around the Barkor, along the main shopping street or on the new plaza. These vary from the spacious and well-stocked to others that are barely more than cupboards opening onto the street. Some shopkeepers are apparently adhering unswervingly to Deng's dictum, 'It is glorious to get rich.' Others have so few goods and appear to do so little trade amongst so much competition, that I wonder how their owners survive.

The loosening-up of the social system is also creating an underclass: those who have no work and those who are involved in shady deals of various kinds. Lhasa has always been full of beggars. There are fewer professional beggars now than in the old days, but there are still faces you see every day and come to recognize: the three children sitting in a row with their begging bowls in the middle of the Barkor; the young man stripped bare to the waist crouched in an attitude of abasement, arms outstretched in front of him, waiting for alms; the woman and her children who scour the restaurants at lunchtime, finishing up the scraps that Western tourists have left uneaten; the two young boys who go round from door to door collecting empty bottles for the few *fen* they will receive on each; the old woman who begs in teahouses and restaurants, pushing past the tables and accompanied by a sheep on a lead.

Other non-workers form a recognizable class of their own, as they do in China, where they are called 'those waiting for work'. These disaffected young men, streetwise, cynical, bored out of their heads, are a new social problem in China as well as Tibet. But here there is an extra dimension to the problem: many of the skilled and semi-skilled manual jobs are given to workers coming in from China. Employers prefer them, apparently, because they are 'better educated, better trained and harder-working'. In the case of drivers, for example, employers will often prefer to employ a Sichuanese or someone from Gansu to drive lorries going east or north out of Tibet, because they will have *guanxi* (potentially helpful contacts) in their homeland. This must lead to a lot of bitterness. China promised Tibet that over a period of time Chinese cadres would be sent home and Tibetans trained to take their places and, as far as we can judge, this really does seem to be happening, albeit slowly. But there is still a lot of immigration at the lower end of the social scale – whether official or not, I can't say. Quite a few of the new immigrants seem to be Sichuanese on the make, who have come into Lhasa on their own initiative to see what opportunities the tourist boom can offer them. But I can imagine that it must put something of a strain on Chinese-Tibetan relations for the young Tibetan men to see newly-arrived Chinese getting jobs, while they remain unemployed. Most of these lads seem to do nothing more harmful than sit around in teahouses for much of the day, smoking and looking bored, but many of them drink, get aggressive and get into fights. You see a lot of fights in Lhasa: fist fights, rock fights, knife fights. I don't think I have ever lived in a place where I have seen so much brawling and quarrelling. There must be unemployed girls too, but they are not so visible: girls don't as a rule frequent teahouses, and they don't hang around on street corners or get drunk or fight.

Morale among these kids is low and some parents are worried that contact with the West in the shape of the Kathmandu hippies, who seem to have found a new haven in Lhasa, may add a drug problem to the drink problem that already exists. Certainly, these young people seem to be turning their backs not only on maoist values, but also on traditional Tibetan values, and are adopting Western clothes, Western music, Western fashions. When I asked why Tibetan young people no longer wore Tibetan dress, the answer was, 'We would feel ashamed.' Partly, I think, because the Chinese sneered at Tibetan dress for so long, but also perhaps because Western tourists have made them self-conscious: being a Tibetan in traditional dress on the Barkor in August must be a bit like being a panda in a zoo. But the main reason is because it's not modern, not fashionable. 'You should be proud of your culture and traditions,' I said, but I felt a kind of hopelessness as I said it. Lhasa seems to me to be poised on top of that slippery slope already descended by so many other countries: the rush into Westernization, the adoption of all the most superficial and least attractive aspects of our culture. How sad and how terrible, was my first reaction. Having managed to survive twenty years of repression, surely Tibetan culture can do without this anodyne Westernization?

But maybe that's sentimentality. Tibetan culture seems so fragile, that one's natural impulse is protective. But cultures can't be fossilized for ever, they must grow and develop if they are to survive and not stagnate; stagnation, after all, was one of the problems of the old Tibet. I just wish that Asian societies could find their own way of developing: one that did not involve turning away from their culture and aping the West. Pop music and trendy clothes are superficial and harmless enough and, talking to my students, I realize what they symbolize: a sense of connection with the outside world after so many years of isolation, a badge of solidarity with other young people of whatever nationality, not specifically Chinese or Tibetan.

Western influences are, however, offering the possibility of worse forms of corruption than just disco and blue jeans. Last year in Lhasa there was a rash of little video-teahouses, advertizing mainly kung-fu and Hindi movies. This year they have all disappeared. I asked a friend why. 'Oh,' he said, looking rather embarrassed, 'the Public Security closed them all.' 'Why?' I asked. 'Well,' he said reluctantly, 'the board outside the teahouse would advertise a kung-fu film, but when you went in there would only be ten minutes of kung-fu.' 'And then?' I prompted. His face had gone pink. 'Well then . . .,' he said, 'a . . . er . . . Swedish film.'

Some of the young unemployed are turning to various forms of petty crime, often connected with the tourist trade. Changing money on the black market goes on quite openly on the streets around the Barkor. The current rate is 140 *yuan* in *renminbi*, or 'People's Money', for 100 *yuan* in *waihui*, or Foreign Exchange Certificates, which are convertible to hard currency. It is actually illegal for ordinary Chinese citizens to possess this currency, but it is impossible to obtain certain imported goods such as Japanese televisions, fridges and cassette players without it, hence its enhanced value.

Others are involved in selling antiques and artefacts, or smuggling them into Nepal. Again, it is illegal to export antiques from

China. This seems ironic when so much energy was expended during the Cultural Revolution on destroying them, but China has belatedly woken up to the fact that it no longer has very much of beauty, antiquity or value left and wants to preserve what it has. When we were in Nepal we were horrified to see how many shops there were selling Tibetan antiques. There are many traders, Nepali and Western, who come into Lhasa on 'shopping expeditions' for the sole purpose of buying antiques and works of art and arranging various complicated procedures for smuggling them over the border. These traders, not content with what they can obtain on the stalls on the Barkor, walk into people's houses and offer what are, to the Tibetans, astronomical prices for family heirlooms: the living-room carpet or grandmother's teapot. How can they refuse? But soon there will be a Tibet denuded of even those familiar and well-loved objects that survived the Red Guards' raids.

Tourism is changing the face of Lhasa, which is becoming more and more Westernized, not in a glossy hi-tech way like Bangkok or Singapore or even, increasingly, Peking, but in an alternative 'World-Traveller' adventurer style. I imagine Kathmandu must have been rather like this in the early stages, and wonder if Lhasa in ten years' time will be another Kathmandu, full of pizza parlours, vegetarian restaurants, cakeshops offering brownies and lemon meringue pie, native crafts adapted to Western tastes, plus all the tourist subculture of drug dealers, dopeheads and black marketeers. There is already one restaurant offering yakburgers and another which promises, but never quite seems to achieve, ratatouille, pancakes and toast. The trouble is that the cook and his wife have not got their supply and demand economics fully worked out and keep forgetting to buy provisions. All we have ever managed to obtain there are noodles and sweet tea. I somehow hope it stays like that.

These travellers claim to want more direct and real experience of a country than that offered by the sterile environment of luxury hotels, so why can't they eat *tsampa* and *momos* instead of demanding lentilburgers and lasagne? Their influence is changing the face of Lhasa much more than that of the affluent West Germans, Japanese or Americans who never really leave their sanitized bubble of luxury hotel and Japanese minibus. They are also putting the food prices up. Shopping in the Barkor, the trader from whom I usually buy eggs suddenly demanded what amounted to a thirty per cent increase. I tried to bargain, and then to buy my eggs elsewhere, but all the other egg-men had formed a syndicate and had put their prices up too. Lhasa is heavily dependent on food supplies and other essentials trucked in from China, and in the tourist season shortages develop while everyone waits for the next truck of candles or tinned fish to arrive.

I suppose all this carping is a kind of cultural Luddism on my part. The tourist boom is bringing increased employment, increased prosperity, and is a window on the world, an end to the frightening isolation of the last thirty-five years. It just seems a pity that travellers cannot experience another culture without changing it in the process. Deep down, attitudes and values remain undisturbed and most Lhasa residents go about their business without really noticing the tourists; the changes are only skin-deep. But skin is the first thing you see, and there's such a lot of it!

Letter six: **Washing Festival**

This week you should all be getting together with your families or friends, taking a tent, a picnic and all your dirty washing and going down to the nearest riverbank for a dip. That's what everyone in Lhasa is doing anyway. This week is called 'Washing Festival' and the riverbanks are crowded with people scrubbing clothes in the river or spreading them out on the stones to dry, then stripping off and wading into the river, soap in hand, or pitching tents and preparing picnics, passing round the *chang* and getting very drunk. No one seems to be in the least prudish about taking all their clothes off and wading into the river completely naked, though most do this where they are not too visible to stray passers-by on the bank, and I got very cross with a group of smirking PLA men out for an evening stroll and a good ogle at the women. Everyone is supposed to go and wash at least once this week, preferably by moonlight, to ensure good health all winter: a sort of 'Autumn Cleansing'. It is really the last chance to bathe before the cold weather starts in earnest.

The date of the festival depends on the appearance at dawn of a special star, which is believed to be a kind of saint who passes most of his time in meditation but who appears at this time to give his blessing and sanctify the waters. The waters thus have the power to cleanse people of their sins and to ensure good health. In the old days the festival lasted about two weeks, with hundreds of tents pitched down by the river and picnicking and merrymaking going on all day. These days the festivities have to be fitted in around work schedules, but there were still a fair number of tents and picnickers along the riverbanks and on Robbers' Island.

This week also saw a festival of a more socialist nature: 'Teachers' Day'. This was, apparently, inaugurated last year. Every teacher in Lhasa got the day off work (presumably the students did too!) and trooped over to the Norbulingka for a mass picnic. Now a picnic is usually the Tibetan idea of a fun day out, but this was a State occasion and, rather as the Tibetan folk dances we saw at Yoghurt Festival had been neutered by their transformation into State-approved art (folk art becomes People's Art which is not at all the same thing), so the chaotic, jolly, boozy Tibetan picnic had become ossified into a rather formal and less spontaneous occasion.

All over the woods behind the Norbulingka, various schools and institutions were putting up their special tents and canopies, white canvas decorated with *appliqué* designs: blue endless knots, brightly coloured flowers, dragons and lions. The most elaborate and biggest of these housed several officials and other bigwigs, all seated neatly in rows around a central table where butter and scarves and various other offerings were placed (to the god of education?). At one end of the tent various important personages got up one after the other and droned on interminably into microphones. Speech followed speech, while outside the tent a queue of schoolchildren in Tibetan dress fidgeted in the hot sun, waiting to give white scarves to the important figures. The Governor of Tibet, a member of the Yi people from south-west China, very smart with swept back grey hair and tightly buttoned cadre's suit, strode around exchanging pleasantries with various groups. His bodyguards followed a few paces behind. Elsewhere, things were more convivial: groups were rigging up canopies in the trees, spreading out blankets on the ground and getting out the food, heating up butter tea on small stoves, fiddling with huge cassette players (this picnic was Westernized as well as Sinicized) and playing chess, cards and *karom*, a Tibetan version of shove ha'penny.

Everyone had set off from the University at about ten in the morning, packed into the backs of lorries. The University has several of these, used for bringing in essential supplies of rice, kerosene, watermelons and other necessities unobtainable in Tibet. (The other day we were issued with thirty kilos of watermelons from Xinjiang. When we said we couldn't possibly eat so many, they just looked puzzled and said, 'That's your allocation.' Fifteen kilos for each teacher in the University! Now every time we visit anyone on campus we know in advance what we shall be offered to eat.) Well, about five lorryloads of festive professors and other teaching staff left the University, but, once in the Norbulingka, everyone dispersed to their own departmental tent or canopy. We had a rather institutional picnic: all university staff had been issued with a standard lunch pre-packed in a plastic bag: two buns, two hard boiled eggs, some dried meat and a lump of sponge cake. The Tibetan picnics looked rather jollier: people were busy building cooking fires, passing around jerrycans of *chang* and unloading various home-cooked delicacies in little tin pots.

We played a few games of chess and cards, then wandered around to check up on what was going on elsewhere. The important people in the big tent had all made their speeches, the children had presented their scarves and now two women were pouring *chang* into a big silver bowl on the offering table as a sort of libation. Then a microphone was produced and tested out with a lot of crackling and whistling and someone stepped forward and began crooning a Hong Kong pop song. The officials continued to look bored and to sip tea. The crooner was replaced first by a group of schoolchildren who performed a folk dance in Yoghurt Festival style and then by another singer. Elsewhere, picnickers were cooking up pots of stew, passing round plates of pickled cabbage and curried potatoes and *tsampa* cakes, and getting high on *chang*.

Wandering around, we made an interesting discovery: the wrecks of the Dalai Lama's cars: two baby Austin Sevens, half hidden by the long grass and weeds in an inconspicuous corner of the park. Brought from India in the 1930s, they belonged to the thirteenth Dalai Lama. They must have been carried in pieces on porters' and yaks' backs over the Himalayas, since no roads existed then in Tibet. Harrer mentions them in *Seven Years in Tibet*. As a young boy, the Dalai Lama used to play with them and drive them around: he once broke one of the headlights and, terrified of his tutor, mended it with melted sugar. Now after decades of rust and revolution, they are quietly rotting away, unnoticed.

We returned to our departmental tent where one or two people were unwrapping their buns and boiled eggs. Then a crate of beer materialized, which began to liven things up somewhat. We had to leave to visit a friend at about four, but the picnic continued on into the evening and it was not until about ten o'clock that five lorries full of singing and giggling people lurched back through the campus gates. It was a very interesting occasion really: almost the reverse of Yoghurt Festival, which was a Tibetan festival in socialist style. This was a socialist festival celebrated in a Tibetan way, though with all the trappings of communist officialdom: speeches, entertainments and mass organization. It also seemed a compromise between the Tibetan way of having fun, which is basically to relax with good food and a lot of drink and to let things happen, and the Chinese way, which is to structure the occasion more tightly. Most Chinese celebrations we have been to, whether dinners or parties, have been quite formal affairs, with chairs arranged in polite rows and every minute of the proceedings filled with either speeches or prepared 'performances'.

The 'Mid-Autumn Moon Festival' party we went to this week was a typically Chinese occasion, with chairs and tables arranged in a square, everyone sitting in place, with glasses of tea, sweets and melon seeds, and a series of songs, *erhu* recitals and dances performed by the students, all introduced by a compere with a microphone. At their best, these occasions are very charming, something like a Victorian evening, with everyone doing their 'turn', having to be coaxed out, blushing and protesting, in front of the audience – a reminder of days the West has forgotten, when people had to make their own entertainment. At their worst, they can be cold and formal, with ritual suppressing spontaneity and getting in the way of real communication.

Nothing formal though about a Tibetan picnic! We have been invited to a few of these since arriving – real ones, not State occasions. Picnics go on all day, and sometimes for three or four days! It has taken us some time to adjust to the time scale. The essential ingredients of a Tibetan picnic are: a tent (these are really works of art, made of white canvas with beautiful and elaborate *appliqué* work of dragons, lions and flowers), small painted wooden tables to sit around, lots of little cooking pots, butter tea, *chang*, various board games, a large cassette player (a modern addition) and – the most important item of all – time. Apart from an initial flurry of preparation putting up the tent and some heightened activity round about meal times, nothing very much happens, and the minutes, hours and eventually the days seem to flow into one another. There is a constant flow of liquid: tea, beer or *chang,* depending to some extent, but not absolutely, on the time of day. People will sit and play the games: there is one like dominoes, there is *karom*, played with counters on a large square board with pockets like a portable billiard table, mah-jong, card games and a game with dice shaken in a leather cup. People drift in and out of conversations. No one seems to talk about anything much; it is enough to be there in the sun with your glass of tea or *chang* and other people all around you. People seem to relax in each other's company very naturally without feeling the need for bright social conversation as we do in the West. With our restless and fidgety Western ways, we at first found this hard to get used to: I sat around wondering when something was going to happen, when people were going to do something, how were we possibly going to get through a whole day of picnic. But we are gradually learning to be more Tibetan in our attitude to time, finding it enough just to *be* instead of doing, enjoying the luxury of letting time wash over us and carry us along with it instead of perceiving it as a void to be filled.

Meals in people's houses tend to be more formal than picnics, with many little politenesses and rules of etiquette, but there is the same sense of expansiveness and leisure. We are met at the gate by a young maidservant and several yapping dogs, and go across the courtyard into the long one-storey building that is the family's main living area. The room is filled with sunlight, the large windows looking south towards the river and mountains. The room is large and sparsely furnished, with an empty expanse of stone floor. In one corner is the family altar: a large *tangka* hanging on the wall above a brightly painted cupboard on which are placed a row of seven brass bowls filled with water – an offering symbolizing the offering of one's pure being to Buddha. Along two walls are benches with cushions covered by faded carpet and, in the angle formed by these, is a small low painted wooden table. A picture of the Dalai Lama, festooned with *katag*, hangs on one wall; a picture of the Chinese party leaders adorns another wall. An enormous stereo cassette player stands on top of a cupboard.

We present our gifts: we have brought *katag*, which we put round our hostess's neck, and a present of fruit and walnuts – we are not quite sure if this is etiquette or not, but when we had visitors, they brought us a present of apples and some tins of pork and mandarin oranges. It is the middle of the afternoon; we have been invited for dinner. The maid brings in a huge thermos of butter tea, and our hostess pours this into small bowls for us. She offers them to us with two hands, one holding the bowl, the other lightly supporting it from underneath – it is considered rude to offer food with one hand only. When you are offered food, it is polite to refuse it at first. You are then pressed to take some, but you should refuse at least three times, while your host continues to insist. It is in fact impossible to refuse anything in Tibet – even if you really don't want any! 'No, thank you', 'No, really no this time' or 'I couldn't possibly' are just taken as extra polite versions of the refusal ritual, and your glass, cup or plate gets refilled just the same. This has sometimes worried us when visitors come to our house for a meal, as we are afraid that they may not like our strange foreign food and may really be refusing a second helping, having found it difficult to swallow the first. On the other hand, they may really be hungry and just be giving a token refusal. Impossible to tell! So we have devised a short cut through the ritual for visitors to our house: after explaining that in England

'No' really means 'No', we then ask them, after the first obligatory refusal, 'English no or Tibetan no?'

Butter tea flows on throughout the afternoon, with gentle chat and perhaps a game of *karom*. Then at some point in the early evening, the butter tea turns to *chang*, and the gentle afternoon atmosphere begins to change. Everyone gets distinctly merry. When your glass is filled you should dip the fourth finger of your right hand into the glass and flick three drops into the air as a libation before drinking. Whoever is pouring out the *chang* will wait for you to drain your glass and then refill it. You can drink the second and subsequent glasses at a more leisurely pace, but every time you look round, the glass seems to have been mysteriously refilled to the brim. *Chang* comes in a variety of containers: in the market it is sold in plastic jerry cans and in the little stalls along the street it is served from these too, but some families still have the beautiful old brass jugs that have been in the family for generations.

Shortly after the arrival of the *chang*, dishes begin to appear on the table. Most meals we have had here have been basically Chinese in form (many small different dishes) and content (stir-fried pork, beancurd, etc), but with some Tibetan dishes such as *momos* or curried potatoes. Sometimes we have had rice with the meal, sometimes *tsampa*, served in a wooden bowl into which tea is poured. You then mix the tea and *tsampa* together with your fingers into a soft dough and eat it rather like bread. We like it: it tastes a little like undercooked brown bread and sometimes has a cheesy taste because of the yak butter in the tea, like a mixture of cheese and mushy digestive biscuits.

After the dishes have stopped arriving, and first your polite refusals and then your real ones have been successively ignored, and you have lost count of how many times your glass has been refilled, and everyone is flushed and merry and laughing, then in time-honoured tradition the dancing begins. Many writers about the 'old' Tibet describe how 'after the meal an orchestra of five or six musicians furnishes the background for two or three women dancers'. Nowadays the cassette players and pirated pop tapes brought from India and Nepal furnish the background for family and friends to dance disco together.

A few weeks ago we went to Tsurpu, a monastery about fifty or sixty miles away up a beautiful long narrow valley full of golden barley with a river in full spate rushing down. There was a small whitewashed village, prayer flags fluttering, at the foot of the valley, then nothing except the occasional horseman along a two-hour ride up a stony track to the head of the valley. We picked up a couple of pilgrims and a lovely old man with a cheerful leprechaun's face who was delivering a sack of yak hair to the monastery.

This is not a Geluk monastery like most around Lhasa, but a much older sect called Karma Kagyu, sometimes called the 'Black Hats', a sub-sect of the Kagyu order founded by Marpa and his disciple Milarepa. The monastery was founded in 1189 by the first Karmapa, who was the first to bring in the practice of finding successive lamas by reincarnation, a custom later adopted by most sects. The monastery was completely destroyed in the fighting in 1959 and during the Cultural Revolution, but now is being rebuilt by the fifty or sixty monks who live there. The main building was finished and one or two others partially restored; on the one nearest the track they were busy carving and decorating the pillars and lintels in intricate patterns. Inside the main temple were old bronze statues of all the Karmapas, or rather of the one Karmapa in all his various incarnations. The monks had had the foresight to bury these before the Chinese attacked the monastery in 1959 and had now unearthed them. In another room were newly-made statues of the founders of the Kagyu order. In the hall below was a vacant throne, waiting for the return of the Karmapa.

A photograph of the last Karmapa, who fled into exile and set up a monastery in Sikkim, is propped up on the throne. The monks showed us another photograph, which they claimed was taken at his funeral. The camera is pointed directly at the sun. Around the sun is a halo and in the sun, clearly visible, is a face strongly resembling the face in the photo on the throne. The monks were very proud of this photograph.

They were looking for the next incarnation now, they told us.

Elsewhere in the temple were butter sculptures solidifying in pails of water and *tsampa* cakes propped up against the altar as offerings. In one room a monk was seated at a sewing machine, putting together long strips of brocade to make frames for *tangkas*. In another room a monk was putting the finishing touches to a huge clay statue.

We ate a picnic down by the river, observed by a group of women who had stopped their work in the fields to come and watch us eat. They gave us butter tea, we gave them tomatoes, which they had never tasted before. On the opposite bank was a huge stone structure like a giant staircase going nowhere, overgrown with grass and weeds. This is a *tangka* wall, where huge religious pictures are hung out on holy days. Further up the mountainside were various retreats and hermitages, now all in ruins.

We went for a walk up the valley: wild scenery of rocks and bare hills and rushing water. On the way down we visited Karmapa's Summer Palace, now an overgrown shell of rocks and weeds, where we were kidnapped by a charming toothless old lady, the self-appointed guardian of the decaying piles of stones, who dragged us all off to see a magic tree. Karmapa's heart lives in this tree, she said, and in 1959 the tree was smashed up by the Chinese, but it grew again. We all had to process around it clockwise and eat some of the bark. The leaves are magic, so we were all given one as a talisman. Magic and Mystery are obviously alive and well in Tsurpu!

Feeling well-protected, we started off down the hill again and picked up a girl and her baby and our old man with the leprechaun face, who were walking back down to the village. The girl had come up to the monastery to ask for blessing for the baby; the old man had exchanged his sack of yak hair for a huge plastic urn full of *chang* and three glasses, and this kept us all very merry all the way back to Lhasa. We expected him to get out at the village, but he decided to come all the way to Lhasa with us. I don't know if it was a premeditated plan or a spur of the moment impulse, or if the effect of the *chang* was to make him feel reckless, but I don't think he had ever been to Lhasa before and when we set him down at the foot of the Potala he was bemused and overwhelmed. We left him clutching his *chang* jug and looking around him in helpless bewilderment like a lost child.

Letter seven: **Namtso and Yerpa**

Our twenty-five Tibetans arrived three weeks ago, and have
proved to be A1 propaganda material all round. The poor things:
their first language laboratory visit, on only their third day – when
they were still reeling from the shock of having two live foreign
teachers, whom they couldn't understand at all – meant they were
subjected to the microphones and lenses and floodlights of the
Beijing National Documentary Film crew, who were making a
film showing the new enlightened attitude towards the National
Minorities, i.e. the people of Tibet. We were a bit annoyed by
all this performance, particularly as we had been told only a
few minutes before the lesson began and had had no intention
whatever of taking the students into the language lab so early.
We muttered things like 'bloody propaganda' and 'who are these
smarmy media people?' under our breaths . . .. However, the
students themselves were delighted by it all, especially the girls,
who had dolled themselves up in (University supplied!) Tibetan
costume, while their boy classmates donned *chubas* (also University supplied).

Two days later, exactly the same thing occurred when another
documentary TV crew arrived, this time from West Germany!
They were making a film about 'New Tibet' and, against our
protestations, we had all once again to troop into the language
lab in national costume and spend an artificial hour in front
of the lenses. By the time a Belgian film crew arrived a
week later, we were prepared. Whatever the language and
propaganda or not (*Hi-Tech on the Roof of the World* or *Mother
China brings Progress to National Minority*), obviously a language

lab makes better television than a boring old chalk-dusty class-room – even though that may be where the real learning takes place!

Our new students are supposedly destined to become school teachers. This is part of a new policy towards Tibet, on the part of Central and Provincial Government, to get more Tibetan teachers into schools. The First-Year Tibetans are mostly country lads from places like Chamdo, Yadong, Gyantse, Xigaze or villages around Tibet, and just a few from Lhasa, the big city, itself. It is not at all clear how they were chosen to be students of English, but after three weeks it is quite clear that some of them are going to find it quite difficult, although some of them are very bright. One problem, immediately obvious, is that not all of our Chinese colleagues feel very kindly disposed towards them. One of them, with the patriotic name 'Beautiful Red', said of the slower ones: 'Well, what do you expect? These Tibetans are all stupid, and they should never have let them come to university!' It's going to be hard to convince *her* of the value of modern language teaching techniques! But I don't think her racist attitudes, so grumpily expressed, are in fact shared by most of her colleagues.

The students are a lively, likeable lot, with good voices – we have an evening English Club, and on song evening they pick up melodies rather faster than the Second Years. They are terribly shy . . . it took ages to get them to raise their voices above a whisper, and so learning their names has taken a long time. This was not helped by the fact that (a) their names are Tibetan which (b) have been transliterated into Chinese characters by the administration and then (c) rendered into *pinyin* (the official system for romanizing Chinese) by (d) administration people who are perhaps not entirely accurate, being either Han-Chinese who don't know Tibetan and/or *pinyin*, or Tibetans who don't know Chinese very well and/or *pinyin*! Added to this is the fact that English has its own system for transcribing Tibetan: thus English system 'Tashi Tsering' may appear in *pinyin* as 'Zhaxi Ciring' and both anyway are only an approximation to the original Tibetan sounds! And added to this is the fact that there seems to be a limited number of names in Tibetan and no apparent fixed system of first names and surnames . . ... Well, at least we do know their faces now. Perhaps we ought to use translations, such as Tashi Tsering = 'Prosperous Long Life', or Dorje = 'Thunderbolt' . . ...

Enough about work. It is now Saturday afternoon, so we'll turn to more relaxing matters – like the weather. It is interesting how rapidly this has changed. It is still very sunny, but out of the sun the temperature has dropped in the last few weeks to the low 40s, and to just above freezing at night. The first real snow has appeared on the surrounding mountain tops at, I suppose, 15,000 feet. The first snowfall was on 15th September, after a night of rain in the valley. This snow did not melt in the sun and has gradually worked its way lower. It is glorious to be in a town, shopping, cycling, going about one's business, in the hot sun, with the glint of white peaks all around. But several nights now we have gone to bed in tracksuits; on a dull rainy day (even though it is called 'Sunny City', it is now the rainy season and you can get nearly 24 hours' cloud cover) you need two layers of clothes; and the cold shower is now definitely a thing to time carefully for when you've been cycling hard or out in the midday sun! Last night, we went over to the Lhasa Hotel to send a telex and have a meal; cycling back hatless in the pitch dark in the drizzle it was bitterly cold. The problem really is the great range between sun and shade temperatures.

We have been on a number of trips out of Lhasa itself since last writing. The first of these, about three weeks ago now, was to Lake Namtso, about sixty miles to the north of Lhasa and apparently 'the highest named lake in the world' (whatever that means). We were actually heading for Damxung, a bleak little settlement of Chinese barrack-style tin-roofed houses, where there was supposed to be a festival at the beginning of the eighth lunar month; but everyone in Tibet seems so vague about dates and times that we were not sure whether we had got the right date or not. ('Coming soon' is the invariable response to any queries about when things will happen.) In fact we discovered that we had missed the festival by a whole week!

So we continued on to Namtso. The road from Lhasa to Damxung retraced the route we took from Golmud when we first came to Lhasa by bus last year. Most of the journey was in darkness that time – we did not reach Lhasa till midnight – so it was interesting to see the road in daylight, and in much greater comfort. The start was misty and drizzly, but as we went northwards the sun came out and glinted on very high snowy peaks to the north. Wild scenery, with lovely gorges running down to the road, and a river parallel to the road with barley fields on either side. At Damxung, we left the road and took a rough track that climbed up over a 17,500-foot pass between two huge boulders strung with prayer flags. From there, we had our first sight of the lake, brilliant turquoise blue stretching endlessly into the distance. We also discovered something strange about distances in Tibet: things look much closer than they actually are. As in a desert, the bright pure light and the vast empty distances play tricks with the perspective. The lake looked no more than a short walk away, but the descent from the pass, down a rough rocky track and across the wide flat grasslands to the shore, seemed interminable. Even when the jeep stopped, unable to go any further because of the boggy ground, we were still an hour's walk from the lake waters.

We lit a fire and cooked up some stew. We had stopped next to a nomads' tent, and the women came out to help us, gave us some dried yak dung (the local source of fuel – wood is scarce in Tibet) and, laughing at our lack of expertise, got the fire going for us with the help of a pair of bellows, which were simply a goatskin (legs and all) sewn up round a short iron pipe. None of us could manage these bellows: it required an extraordinary circular motion to trap air in the goatskin and then expel it, all in one movement. Our clumsiness produced great hilarity.

We were invited into the tent for pre-lunch drinks and snacks – of butter tea and roasted barley. The black tent was made of loosely woven yak hair; it seemed incredible that the wind did not come whistling in – it was quite warm and cosy inside. There was a bare earth floor, blankets, and cushions round the edge, a smoky yak-dung fire in the centre. We gave them mugs of stew, which they did not like at all, and some tinned pineapple, which they were very wary about accepting, but which, when they were finally coaxed into trying, proved a great hit. Through a friend who speaks some Tibetan, we were able to ask some questions. 1,500 people and 3,500 yaks live on the plain around the lake. During the six winter months, they cross the lake to the warmer northern side. There is one metre of snow in winter. It takes three days to cross the frozen lake, and a week or so to walk all round it.

After lunch, we walked down to the lake, across the water-logged grass. Herds of yak grazed in the distance. I love yaks, they mince along so delicately, like ladies in huge shaggy fur coats and high heels. And when they run, they turn into flying carpets. There were also marmots, sitting up and whistling, or scurrying for their holes, and smaller animals we believe were pikas. Down by the lakeshore, there were terns, and swifts flying low over the water, and plover-sized birds with buff backs, white faces and brown and white striped wings. They waddled rapidly along the shore, or flew in spurts. The turquoise of the lake, the olive-green grassy plain, the bare brown mountains capped with brilliant white snow and the bright blue cloudless sky made a vast and unforgettably vivid landscape. When we returned from the lakeside, the yaks had been milked and the nomads presented us with a big pot of warm frothy yak milk – delicious!

A week or so ago, the University gave us a jeep to go to Yerpa, about forty miles north-east of here. They have promised us an excursion every two or three weeks. We are on very good terms with the driver, who enjoys these Sunday trips as much as we do, since he is quite devout and taking us out gives him a chance to go to temples he has never seen before. He brings along several members of his family, with their picnic and thermoses of butter tea, and butter-lamps or jars of butter as offerings, and all this turns our Sunday tourism into something of a pilgrimage or holy day. Appropriate for a Sunday!

To get to Yerpa, we took the Ganden road east out of Lhasa, crossing the river just near the University, and followed it along its southern bank till we came to the big suspension bridge, Taktse Zamchen, put up by the Chinese two years ago. We recrossed the river on this bridge, swaying and skidding as the iron carriageway was quite slippery in the rain. Across the river was a rough stony track, running back towards Lhasa for some of the way, then turning off north into the mountains. Gradually, we left the cultivated valley with its fields of golden barley and hay along the river, poplars slowly turning yellow, women harvesting in the fields, and lines of young trees with circular stone walls around their bases to protect them from animals, and wound up past a small village to a stony desolate valley. The road became extremely rough, broken up here and there by landslides, and we admired the driver's skill and crossed our fingers as he negotiated broken bridges, streams, gulleys and rockfalls. Higher up, the valley became greener, sheep and goats were grazing on the hillsides, and the mountain tops drifted in and out of the cloud and mist. We passed the ruins of Yerpa monastery above us on our right, and drove on up to the head of the valley, where we stopped a little way below the snowline.

Loaded up with picnic, thermos bottles and butter-lamps, we trekked back along the mountainside above the narrow valley towards the ruins of the monastery. Above us were fantastic rock formations, pinnacles, crags, worn into towers and arches by the wind and weather. On the other side of the valley, snowy peaks appeared momentarily and disappeared back into the clouds. It was cold up here, and we became quite breathless with the climbing. We walked back first to the ruined monastery. The Red Guards had made a pretty thorough job of smashing this up: a few low walls and crumbling stones indicated the ground plan, weeds and grass had grown over the stones and carpeted what had been the monastery floors. A few goats were grazing where monks once chanted, and a nomad had pitched his tent using one of the higher walls as a windbreak. From here, we could see right back down the valley to where it joined the Lhasa valley, its bright blue river and golden fields in the sunlight below, while mist and drizzle swirled around us. The whole valley and mountainside where we stood was littered with ruins: stepped pyramids and crumbling stupas overgrown with weeds.

Above us on the mountainside were numerous large holes and caves and small stone buildings built directly into the side of the mountain. Most of these were little cave temples, still maintained and inhabited by hermits. We climbed further up the mountain in a slow procession from one cave temple to another, leaving offerings of butter to fuel the butter-lamps, and *tsampa* flour and money. One temple was constructed around a brightly coloured rock painting of Buddha, another cave had beautiful though faded murals of a dancing three-headed god, and a very serene Buddha. One was like a miniature stone fortress built into the mountain, and above it was a temple with a roof and tower. One large cave, festooned with prayer flags, was filled with the crumbling remains of what must have once been a huge Buddha statue: only the head was intact and two huge eyes stared watchfully out of the rubble. Other caves were dark, small and buttery. One or two hermits sat cross-legged on the floor, chanting prayers, beating *damaru* drums, ringing bells, burning incense. Men and women, sometimes indistinguishable, wore dark purple robes. Our driver and his family carried lighted butter-lamps from cave to cave, mumbling prayers and pouring a little of the melted butter into each of the temple lamps as they went. We asked how long the hermits had been there. Yerpa had always been a very holy place and hermits had always lived in the hill caves, it seemed, though the destruction of the monastery and of the big Buddha inside the cave took place in 1959. No hermits had lived up there through the Cultural Revolution, when all religious activities had been suppressed. One old man had been living in his cave for nine years, summer and winter alike, eating only once every three days. It must be bitterly cold in winter.

At the top temple Tsering and his family collected bundles of juniper twigs and, lower down, from a cave which served as a kitchen, they borrowed a kettle of hot water and a big butter churn. We all sat down on the hillside, near a crumbling, overgrown stupa, and shared a picnic of eggs, yoghurt, flat bread and butter tea. Sheep, goats and yaks grazed all around us. On a far hillside below, women were singing as they worked; from above came the faint sound of chanting and the ringing of bells. The bleating of the sheep echoed across the valley. We saw hoopoes, redstarts, wagtails, rabbits and the pikas and marmots that we had seen at Namtso. Just across from where we were sitting, on the side of a small hill, the prayer *Om Mani Padme Hum* had been laid out in Tibetan letters in small white stones. This hill, called Lhari, was small and rounded, and shaped rather like twin breasts: prayer cairns surmounted the twin humps and prayer flags, like a line of washing, were looped from one mound to the other.

When we had finished our picnic and returned the kettle and churn, we all made for the top, Tsering and his family with the bundles of juniper strapped to their backs. On the way up, we passed a sky burial site. In a country where wood is so scarce, and the ground is often frozen for a good part of the year, it is not practicable to bury or cremate bodies, and the Tibetans practise what is known as Celestial Burial: the body is cut up into small pieces and left for the vultures. This is considered an act of compassion, as other creatures are nourished by the remains.

At the top of the hill, our companions lit a fire of juniper on each peak, walking round the smoky fragrant fire three times clock-wise. They then threw a handful of *tsampa* flour into the flames and solemnly stood in line, a handful of flour in their right hands. Hands outstretched, they uttered three long notes (it sounded like 'So-o-o-o-oh') and then with a triumphant shout, threw all the *tsampa* into the air (like the ritual we had seen at Yoghurt Festival).

We then made our way back down to the jeep and started off on the drive home. We followed a different route, staying to the north side of the river, taking a very rough road to the top of a small pass where the rocks looked like solidified mud or lava, and had a stunning view along the Lhasa valley: the deep blue river, the golden fields and the bare brown mountains sweeping up from far valley floor.

In *Daughter of Tibet*, the author talks about Yerpa as a 'most holy place' to which Lhasa people often made pilgrimages, and she mentions a legend (or perhaps it is a piece of Tibetan history – it's sometimes difficult to tell the two apart), connected with Yerpa during the reign of a Bad King in the ninth century. This king, Langdarma, was opposed to Buddhism and sealed up the main Buddhist temples and broke the images. A hermit from Yerpa called Lhalungpa decided to do something, and determined to kill the king. He set out for Lhasa wearing a black hat and black coat, riding a white horse covered in charcoal, with his bow and arrow hidden in the long sleeves of his coat. In Lhasa he found the king in front of the Jokhang. Prostrating himself before the king, he shot an arrow into his heart, then mounted his horse and rode straight for the river, where he forced the horse to swim across to wash off the charcoal. Then, turning his coat so that the white lining showed, Lhalungpa galloped back to Yerpa and hid in his cave. Everyone searched for the king's murderer, but no one could find a man in a black coat on a black horse.

The king, incidentally, had horns on his head and a black tongue, which proved that he was a wizard; and he initiated the custom of Tibetan men putting their hair up in plaits with red ribbons, to hide the horns. Ever since his day, a Tibetan greeting has been to scratch your head and put your tongue out, to prove you have neither horns nor a black tongue. Walking in Lhasa today, a friendly smile at an old lady will often be reciprocated by an outstretched tongue!

Letter eight: **Lhasa Profiles**

We have met a great variety of people since our arrival here, some through our work, some socially, others more formally at official functions or more superficially in the town or on trips out. Here are a few pen portraits:

An old monk at Ganden shuffles around, prepares tea for us in little wooden bowls. He was at Ganden before its destruction in 1959 and was subsequently sent to do manual labour in the countryside for over twenty years. Some of his fellow monks were imprisoned, some died in the Cultural Revolution. Others were forced to marry and become members of the laity, and a number fled to India. He returned to Ganden when the rebuilding started. We comment on the progress of the rebuilding, funded mainly from private sources. 'We will rebuild it all,' he says, 'even if it takes twenty-five years.'

A very old lady, thin and frail, dark gentle eyes in a lined face, hair pinned up in plaits. She wears a long Tibetan pinafore dress and striped apron. The daughter of a noble family, she was married young. As a young wife she had little to do but attend parties and dinners, fuss over clothes and jewellery. I cross a courtyard, climb a ladder to her living room where we sit on carpet-covered cushions, the afternoon sun spilling in through the windows. She serves me butter tea and wind-dried apples and shows me photographs of their family, their former house, their country estate, herself resplendent in silks and jewellery. In some photographs a section has been cut out, a figure is missing. I learn later that this is their daughter, who was killed in the Cultural Revolution. The family, like all the nobility, suffered badly during those nightmare years: her husband was imprisoned, she came home one day to find him missing and for a long time did not know where he had gone. She herself was ridiculed and humiliated, paraded around the Barkor with a dunce's cap and a placard round her neck by groups of jeering Red Guards, possessions and jewellery confiscated, forbidden to practise her religion. Now, she says, life is sweet again for them; her husband, released from prison and rehabilitated, has a good job, they have this lovely house, they have received some compensation for possessions stolen during the Cultural Revolution, they can once again practise their religion without fear. But walking home from her house, all that evening and for many weeks afterwards, I am haunted by the spectre of the missing figure in the photographs.

Two pilgrims from east Tibet who have made the once-in-a-lifetime pilgrimage to Lhasa, walking some of the way, hitching lifts on lorries, tractors and donkey-carts for the rest. In Lhasa, they are terrorized by the traffic, intimidated by the shopkeepers and embarrassed and humiliated by the city slickers who jeer at their peasant's clothing.

There is a small girl living in our block, possibly eleven or twelve years old. Every time we see her, she is working: a small baby strapped to her back, a toddler stumbling after her, clutching her skirts, carrying a mountain of washing to the pump, chopping firewood or returning from town with a heavy basket of shopping. She has a sense of responsibility beyond her years and often looks after us too, knocking at the door to tell us it's raining and we had better take in the washing, or retrieving articles of clothing that the wind has blown off the washing line. I assume she's an unfortunate elder sister who is taking more than her share of family duties, until I meet others like her: child-servants, usually girls from poor families in country areas or orphans brought by relatives into Lhasa to find a family that will offer food and lodging in return for household duties – a sort of unofficial *au pair* service for the homeless.

At a friend's party, a young man dressed in tight blue jeans and black leather jacket is dancing with abandon. Later I see him chatting up three giggling girls with very Western-style panache. Intrigued, I try to find out more about this Tibetan Casanova, and discover that he was found at an early age to be a reincarnation of a high lama. During the Cultural Revolution, however, his monastic education left something to be desired, and by the time the more liberal eighties arrived, when he could have rejoined his monastery, he had decided that life outside the cloister had more attractions. 'More like a reincarnation of Don Juan,' I say, watching him persuade one of the girls, blushing and giggling, on to the dance floor.

At an official teachers' reunion, we are introduced to an old lady who teaches English. She speaks very formal, very correct Indian English; the English of half a century ago, of the British Raj. The daughter of a noble family, her parents sent her to school in Kalimpong, a convent school where she wore English school uniform and attended church services, but never lost her faith in Buddhism. Twice a year she would make the long journey back to Lhasa across the pass at Kalimpong. As I talk to her politely between official speeches, the image of a young girl with bright dark eyes and long plaits in an English school gymslip takes shape in my mind and gradually becomes superimposed on the figure in front of me.

Two Tibetan exiles from Nepal, businessmen, smart in Western suits. How sophisticated they seem, how worldly, compared to the Tibetans we have met here, where even those in important positions seem curiously innocent, unworldly. And how angry they are, how bitter! These exiles were children when they left Tibet. One of them left with his family. The other, a novice monk when the fighting broke out in 1959, left on foot with his teacher and a small band of novices, crossing the high passes through the snow, arriving in India exhausted and ill, without knowing what had become of his family. He did not find out for over twenty years. He returned to Tibet in the early eighties to see his mother and sisters. Up until that time, he did not know if they were alive or dead, and they did not know what had become of him. I try to imagine the anguish of exile, of being separated from your country, your family, your friends, with no way of knowing what was happening to them, feeling impotent and frustrated, unable to do anything except feed on your own fear and anger. A friend described to me how she felt, when, allowed to travel to Nepal to be reunited with members of her family who had fled to India in 1959, she met her sisters and cousins at the border. 'We were all crying,' she said. 'I did not know who was my sister and who was my cousin but I was crying and crying.'

In a dingy teahouse near the Potala the long tables are filled with young men playing cards, dice and *karom*. Teahouse society is not for women. One or two girls do circulate, however, topping up the cups with tea from large thermoses, while the men slap down cards and shout. We fall into conversation with a morose young man at an adjacent table. He gestures angrily at the cups, the thermoses, the noodles and rice that his companions are eating. 'All from China,' he says 'everything is from China here. Chinese food, Chinese products, Chinese people. They take our jobs and we have to buy their goods. They killed my grandfather. They look down on us. They tried to destroy our culture. They tried to kill our religion. Now they allow us a little more freedom and they expect us to be grateful.' 'What do you want?' we ask him. 'What do young people in Tibet want?' 'I want to choose my job. I hate my job. I hate my unit leader. I want more chances. I want to study. I don't want to be always afraid. I don't want to be looked down on. I don't want to be . . .' He is so choked with feeling that he cannot find the word. Instead he throws the stub of his cigarette on the floor and grinds it beneath his heel: an eloquent gesture. He is, I realize, angrier than anyone I have ever met before, with an anger that has been choked back and swallowed so many times that he is nearly bursting with its accumulated intensity. How many more are there like him, filled with that powerful mixture of personal grievance and national sorrow, like an unexploded bomb?

The son of a former landowner and his wife now live in much reduced circumstances in a tiny two-room flat. But old habits die hard. He, his wife and son live in the main room which is simultaneously bed- and living room; the other room, the kitchen, is occupied by their serving-girl, who works there by day and occupies a makeshift bed in the corner by night.

An old man who used to be a tenant farmer on a noble's country estate talks to us about the arrival of the Chinese in 1950. 'They were polite and decent,' he says, 'and we were optimistic at first. We thought perhaps they would bring a better life for us. I welcomed them. Yes. But later . . . in the Cultural Revolution . . .' He shakes his head sadly, unable to finish the sentences.

A young man with a vacant expression can often be seen loitering in the Barkor Square or sitting alone in the teahouses. They say he 'lost his mind' in the Cultural Revolution, and now, unemployable, he strays aimlessly around the streets of Lhasa, a lost soul.

Our students, Tibetan or half-Tibetan, who were born into and grew up during the Cultural Revolution, are sinicized in ways I wonder if they themselves suspect. It's not only that they often cannot read or write Tibetan and that those coming from different parts of Tibet sometimes use Chinese as a common language, but that some of them, particularly the girls, have a very Chinese orderliness, acquired I imagine in a Chinese classroom rather than in a Tibetan household. Their shyness too – again particularly the girls' bashfulness – strikes me as conforming to a Chinese ideal of womanhood. And their shyness about sexual relations is something that strikes me as very Chinese. All writers about the old Tibet describe, usually with some surprise, the free and easy behaviour of the Tibetans. Our young students giggle and blush if the word girlfriend or boyfriend is mentioned, are very coy about admitting if they have one, and will not be seen so much as holding hands in public. There is another overlay, now, of Westernization, though this is very superficial: an interest in clothes, make-up, pop music. Underneath, attitudes are more Tibetan: that lovely Tibetan sunniness, a delightful bubbly sense of fun and general enthusiasm for life. Some have a fairly relaxed attitude to work, though some, particularly the girls, have absorbed the more serious Chinese work ethic. They have a very natural grace and courtesy, though some of the lads from east Tibet have a kind of wild untamed quality very different from the girls' Chinese tidiness: it's difficult to get them to sit still, concentrate, come to lessons on time, remember their homework. There is also a real difference in poise and sophistication between those who come from Lhasa or Shigatse, the big towns, and those who come from the country; also between those from noble families and those from peasant families. Without knowing their origins, I can guess from gestures and mannerisms and am surprised that, after thirty-five years of communist rule, these young people who never knew the old society still retain its traces. For many of the students, it's the first time they have come into contact with young people from different parts of Tibet, and they too are surprised by some of the differences, not only in dialect but also in customs. One student, speaking of his friend from Chamdo, said, 'When I first met him, I was very surprised because he offered me a cup of coffee with only one hand, not two, and he didn't use the polite form when he asked me to drink, he just said "Drink!" I thought, "This is not polite."'

A former monk owns one of the little shops on the Barkor. He must be an astute businessman, for the shop is in a prize position and the rents are very high, so he has to make quite a profit just to meet his overheads. The little shop is always crowded out with a mixture of tourists inspecting souvenirs and Tibetans fingering the bales of brocade and woollen cloth. I wonder how his talents would have been put to use in the monastery.

Chinese expatriates: two new arrivals, young girls newly graduated from Hangzhou, starry-eyed idealists, they have volunteered to come to Tibet as teachers to 'help the development of this backward region'.

Two colleagues, young men, bored to tears on a Saturday night, arrive on our doorstep with bottles of beer and a bag of peanuts. 'We felt lonely and homesick, so we thought we'd come and see you,' they explain. They are here, unashamedly, for the money (twice the salary they would get in China) and for the greater freedom a posting to Tibet gives them: long holidays, a chance to travel. 'Every time I go home on leave,' says one who comes from the far north-east, 'I plan a different route and take my time over the journey. That way I get to see a lot of places I would never have the chance to see otherwise.' We get out the cards, open the beer and play bridge.

The old man at the Sichuan restaurant has been here since the 1950s, and is married to a Tibetan. His son and daughter-in-law manage the restaurant for him now, while he sits in the corner, grandchild on his lap, or serves the customers with beer or *chang* from an old kettle. 'He is Tibetan now,' the other customers say, 'we think of him as Tibetan.' There is often singing in the restaurant; once, while we are there, an old man is persuaded to do a Tibetan tap dance. An old plank is hauled out of the kitchen and he performs on this to a cassette of Tibetan music, while the other customers sing and clap.

A colleague has been paying a lot of visits to the doctor recently. One day he drops in to see us and announces with scarcely concealed glee, 'There is something wrong with my heart.' We look at him with concern, stammer condolences, ask if it's serious. With evident delight he tells us that the wall of his heart is some fractions of a millimetre too thick, that the condition is potentially dangerous, and that he will have to go back to China. Understanding dawns: the discovery of this heart condition means a return to his home town where he will be reunited with his wife and baby son.

One day returning from a shopping expedition, we run into Mr Ding, the philosophy professor from Peking who came with us on the plane. He is wobbling along rather precariously on a borrowed bike. We stop and talk; he wants to know where the main shops are. We have been in Lhasa six weeks now. This is the first time he has ventured off campus.

At a party for teachers given by the Tibetan Educational Bureau, we meet a middle school teacher who tells us that Tibetan children are less intelligent than Chinese children: 'Their minds work more slowly.' We suggest that if Chinese children had to study all their school subjects in Tibetan, their minds might work a little more slowly too. She doesn't seem convinced by this. 'Tibetans are very backward,' she says, 'their cultural level is low.' We tell her that in many universities in the West there are departments devoted to the study of Tibetan culture, and ask if she has ever thought that *she* might learn something from Tibetan culture. She doesn't appear to understand the question. 'The cultural level is low,' she repeats, 'they must learn from our advanced culture.' At the same party a head teacher is lamenting how slowly the Tibetan children in his school learn Chinese. We ask if he speaks any Tibetan. 'No,' he says. 'Well, maybe two or three words.' How long has he been here? 'Eight years.' Has he ever tried to learn Tibetan? He too seems surprised by our question. 'Tibetan is useless,' he says flatly. How widespread this attitude is we can only guess, but we find it particularly upsetting to find such sentiments among teachers, who have such power to pass them on implicitly along with the Maths, Geography or Chinese that they are teaching.

After these depressing encounters, we are happy to meet an artist from Sichuan who came to Tibet because he 'had a dream of the clear light there and the brilliant colours'. The brilliant colours glow from his paintings, where motifs of prayer flags and stupas and *mani* stones whirl together in abstract patterns or figure in dream landscapes as strange as Dali's. The contrast between the richness of his imagination and the poverty of spirit that we encountered at the party that afternoon could not be greater.

I am on friendly terms with the owner of one of the little local shops – something between a stall and a shop, little more than a cupboard in the wall, with lock-up shutters. I buy bread rolls, peanuts and beer from him because he is cheerful and chatty. A Sichuan Chinese, he has been living in Lhasa for twenty years, is still homesick for his hometown and dreams of going back.

I am surprised to learn that a couple at the middle school down the road, whom I had assumed to be childless, in fact have two children, who are both living with their grandparents in Guangzhou. Their parents see them once every two years. To bring them up in Lhasa would, in their view, condemn them to an inferior education and a life of exile.

At an official reception we meet a young Chinese with a mission. He wants to write a book about Tibet 'to tell the Chinese people what Tibet is really like'. 'What do you want to tell them?' we ask him. 'People in China know nothing about Tibet. All they know is an old film they have seen called 'Slave'. They think Tibet is dirty and primitive. And they think the Tibetan people are savages. We must stop thinking like that and learn to respect their culture.'

Two young PLA soldiers from the barracks by the river, raw new recruits, mooch along the embankment for an evening stroll, an evening smoke. They look unutterably bored. One of them picks up a pebble, throws it into the river, but even this action is lethargic.

Letter nine: **Work and Worthy Speeches**

Are you sitting comfortably in your chintz armchair with its lace antimacassar, glass of *maotai* ready for the toast? Then I'll begin: 'The Tibetan people are feeling very delighted and joyful after thirty-five years of socialist rule . . . it is the best time for them since the Peaceful Liberation of Tibet by the People's Liberation Army . . . we thank everyone here who is working hard to construct socialism and to modernize the Autonomous Region . . . the workers and peasants and herdsmen, the workers and fighters of the People's Liberation Army, the members of the armed police force, and our foreign friends who are helping construct the New Tibet and promote friendly ties among all nations . . . *Gan Bei!*' – at which we all raise our glasses (of *maotai*, or sweet red wine, or beer, or orange fizz, or mineral water) and wait for a line of officials to come down and clink glasses with '*Gan Bei!*' or 'Bottomer Supper!' This was part of a stirring speech made at the Provincial Foreign Affairs Bureau buffet just before National Day (1st October), to which all resident *waiguoren* working for the Motherland were invited. First, what exactly have we (along with our comrades the herdsmen and armed police) been doing here to make the Tibetans so 'delighted and joyful'?

We teach six days a week, seeing the First and Second Years every day, and teacher training on two afternoons. It's not exactly strenuous, but then perhaps the most important part of our work here is to set up a materials bank (books, cassettes, etc) in a way that will be usable after we go. We have a syllabus to write, and a self-study listening centre to organize with the technicians in the lab. Our colleagues say we 'work very hard' –

but as normal Chinese university teachers only teach eight hours a week, and as up here there is an 'altitude allowance' of two hours, so that most of them do only six – our fourteen or fifteen hours a week *is* heavy! Middle school teachers here do ten or twelve hours. Compare that with teachers in Britain! We are starting a series of 'open lectures' for staff and students, on general topics like 'Introduction to Britain', 'Europe', and so on. It will be interesting to see who comes, and what questions they ask.

We had two days off for National Day: the Wednesday and Thursday, 1st and 2nd October. We decided to go to Samye. This is, or was, the oldest monastery in Tibet, founded in 779 by Trisong Detsen, one of the very religious early kings, after he had invited a sage-magician called Padmasambhava up from India. The monastery was built by demons, so the legend goes, whom Padmasambhava compelled to haul stones and wood from the rivers and forests to construct the buildings. The new temple was unpopular with the Tibetan aristocracy of the time, who saw it and the creation of a new monk class as a threat to their power. They clung mainly to the old pre-Buddhist religion, an animistic faith, called Bön. They were right about the change in the power structure: the landowning families of the district had to provide the monks with income, food, butter, paper, cloth and ink, and were subject to the monks, rather than to the king. Special laws were enacted which placed the monks above the law, and anyone harming a monk was severely punished: a dirty look could mean having an eye put out!

Samye is where the great debate took place that determined the course of Tibetan Buddhism, between Chinese Chan Buddhism (like Zen) and Indian Buddhism in the Mahayana tradition. The latter emphasizes a moral code of good and bad deeds leading to an accumulation of knowledge and merit through successive existences; the Chinese tradition lays greater emphasis on meditation and 'salvation' through sudden flashes of insight. The debate (in 792) was carried out between two learned monks, one from China, the other from India, and the verdict finally went to the

Indian; this has influenced the development of Tibetan Buddhism ever since, although there are some Chinese influences.

Samye was designed as a representation of the Tibetan view of the cosmos; the central temple represented Mount Rirab, which the Tibetans saw as the centre of the universe, and four pagodas around the temple, glazed in white, blue, red and green respectively, represented the four continents surrounding Mount Rirab. Smaller temples between the pagodas represented the islands between the worlds, and two large temples to north and south represented the sun and the moon. The whole complex used to be a small town of 108 temples. Now the great main temple, which used to have three storeys in different architectural styles, has only two, without the roofs. The murals which adorn the cloister walls have been burnt and mutilated: some of the figures have had their faces gouged out, presumably by Red Guards in the Cultural Revolution. The four pagodas, which must have been a stunning sight with their different coloured glazed tiles, have all been razed to the ground, and we saw some broken green tiles, perhaps relics of the green pagoda, used to decorate walls and houses. Many of the temples have been knocked down and some are being used as granaries and storehouses. One we peeped into had horses stabled in it, and another was a carpenters' workshop. One dusty, empty shell of a temple had Mao pictures pasted up over the murals.

But the main central temple was a hive of activity. In the square outside, stonemasons were chiselling away at blocks of stone, and women were carrying them up a rickety gangplank, built against the side of the temple, to the upper storey. Down in the cloister, a group of workmen were hammering away, making masks out of beaten copper, while upstairs carpenters were sawing roofbeams and carving the beam-ends into intricate patterns. The monks were engaged in gentler occupations. A couple were busy with sewing machines making bright cloth-hangings and brocade-surrounds for *tangkas*. A group of novices were sitting in a merry circle with thermoses of butter tea and biscuits, cutting up sheets of prayers into long strips to go inside prayer wheels. In another room, a monk was operating a wood-block press to print the prayers. It annoyed us slightly to see the comfortable looking and perfectly able-bodied young monks doing nothing more strenuous than wield a pair of scissors, while around them aged peasant women, bent double under the weight of the stones they were carrying, struggled up the swaying gangplank!

Inside, the Chanting Hall of the main temple was in quite good condition, though dark and buttery, lit by the flicker of butter-lamps through the gloom. One thing that always strikes us about Tibetan temples is the combination of bright colour and gloom. The walls are painted with murals in gaudy primary colours, embroidered cloths and *tangkas* hang from the ceiling, the pillars and roof beams are decorated in red and blue and gold, and various gilded and painted statues line the walls: but the general effect is sombre, with colours glowing dully through the darkness. In the older temples they are overlaid with a thick layer of grease and smoke from the butter-lamps, which makes the colours rather muted.

One chapel we went into had huge figures, two or three times lifesize, lining the walls. Because these clay statues are painted and dressed up, they look like huge, rather frightening dolls. They surrounded a huge gilded Shakyamuni statue. Another chapel was very sinister: very dark and murky, with huge statues completely draped in cloth and brocade. Apparently their faces were draped because they were too frightening to look at! A clay mask – not, apparently, scaring enough to be covered, but still quite terrifying in the gloom – grinned from a pillar. As our eyes got accustomed to the dark, we made out other horrors: a huge snakeskin coiled around a pillar, animal skins, chain mail, vicious-looking weapons, yak horns . . .. The atmosphere in the chapel, these half-glimpsed objects in the twilight, the overpowering cloying smell of rancid butter, the claustrophobic darkness, were all too much for us, and we fled!

The last chapel we looked into was not really a chapel, more a sort of large cupboard. A monk took us outside the Chanting Hall and opened a door in the wall which swung open to reveal a statue of Chenrezi. This statue was surrounded by a halo of arms and hands in relief against the wall of the chapel-cupboard. Each hand had an eye in the palm. On the upper floors of the main temple were faded, beautiful murals, and a little chapel with a statue of a fiercely grinning Padmasambhava with a row of skulls transfixed on his sword, rather like a skewer of kebabs.

The journey to Samye is worth doing in itself. We had a wonderful driver, a friendly young man called Tenzing, who, halfway there, asked if we felt like a cup of tea. We said why not, and he said, 'Well, actually, my aunt lives near here, I just thought we might drop in on her . . ..' So we all went for tea with his aunt. She lives at one of the villages near the airport and her small bare room was decorated with old airline calendars and pictures of Deng Xiaoping or Mao being greeted with flowers on a runway somewhere. She heated the water for the tea on a small solar heater outside her front door, and then pounded the tea and butter together in an ancient wooden churn. We spent a very pleasant half-hour, and I'm actually getting used to butter tea now! It is all right as long as you don't think of it as tea – I try to imagine I'm drinking a rather salty soup.

The road from Gongar follows the Yarlung Tsangpo (Brahmaputra) river, and from there on the scenery gradually changes, becoming more arid and desert-like, with very bare sandy mountains sweeping down to the bright blue river. The colours are simple: brown, the brilliant blue of the sky and river, and white snow gleaming on the mountain tops. Between the mountains and the road, there are dunes and small table-top hills eroded into strange shapes, like Badlands in the Wild West. To get to Samye you have to cross the Yarlung Tsangpo. This meant saying goodbye to Tenzing, who went back to spend the night with his aunt.

We boarded a small boat filled to the brim with pilgrims going to the monastery, and traders with sacks of flour and cans of oil. The boat takes an hour to cross the river, which requires very careful navigation because of shoals and sandbanks. A couple of old ladies helped, by counting their rosaries and praying us all the way across. Safely disembarked on the other bank, we waited around in the hot sun with everyone else for a lorry, which eventually materialized out of a cloud of dust. We all piled into the back and chugged off down the bumpy sand track, clinging on to the sides as we jolted over rocks and forded streams. Rounding a bend, we passed the five white stupas we had seen from the air as we came in to land at Gongar, two months ago.

Samye is a kind of oasis in the midst of all these brown mountains and sand dunes. Last year, we had to walk to the monastery from the boat: a very dry and dusty walk, through rolling dunes, with occasional patches of bright purple flowers. I remember the texture of the air changing as we arrived at a grove of willows bordering the stream that runs past the monastery: much thicker, heavier, damper, and sweet-scented.

We had a good view of Samye and the surrounding country from a hill just east of the monastery. This is a holy mountain, whose name sounded like 'Highbury', but I suppose was 'Hepori' (*ri* means mountain). There is a chapel on top, and festoons of prayer flags looped from crest to crest. From one side you could see the monastery spread out below, temples, courtyard houses, stables, barnyards, piles of hay in the yards and in the fields surrounding the village. Women were in the fields, threshing: we could hear their songs as they worked. A stream winding through the fields, willow trees in clumps along the banks. Flights of birds: hoopoes, wagtails, magpies. Beyond the oasis of cultivated fields were bare, wrinkled, craggy mountains. On the other side, away from Samye, there was nothing but the brown of dunes and mountains, and the blue river straggling in several streams and rivulets across the wide valley floor.

We had with us an old black and white photograph of Samye, another of Harrer's taken in the 1940s, which showed the view from the same point on the same mountain, and we were able to compare the former monastery with the present place: a lot of destruction and a lot of infill – all available space between the temples has been turned into a maze of little courtyard houses. Some of the encircling wall is still visible, but in other places it has been knocked down, or swallowed up in the closely packed houses.

There was a party of pilgrims on top of the hill, not seriously pursuing their devotions but getting very merry on *chang*! We were welcomed into their midst, took a souvenir photo of them for posterity, and were liberally plied with *chang*. We reached the bottom of the hill in a rather worse state than when we went up, and the steep sliding descent was not the only reason our knees were shaking when we reached the bottom. Tibetan hospitality is impossible to refuse: if you are not drinking fast enough, or just seem to be toying with your drink, you will find the glass being raised to your lips for you.

Back in the village we concentrated on getting a bed for the night. There is a little courtyard hotel in the monastery, guarded by a veritable witch of an old lady. Half-sozzled most of the time, her vocation in life seems to be to try to stop you getting a bed by any means possible. She actually drove two foreigners out with a stick on one occasion. Luckily, our new friends the pilgrims were in her good books, and they succeeded in getting us a bed. We were by now exhausted and tumbled into bed as soon as it was dark, but the pilgrims stayed up most of the night, making a fire, boiling up potatoes and yak ribs, singing and passing round the *chang*.

The next morning we had a rather odd breakfast of tinned Chinese pineapple and Nepalese glucose biscuits by the bank of the stream beneath the willows. We were near a small stone bridge at the entrance to the village, and the boy shepherds were driving their flocks out up to the mountain pastures, busily spinning as they walked behind the sheep and goats.

We caught the shuttle-lorry again as it went down to the riverside to pick up passengers and cargo from the boat, and met Tenzing – and a jeep-load of his relatives – on the far bank. His aunt had decided to come for a ride too, and so had her daughter and friend, and her friend's friend. They had brought a big picnic, and thermoses of tea, and jars of butter for the temple lamps. We wanted to go to a temple not far away called Mindroling, and when they suggested going along to another one too, we were delighted. Mindroling is the only

Nyingma, or 'Red Hat', monastery left in central Tibet. It is set in a beautiful valley running at right angles to the main Yarlung Tsangpo valley. We walked up a gently rounded hill which runs up to a jagged crest surrounding the monastery, and saw a patchwork of green and gold fields along a dried-up sandy river bed. Harvesting was still in progress here, though at Samye it had all been gathered in. Women were busy harvesting in some fields and gleaning in others. Tenzing and his extended family had a big picnic ready for us when we came down from the crest.

The other temple we visited was one of the nicest we have ever seen, looking more like a manor house than a temple. Dunbu Chökor, in the village of Chitishö, was mainly intact, although some of the side 'chapels' were destroyed. The walls were covered from floor to ceiling with beautiful swirling murals. A friendly monk, grinning from ear to ear, showed us round, and was particularly proud of some tinted photographs of the Sakya Lama, who visited this Sakya temple when he was twelve years old.

After Chitishö, we all dropped in on 'Aunty's' friend's mother, who lived nearby, and consumed vast quantities of home-brewed *chang* in the main room of her little courtyard house: beaten earth floor, bed in one corner, low stools to sit on, and a huge basket of wool ready for spinning, with a pump in the courtyard for water.

Letter ten: **Some Cultural Events**

Usually, the University gives us tickets for anything that happens to be going on in the campus auditorium – films, dances, talent contests and so on. But this time they didn't. We heard that there was going to be a 'cultural event' that evening, and enquired what it was. 'Oh, do you want tickets?' they asked, 'we thought you wouldn't be interested as it's all in Tibetan.' It turned out to be a modern Tibetan social drama – we didn't understand a word of course, and not much of the action, which was fairly complex, but the social types were clear enough and the evening gave us some very interesting insights.

The play seemed to be about the Generation Gap in various forms. The main character was a distinctly modernized and Westernized Khampa – one of the tall, warlike people from the east of Tibet. Often to be seen round the market place, they have a more aggressive reputation than the central and western Tibetans, and wear long daggers, which they are quick to whip out if provoked (or drunk, which they frequently are). This cross between a Khampa and a Hell's Angel roared on to the stage on a motorbike and strode around in his black leathers wearing a Walkman headset, which sat rather uncomfortably across the thick coil of hair and the red silk tassel. After a few minutes strutting round and humming some Hong Kong style pop tunes to himself, he then pursued a girl across stage and proceeded to rape her behind a *chöten* (at least, she emerged dishevelled and weeping, so we presume that's what happened!). The rest of the play consisted of various confrontations: a tearful one between the girl and her parents, who obviously considered her dishonoured by the episode; an aggressive one, involving a knife fight between the Khampa and the girl's boyfriend, a straight, sober, serious type in a Mao jacket; a few shouting matches between the Khampa and his parents (traditional Tibetans: father in long black coat, mother in long pinafore dress with striped apron, hair in plaits); and an ideological confrontation between Authority, in the shape of some dignified elderly Tibetans in cadres' jackets, and the Younger Generation, mostly in Western style jeans and pullovers, who didn't seem to be doing anything more daring than gyrating to the strains of Hong Kong pop from an enormous cassette player. Authority was distinctly disapproving, anyway.

What a strange blend of Tibetan, Chinese and Western culture the whole thing was! Khampas with motorbikes and black leathers, rape behind a *chöten*, a traditional Tibetan picnic with thermoses of tea, pots of stew and gaily decorated tents, which dissolved into a disco party . . . and a strain of dour socialist moralism pervading the whole performance. 'Too much imbibing of Western culture leads to loose behaviour' was clearly the message: black leather + disco = rape. And yet the play was much racier than anything we have ever seen in China: quite a lot of grabbing and fondling went on (even in front of the *chöten*!) and the audience seemed to lap it all up.

The second 'event' was totally Tibetan and, as far as I could judge, uninfluenced either by Western fashion or by bureaucratic notions of what People's Art should be. This was a dance drama: a fantastic blend of colour, music, action and sheer spectacle, and it took place at Sera monastery, about forty minutes' cycle ride north of Lhasa. I went alone, as Charlie was teaching. In the old days there were travelling troupes of actors who would stage these dramas, known as *ache lhamo*, at monasteries or great noblemen's houses, and people would come from miles around to see them. There was a fairly limited repertoire of plays, all religious in nature. These performances were, of course, banned, along with other manifestations of Tibetan culture, during the Cultural Revolution, when the only performances allowed were Madame Mao's 'Eight Revolutionary Model Operas'.

This was a whole day event, starting at around 11 o'clock in the morning and still going strong at 7 o'clock in the evening. The idea is: you bring your family and all your friends and relations, well equipped with blankets and cushions to sit on, and umbrellas and awnings to keep the sun off, and a huge picnic, with pots and pans to cook in and a supply of wood to make a cooking fire, and, most essential ingredient, a huge jerry can of *chang* to provide general merriment. Then you stake out a pitch and encamp yourselves, preferably under the trees around the arena where the dancing is being held. Thereafter the dancing is mainly a background to a day-long party and, though your attention may drift in and out of the action, it is secondary to the food and drink and chat and even the odd snooze. It is the Tibetan equivalent of a cricket match, I suppose. Here again, I didn't have a clue what was going on – and no one I spoke to seemed to have much idea either, although one old man told me it was a historical drama about a Muslim invasion of Tibet. That didn't enlighten me much, but not knowing what it was about did not detract in any way from my enjoyment – I was enthralled. After eight hours, however, my attention was beginning to wander, and that, coupled with black clouds looming overhead, was why I left.

I got there at about 10-ish, and staked my claim to a piece of ground on one side of the large arena marked off for dancing by a wire fence. A family next to me made room on their blanket, and offered me roasted barley and *chang*. Not much was going on; testing of microphones, a few people looking important and bustling around, rows of monks seated on cushions on the ground opposite us, a nearby family brewing up butter tea, a woman with turquoise earrings and immensely long plaits feeding a quilted bundle of a baby. Two old ladies in front of me had brought their grandchildren and a huge jerry can of *chang*, so they were quite happy. Other people were passing the time by telling their rosaries and muttering prayers to themselves.

Suddenly, the dancing began to the clash of cymbals and the beat of a big drum. There were two teams of dancers in the first part: men in rich brocade costumes with painted devil-like masks, and women in brightly embroidered dresses with long sleeves and fan-shaped headdresses. Two men with long coats over baggy trousers and curly-toed Tibetan boots and looking rather like Muscovites also made an early appearance. They wore their hair in a long plait down their backs.

There were two main phases to the dancing: everyone would stand in a circle and all sing together, or stand and watch while one sang solo. Then everyone would whirl round in a circle to the clash and bang of cymbals and drum. This pattern continued throughout the eight hours. Sometimes there was an interlude of dialogue or of slapstick comedy. Strangely, though no one I asked had seemed to have much idea of what the play was about in general, they all seemed familiar with the comic interludes and would often recite the dialogue along with the actors.

It was the costumes and the array of characters that made it all so fascinating, and the sense of holiday and occasion – all these people out for the day, enjoying the sunshine, the *chang* and the spectacle. Trying to work out what on earth was happening kept me pretty busy too! After about an hour of dancing and duetting between the masked men and the fan-shaped ladies, several more characters made an appearance – and new characters kept on appearing throughout the play. As soon as I had advanced a theory about the identity of one character, he or she would disappear and someone I had never seen before would arrive to take his place. In the end I gave up interpreting, let my senses take over, and just enjoyed it as a visual treat.

There was a King figure, with white mask and long black beard, in silver brocade robes and a turban. He had two turbanned attendants in long flowery robes. There were some men in yellow, with flat red hats with fringes, a blue-robed, domed-hatted man, and a very aristocratic-looking lady with an elaborate Y-shaped headdress made of silver. Best of all was a villain, who looked like a combination of a pirate and a terrorist, with a knotted headscarf and big curved dagger. Instead of a patch over one eye, he wore a black hood with cut-out eyes and mouth. The hood was, rather incongruously, trimmed with rabbit fur – a fashion I haven't noticed among Western villains! He was something of a comic villain though, rather less wicked than funny, and he provided light relief, with a lot of slapstick tripping up of other characters and poking them in the buttocks with his dagger.

Then there were Three Men in a Boat, or rather Two Men and a Parrot in a Boat. The boat was simply a long strip of material painted with waves and jumping fish, which they carried round themselves, and walked inside, pretending to row with plastic paddles. The two men got out, the parrot stayed in the boat. After some whirling and stomping, they got back in again and rowed off. On their homeward journey, they were attacked by giant spiders with huge mouths and floppy waving legs. A new character, with yellow robes and a hairy face, arrived and had a comic duel with the pirate-terrorist. A woman with a snake headdress made a brief appearance. The men and the parrot arrived again in their boat, and this time carried off the blue-robed, dome-hatted official. The snake-lady gave him roses as a leaving present. On the homeward journey they were again attacked by spiders; it seemed to be a routine occurrence. When they reached land, the men climbed out of the boat and strode off, leaving the parrot to fold up the boat and carry it off stage with the oars.

At this point in the performance a group of Chinese cadres arrived in a big black car, and presented white scarves to all the dancers, who continued their dance uninterrupted. The bland-faced dignitaries in their grey cadres' jackets looked very strange, threading their way through the brightly costumed dancers. Scarves presented, they got in their car again and drove off. Not interested in watching the performance? Or was their schedule for the day so crowded that they couldn't fit it in? At various points in the dance, two men in charge of refreshments carried butter tea in bowls to the dancers and musicians, who drank it there and then, on stage. At one point, sweets and apples were distributed all round! Just as I thought the whole thing was drawing to a close, several new characters arrived. These had long coloured hair like punks and clown-like costumes. There was a black one, carrying a pink balloon, then a red one, a yellow one and a white one. They all carried balloons and wore bells on their costumes, like jesters or Morris men. The whole thing was reminiscent of a strange mixture of different art forms: a little like Chinese opera, a little like *Commedia dell'Arte*, a little like mummers – but mostly like nothing I have ever seen before.

We have also had a couple of Western 'cultural events' as part of the English Club that we have started, and it was interesting to see reactions. The first was a video of Zeffirelli's *Romeo and Juliet*. They loved it! And not only because of the universal theme of adolescent passion, which of course went straight to our young students' hearts, breaking down any cultural barriers on its way. There was audible sniffing and quite a few wet eyes in the scene at Juliet's tomb. But, in a curious way, there seemed less distance culturally between Shakespeare's England and twentieth-century Tibet, than between Shakespeare's England and its twentieth-century counterpart. Scenes with gangs of youths in medieval dress, feuding aristocratic families, messengers on horseback or monks in their cells seemed totally natural and in the order of things to our young Tibetans, much less of a cultural barrier than to a comparable group of adolescent English kids. Strange to see two cultures speaking to each other so directly over a gap of four hundred years and through a video machine!

The other Western 'cultural event' was a series of slideshows we gave for our students and the Arts Department, which we rather pretentiously entitled *Western Art from Botticelli to Bacon*. (You find yourself in this sort of situation when you are the sole available interpreter of your culture, alone in a foreign country armed only with what you brought in your twenty-kilo baggage allowance.) But it was fascinating to see the reactions of staff and students to our motley collection of slides: such fresh and spontaneous perceptions, as if the pictures were speaking directly to them with no barrier of tradition, history or preconceived ideas, although something like Mondrian's abstract painting in primary colours must take on its own symbolism for Tibetans, for whom each colour has a meaning. 'What did you like best?' we wanted to know at the end. 'Dali and Chagall.' We were a little, but not altogether, surprised: those images speak very directly to your subconscious – images of dream, of fantasy, of escape. And the landscape in Dali's paintings is no weirder than some Tibetan moonscapes, the juxtaposition of images in Chagall's paintings of flying people or green horses, no stranger than some temple murals of holy men and deities floating in the clouds.

For some time now we have been trying to learn some Tibetan and are having informal lessons. Knowing we will not be here long enough to become fluent, our aims are fairly limited. We really just want a few phrases for shopping – especially for bargaining! – and a few conversational interchanges: names, jobs, where people come from and so on. We also find it interesting to gain some insights into how the language works. We find it very difficult! Whenever we try to say the word for 'I' (*nga*) our students dissolve into giggles and tell us we are really saying the word for 'fish' (*nya*). Even when they pronounce both words for us, slowly and carefully, we can't hear the difference. And then we can't work out whether the language is tonal, like Chinese, or not: no one seems quite sure, or able to tell us what to do with our voices or where to put our tongues. It seems to be, we have concluded, *slightly* tonal! The difference between two words in some cases seems to be the difference between a falling and a rising tone, in others it seems to be the degree of aspiration. So much for learning from native speakers with no textbooks or formal guidance! The one book we managed to acquire in London before we left, called *A Guide to the Colloquial Speech of Tibet in a Series of Progressive Exercises*, was published in 1879 by a 'learned lama' and is full of such unhelpful phrases as 'Are you my uncle's servant?', 'I have got the girdle of your friend's sister.', 'The modes of divination practised are two in number.', 'The soothsayer's wife cannot prepare good beer.', 'Do the people of your country smoke ganja or opium?' and 'Put your sword back into its scabbard.'

And then it seems to be two or even three languages that we have to learn, not just one. Tibetan traditionally had two main forms, sometimes three, each with a different vocabulary, depending on the status of the person you were addressing. In the

Cultural Revolution this tradition was frowned on as bourgeois and attempts were made to eradicate the 'honorific' language, which is now disappearing, especially among younger people. One friend's father, an extremely aristocratic and dignified old man, who teaches a group of teenagers in the afternoons, complained that they couldn't understand what he said when he used the 'honorific' language, yet he felt it was disrespectful to use the less polite forms when addressing them. We seem to have to learn two Tibetan words for every English one. It is not just a matter of *tu* and *vous* or *Du* and *Sie* – there are completely different sets of vocabulary, depending on context, on who you are, and on who your interlocutor is. So, for example, you use the word *paleb* for bread when buying it in the market, but if you are a host offering bread to your guests, you must use a different word, *shepa*. The same with dumplings, which are familiarly called *momo*, but in polite society must be re-christened *shemo*. If you ask someone's name, you should use the polite word for name, *tsen*, but if you talk about your own name, you need not (or maybe must not) use the polite form for your humble self: you talk about your own *ming*. At the end of a lesson, the girl students would often say to the boys '*Dro-ge*' meaning 'Let's go,' but at the end of one lesson the boys said '*Te-ge*' as they stood up to leave. 'Hey,' I said, 'I thought *dro-ge* meant "go".' 'Oh,' one of them explained, 'I was talking to the girls. If I talk to a girl, I should be very polite.'

To add to our confusion, people in different parts of Tibet naturally have different dialects – we had students from Lhasa, Shigatse and Chamdo, who all spoke different forms of the language, and they would often disagree about what was right and what was wrong when correcting our Tibetan. I gather that the language of the Tibetans-in-exile has diverged from mainstream Tibetan and that Dharamsala Tibetan has its own idiosyncrasies.

One big difference must be that many Chinese words have become incorporated into Tibetan Tibetan for words and concepts that didn't exist before 1950, whereas Dharamsala Tibetan uses Indian or English words. Some of our Tibetan students from different regions of Tibet found it easier to talk to each other in Chinese – all their schooling had been in Chinese, so in some cases and on some topics they were more fluent in Chinese than in Tibetan. I tried to find out which topics they felt more comfortable on in Tibetan, and which in Chinese. It seemed that they felt more comfortable on intellectual topics in Chinese – indeed there were some topics, like science and mathematics, that they felt they wouldn't be able to talk about at all in Tibetan.

What about feelings? Could they express those best in Tibetan or Chinese? Tibetan, they thought, although one student said he could express himself better in writing than in speaking, and he had never learnt to read or write Tibetan (indeed, he wrote his diary in Chinese). What a terrible thing, to be cut off from your own language to such a degree! The student in question was an avid reader, and his facility in Chinese had given him a window on the world through access to world literature translated into Chinese. I was amazed at what had been translated and how widely some of the students, who had never left Lhasa in their lives, had read: Zola, Tolstoy, Hemingway, Dickens, Lawrence, the Maigret stories, even Sartre and Freud! More is being translated into Tibetan now, but the range is very limited.

These days, there is a policy to teach the mother tongue in schools, but our young students, born into the Cultural Revolution when any divergence from the Chinese norm was rigorously suppressed, had been discouraged from learning their own language. One student even said that his parents had spoken Chinese to him at home, because they thought it would be better for him. When they were on their own, I continued to question them, what did they think in, Chinese or Tibetan? Tibetan came more naturally, but sometimes their thoughts would drift into Chinese. I have noticed that happening a lot in conversations, too, which sometimes seem to switch from one language to the other, almost without the participants being aware of it. I want to know if thoughts ever get lost between the two languages and how the intellectual/emotional split that seems to exist for them between the two languages affects their thinking.

Letter eleven: **A New Hotel and an Old Monastery**

Things are changing fast here: maybe the Fifth Modernization should be known as the 'Holidayinnification' of China. It is perhaps time to tell you more about the modernization of Tibet, the demystification of it, the 'Invasion of an Alien Culture' – Tourism.

While we labour away up here for Education, with our comrades the herdsmen and armed police, there are several other Westerners also beavering away in their own fields. A very interesting group of people: some are also teachers, employed on local contracts by various work units on a temporary basis; the others work at the Lhasa Hotel. This was being built when we were here in 1985, opened and closed again several times in its first six months, and is now functioning properly. Holiday Inn are in charge, but won't put their name to it until they consider it meets their standards. The staff are a mixture of local Tibetans, mainland Chinese, Hong Kong Chinese and European managers. There was great competition for jobs there among local people when it first opened, until the rumour went round that the jobs involved too much hard work.

For someone in the hotel trade, it must be very challenging to work there. For the package tourist it ensures comfort, and recognizable food and oxygen on tap in the bedrooms in case of altitude sickness on arrival; for Mother China it means an influx of foreign exchange. For us it offers the occasional treat of a good meal and from time to time the unexpected bonus of a food parcel: unused rations left behind by an Everest expedition: treasure troves of Mars Bars and processed cheese. A room costs the individual tourist 70 or 80 *yuan* a night, but climbing expeditions pay about 400 *yuan* – the hotel gets its 80 *yuan* and CITS, the China Travel Service, collects the rest! The hotel has two restaurants, a bar and a disco. I suppose Harrer and Aufschnaiter would not approve. And certainly Chairman Mao must be turning over and over in his mausoleum! The managers and staff trainers have had a hard job trying to get untrained and unskilled Tibetans, naive in the ways of the outside world, to understand what Western tourists demand for themselves in the way of creature comforts, service and hygiene.

For the Tibetans it must be a strange world indeed, full of such undreamed-of luxuries as carpeted floors and hot running water and peopled by odd beings who could have come from another planet, with their electronic cameras and wallets bulging with money, and their extraordinary needs for things like clean sheets and spotless bathrooms. Even we, after only three months here, get culture shock every time we enter the lobby! Most of the staff have barely adequate language skills, let alone hotel skills of the kind your average tourist now expects. We overheard the following dialogue in the lobby the other day. 'What time does the coffee shop open?' 'Coffee shop over there, turn right.' 'No, what time does it open?' 'Open?' 'Yes, what time?' 'It's five o'clock.' 'No, what time does it open?' 'Open?' 'Yes, the coffee shop.' 'Coffee shop over there, turn right.' 'But it's closed, what time does it open?' 'Coffee shop close now. Please try later.'

One way of seeing that Lhasa is no longer the place it used to be is to climb our local mountain, *Bumburi*, which means 'Flower Vase Mountain'. It is a 'good' mountain, and the top beckons every time we look out of the window. It rises from the other side of the river and for some weeks we had been looking at it through binoculars and trying to work out the best way to the prayer flags which flutter between the crags at the summit. One Sunday in mid-October we started out and to our surprise found it was a much shorter climb than it had looked – steep and a scramble in some places, but not more than a morning's walk.

The view over the Lhasa built-up area, and up and down the valley, is spectacular. As you climb, the Potala grows and grows to dominate the city and then it too shrinks as it is dwarfed by the surrounding mountains. From Aufschnaiter's map of the city, made in the late 1940s, I suppose, you can see just how much the place has grown and changed character. The old Tibetan town around the Jokhang temple is hidden in a twentieth-century town-planner's dream of concrete and grey jerrybuilt three- or four-storey junk! It is hard to identify the Jokhang even, with its gold roof ornaments. What stand out are the Holiday Inn far over to the west, near the Norbulingka; the TV mast on top of Chakpori; the new Tibetan Hospital (four storeys); and the number of PLA sites all around on both sides of the river, plus two incongruous-looking satellite dishes north of the University. Arrays of radio masts on the outskirts. Massive snow-dusted mountains in every direction. The lazy curls of the river, its islands with Tibetans washing and picnicking. Rumbling dust clouds of lorries on the main road. Barking dogs. The bright, bright blue sky and dazzling sun. And (a wonderful lack of modernization here), no pollution haze at all. Far off to the north, Sera monastery at the foot of its steep mountain, and far off to the west, the white gleam of Drepung monastery and even at this distance you can make out the huge rock paintings beside it.

Vultures circled over us, curious ravens swooped near and croaked at us. We stood on top, ate eggs and biscuits and 'Lucky' chocolate, and gazed at the immensity of the view – mountains in every direction, dry desert colours, rock strata clearly visible as there is so little vegetation. And the capital spread at our feet, a world-famous city now twice or three times its original size and still only the area of a small market town. The next mountain down river, westwards, opposite the Potala, is apparently a 'bad' mountain (a Tibetan friend said 'because it blocks the view from the Potala'). In the old days, the Tibetan army used to shell it once a year to keep the bad spirits in order. Quite easy target practice!

Another new trend in Lhasa seems to be an increase in crime. This is happening elsewhere in China too, and harsh measures are being taken to deal with it. A few weeks ago a colleague who lives opposite the sports stadium saw a convoy of trucks full of armed police arrive – there was going to be an execution after a large public gathering for the sentences to be proclaimed. Apparently, two Chinese crooks had lured two Tibetans into a trap near a cave outside Lhasa. Some illegal goods were to be exchanged for cash. The Tibetans, suspicious, took along sacks full of paper instead of money, and were murdered by the Chinese.

There are quite often violent incidents in Lhasa streets, too – often racial in origin. One evening we were cycling back late through the old town and ran into a glare of floodlights, a gawping crowd and a group of police, who were examining a wicked foot-long knife by the side of the road. There had been a knife fight involving Tibetans and Chinese, and one man had been killed. Once, when wearing Chinese greatcoats and cycling home in the dark, we were stoned by Tibetans, who were perhaps drunk or perhaps thought we were connected with the PLA barracks further along the road. Lhasa is not quite downtown Manhattan, but it isn't the peaceful Buddhist paradise of myth either.

The atmosphere here is nowhere near as grim as during late 1983 and early 1984 (the 'Spiritual Pollution' period); viewed from the outside, it all looks bright and hopeful, but there is a campaign going on at present, called 'Spiritual Civilization'. This seems to be a move to make people more 'responsible' and to have 'a correct idea' of their duties to State and Party, while at the same time keeping the opening up of minds and manners to a more 'Western-style' economy. In other words, it is fine to make money and develop modern lifestyles, but politics comes first, and you cannot simply take the blue jeans and pop music without the responsibility to society at large. In practical terms, it meant for our university colleagues several additional long boring meetings (some old buffer reading unintelligibly from an interminable official report) of over two hours each late in October, and an injunction 'not to bring your knitting along to Thursday afternoon Political Study meetings!' Our Section leader said aside to me: 'Too many meetings, not enough work!'

Our Tibetan driver, who has taken us on most of our 'outings' so far, was a little nonplussed when we suggested going to Talung one Sunday. We showed him a map, and he shook his head and said it was too far. We knew he was going north for two or three months very soon. (This was something to do with getting a truck repaired in Lanzhou, which seems unlikely, but then this is a country where the University will send a truck all the way to Hebei Province, south of Peking – a journey of at least three weeks – just to buy and bring back a truckload of pears with the result that each university teacher, including us, was given ten pounds each of deliciously just-ripe pears as a gift!) So we reminded him that he wouldn't be here to go on any more trips out of Lhasa with us. He pondered, and then agreed.

The result was that the following Sunday, at 7 a.m. in the freezing dark, we climbed into his Toyota Landcruiser with about nine other people – his family and friends. In the starlight it was difficult to make out exactly who we knew and who were new. But the dawn brightened over the jagged skyline as we headed east along the river, past Ganden (its ruins like broken teeth on the ridge above), and faces appeared smiling, offering sweets, cigarettes, biscuits, cakes. It is really nice to organize a trip, knowing a lot of Tibetans are overjoyed to get the chance to come along too, to visit places they have only heard about, like us. Doing this on a Sunday seems especially right, going to temples on a combined pilgrimage and tourist jaunt.

It is wonderful to set off before sunrise, and watch the dawn come up: first, a cold blue light behind the mountains, making them look like cardboard cut-outs or a stage set, then a delicious rosy glow on the snowy peaks, finally the whole valley flooded with gold as the sun fills it. We followed the Lhasa river for a while and then branched off northwards into a wide fertile flat valley. As we drove along the river, we startled flocks of geese or duck: gold body, white wings with black tips, which we think are Brahminy duck. We have been inventing names for all the unfamiliar birds we have seen. We have the 'whatear' which looks something like a wheatear, but we are not sure; the 'postman bird' in its smart uniform of black and pillar-box red which I believe is Hodgson's redstart; the 'sparrobin' and the 'strawberry ice-cream bird' (the exact colour of a pink ice), which must be a rosefinch.

The harvest was all in; straw stacks in courtyards, fields fallow or freshly ploughed. Later in the morning we saw men and women at work threshing the grain, either by beating sheaves against a board or by driving a team of four or five horses round and round to trample the grain. In village courtyards, women were winnowing, tossing the grain up and down in large round flat baskets. Threshing seemed to be mainly men's work, winnowing mainly women's. But at eight o'clock in the morning everyone appeared to be asleep (Lhasa is made to run on Peking time, so by the sun it was really only six o'clock). Trees were bare. A ground frost diluted the colours of the earth, turned the rich brown of the ploughed fields to grey, and the yellow stubble of barley straw to cream. Streams were frozen. We passed nomad encampments, the people still asleep inside the tents, their animals, tied together by the legs to prevent them straying, dozing nearby.

The valley was quite densely populated, with permanent settlements as well as overnight camps: small villages enclosed within a perimeter wall, the houses low and solid, trapezoid in shape, with the base wider than the top, the walls sloping inwards, giving them a massive appearance like miniature fortresses. Each house is enclosed in its own courtyard. There are prayer flags and bunches of twigs on every rooftop. Round flat pats of yak dung were plastered to dry on the walls. We stopped briefly in two of these villages to let passengers off to visit parents for the day.

In one village every home was equipped with a solar reflector, with a small device for holding a kettle. In another, a young girl had been up early, out gathering yak pats – a more traditional source of heat – and was returning with her collection piled up in a triangular wicker basket strapped to her back.

The outer walls of the buildings were all decorated with a pattern of wavy lines made by scraping the mud with twigs while it was still wet. Near Lhasa, the mudbrick villages were all whitewashed, but as we went further up the valley, the red earth villages were painted in more fanciful colours, duck-egg blue, green and yellow. When we looked across at the other side of the valley we saw the reason for this: I have never seen mountains like them, swirling, multi-coloured strata of rock in wavy lines and circles, in Neapolitan ice-cream colours of dairy yellow, pink and pistachio green. They looked like enormous confections from a giant ice-cream parlour: tutti fruttis, knickerbocker glories, strawberry surprise. Further up the valley, the colours were even richer, mountains striped in maroon and gold, or purple and green, and capped with snow.

At the head of the valley we began our climb up into the snow-fields, startling a flock of small greyish birds and a couple of snow-cock as we rounded a corner. The road wound steeply upwards, snow banked up high on either side, until coming round a bend, we nearly ran into the back of a lorry which had stalled on a steep gradient: the only vehicle we had seen en route. We all got out to help. Walking down the road, I startled – and was startled by – an enormous blue hare! Huge ears! Thumping great back legs! Dusky blue coat, long and thick for winter. Back up the hill, the men had cranked up the lorry and it had eventually started, groaning painfully, up towards the pass. We piled in again and followed.

In Tibet, you have to shout as you reach the top of a pass – perhaps to scare off any evil mountain spirit that might be lurking there, or perhaps just out of sheer exultation at having made it and seeing the view before you. Anyway, everyone yelled at the tops of their voices, and then we got out at the prayer-flagged pass, surrounded by snowfields. There was an icy glistening crust, so hard you could walk on it – but if you broke through, you were in up to your middle. The pass must have been at 17,000 feet or so, the air very thin and bitingly cold, despite the bright sun. Below and beyond was a bare brown valley, olive-green-gold mountains rolling away into the distance. The thin air, the pure light, the vast distances, all make you feel as if you are floating. No wonder the monks used to claim they could fly or move at supernatural speeds: in Tibet you feel supernatural just being here! The road now descended steeply, crossed a stream, and suddenly we were at Talung.

There is not much left of this once very important monastery. It was the head temple of one branch of the Kagyu sect and was founded in 1178. Now, just the shell of a huge red-ochre central temple stands beside the stream, surrounded by rubble. Higher up, some rebuilding was going on and there was a small sunny courtyard with a little temple, living quarters and a kitchen for the monks, of whom there are thirty-six or so. We had our picnic in this courtyard, the monks brought us butter tea, and we were soon surrounded by a crowd of onlookers. The small temple was being painstakingly rebuilt, and had a set of bright new murals.

After lunch, there sadly not being much of the monastery left to explore, our driver organized a walk up the hill behind the temple. One of the nicest things about these Sunday expeditions is that, although the trips are always made at our instigation, somehow the tables get turned on us, and we end up feeling as if we have been invited out on a family outing. Tsering, our driver, always has things organized; when to set out, where to stop on the way, the exact spot to have a picnic, a tour of the temple, tea with the monks and an afternoon walk. We end up feeling that *he* planned the trip and is proudly showing us round his country!

From the top, there was a lovely view down the sunfilled valley: snowy mountains all around, sheep and horses grazing on the olive-green mountainsides, a stream bubbling through a small village at the foot of the hill. There was a large, rather sumptuous building at the near end of the village, and we asked if it was another temple. Tsering said no, it was where the lord of the manor used to live. I wondered who lives there now, probably some Party cadre, the latter-day lord of the manor . . . *plus ça change*.

On the drive home, in beautiful golden late afternoon light, we hit 'rush hour': train after train of yaks, horses, donkeys, flocks of sheep, all being driven home to base. We stopped to pick up the two morning passengers and were treated to two parties, one after the other. In the first house, this took the form of a supper of boiled mutton, cabbage and noodles. Tsering scorned the noodles and called for a bowl of *tsampa* instead, which he mixed up and rolled into balls with his fingers. All washed down with *chang*, though we were also made to drink eggcupsful of *baijiu*, which means, literally, white spirit. One of our companions got extremely drunk, downing about fifteen or sixteen glasses. At the next house we were all invited in, and given yet more *chang*, after which our friend collapsed in a heap on the back seat and snored loudly all the way back to Lhasa.

Letter twelve: **Two Journeys – Real and Remembered**

One of the nicest things about our weekend trip to Shigatse early in November was that we were accompanying two friends for part of the way on their journey back to the Nepalese border. They had had an enforced wait at the border because of a landslide and their time with us was very brief. To spin out the time together we managed to swap Saturday classes and set off with them, hoping to get the bus back in time for Monday morning – a gamble that paid off. Last year we made the same journey all the way to the border in a lumbering Chinese minibus, and it was interesting to compare notes.

The first part of the route towards the bridge over the Yarlung Tsangpo is a tarred road, but from the bridge onwards the road is an unmade track the texture of talcum powder, switchbacking up over the Kamba La pass. This road is so dusty that travel along it invariably produces a sore throat and cold. What you think are ribbons of mist in the early morning chill are in fact dust clouds hanging in the air, barely moving in the stillness. Grinding up through the sand, you can see far below you, through the powdery haze spun up by the wheels, the Yarlung Tsangpo valley: the brilliant blue river flowing into a dozen shoals and channels between brown sandbanks, the summer gold of the fields transformed into brown stubble. Skeins of bright prayer flags signal the top of the pass and, getting out of the jeep, you cannot tell if it is the shock of the thin cold air or the view stretching below that takes your breath away. The huge lake of Yamdrok Yumtso is nearly 15,000 feet above sea level and as complicated in shape as an octopus, tentacles curling in all directions around the base of the snowy peaks that surround it. It is the third largest lake in Tibet and, once you have descended the pass, the road follows its shores for a couple of hours before branching off over the Karo La pass to Gyantse. There is plentiful birdlife: geese, ducks and divers skimming the water with their wings, light bouncing off the ripples in silver drops.

The road diverges from the lakeshore and begins to wind up the Karo La. This pass is higher than the Kamba La, though without the sweeping views. Here is an expanse of snowfields on either side and a huge glacier that rolls down to the roadside in a chaotic jumble of ice-falls and crevasses. This was the site of a battle between the Tibetans and Younghusband's British and Indian troops in 1904.

This expedition must be one of imperialism's odder exploits. The expeditionary force was sent by Curzon, ostensibly to force the Tibetans into granting trade concessions to Britain, but with the deeper motive of counteracting what was thought to be Russian influence. The force marched from Sikkim to Lhasa, where they extracted a trade agreement and a large indemnity. There are interesting accounts of the expedition written by Younghusband and Landon, who are obviously fascinated by Tibet, but who have not a trace of guilt at their invasion: to them it seems like a gigantic adventure of the kind every schoolboy dreams of.

The execution of the expedition seems to have been as eccentric as its conception, with the British imperturbably feasting on turkey and plum pudding at some improbable altitude on Christmas Day (the Christmas champagne unfortunately was undrinkable, having frozen in the bottles), and alternating between shooting the poor Tibetans and teaching them to play football. The description of the eventual signing of the treaty seems typical of the shambolic nature of the whole undertaking. The British army in their heavy boots found the ascent of the glass-smooth incline leading up to the Potala somewhat difficult and were reduced to crawling up crabwise, grabbing on to the parapet. Once inside, there was quite a festive atmosphere: tea and various delicacies were served with the Tibetans laughing and joking, while the British, as one officer recorded in his diary, 'were a rowdy lot and made a beastly noise.' The exit of the British army was even more undignified, with officers skidding and slithering down the ramps while the Potala monks all crowded to watch, splitting their sides with laughter. There can hardly have been a treaty signed with less dignity in the whole history of international relations.

Despite the 'wizard prank' schoolboy adventure nature of the expedition, some pretty serious fighting did go on. The poor Tibetans were armed only with antiquated muskets and charms against foreign bullets, and a battle near Gyantse left seven hundred dead. To block the British advance on Lhasa, the Tibetans built a wall across the Karo La, six feet high, four feet thick and eight hundred yards long. The pass is roughly funnel-shaped, with cliffs rising steeply on either side, so British and Indian troops were forced to climb up the mountain on either side of the wall, whereupon the Tibetans retreated and the British broke down the wall. It is a suitably grim place for what was apparently 'the highest battle in the world'. Tibet is full of superlatives.

From the Karo La, the road descends through contorted mountains, brown and orange in streaks, the product of tremendous forces pushing up through the earth, twisting the rock like barley sugar. Coming down out of the range of mountains we reach what Younghusband et al call 'the Plain of Milk': a wide flat valley floor, which, when we first made the journey, was bright with the yellow of mustard fields and the green of new barley, but now is the dull brown and grey of earth and stubble. This is both a trade route and a route to the high pastures, and we pass herds of yak, caravans of donkey carts and nomads with their sheep, many of the men spinning as they walk behind their flocks. Tents are pitched, yaks hobbled and divested of their packs, grazing by the roadside. The way is littered with the crumbling ruins of villages, forts, monasteries, and from time to time we pass slogans laid out in white stones on the hillside. Those Cultural Revolution slogans promising 10,000 years to Chairman Mao are now disintegrating, their stones tumbled out of place or overgrown with grass, while on other hillsides fresh new white stones spell *Om Mani Padme Hum* in Tibetan letters.

The fort of Gyantse, crumbling on its hillside, is visible a long way off across the plain, partly destroyed by the British in 1904 and further damaged in the 1960s. A more cheerful sight is the Kumbum, a huge temple-stupa that dominates the little town. Built by Newari artists from Nepal in the fifteenth century, it is quite different in style from most Tibetan temples. In shape it is like a pile of children's building bricks, of enormous size and gorgeously decorated, crazily heaped on top of each other: square ones arranged in a pyramid of tiered steps for the base, then a huge cylindrical one balancing a cube from which Buddha's all-seeing eyes painted on all four sides stare out, melancholy and heavy-lidded, over the plain of barley. Above the staring eyes is a crown of golden rings, each smaller than the last, tapering into a cone and topped with an overhanging parasol of gold filigree. Its shape on a vast scale echoes the many small stupas or *chötens* dotted around the Tibetan countryside. The *chöten* is a universal symbol of Buddhism, like the cross for Christians, representing the path to enlightenment with the different parts representing the stages of enlightenment. *Chötens* were often used as tombs to hold bodies or ashes, or built for merit by individuals or to commemorate events. Built of stone or mud brick, they are a focal point in a Tibetan landscape: one crumbling on top of a mountain, scarcely distinguishable from the peak it crowns, a whole row in front of a temple, a solitary one in a wide flat valley, silhouetted against the mountains behind.

Behind the Kumbum is a monastery which in the old days used to stretch all over the hillside, but which is now mostly rubble. A large Chanting Hall is still standing and about twenty monks live in a dormitory nearby. Restoration of the monastery does not seem to have progressed very far since we were last here. The town, in contrast, is almost unrecognizable. In 1985 the whole place was one huge muddy building site; the main street a long stinking puddle and the air full of songs chanted by gangs of workmen who were building a whole new double row of houses. We squelched our way through the mud and puddles and listened to work songs and admired the old work styles: two women digging a trench with one spade, one holds the spade, the other tugs on a rope attached to the metal part in rhythm with her digging. Work gangs were shovelling mud, and everywhere were those beautiful songs which turn work into a celebration. Now one whole street is complete and gaily painted houses line a little market with busy stalls. There are more hotels and restaurants too. When we came through last year there were only two truck stops to stay in. One, it was rumoured, had water, the other did not. We unluckily chose the wrong one and had to fight for one thermos of water between seven of us, though we did get water later – bucketsful of it pouring through the leaky roof in the night. The walls and the door were not pry-proof and practically the whole of Gyantse, it seemed, came to watch us as we ate in the room (no restaurants then) and got ready for bed. Gyantse is still little more than a village, clustered round its mouldering fort on the hill and its wonderful staring stupa, but it looks a lot more prosperous than it did a year ago. The monastery, though, continues to crumble away in the background – which gave us food for thought on the relative values placed on religion and commerce in modern Gyantse, as we sped across the plain to Shigatse.

The huge plain is fertile barley land, now bare and brown, but in midsummer last year the whole plain was a gently swaying gold-green. We broke down here last time on an apparently deserted stretch of road. In no time, two or three faces materialized at the windows of the minibus. Where did they come from? We couldn't see anyone working in the fields, still less a village or nomad encampment. Soon the faces were joined by two or three more, then seven, then eight . . . soon there were thirty or forty people standing around; ragged muddy children with even smaller children strapped in bundles on their backs, apple-cheeked young girls, hair tied up in headscarves, herdsmen in grubby *chubas* and felt boots, toothless old grannies, and a wonderful old man with a bewildered and incredulous expression, looking utterly baffled by life, the kind of expression you would have if you were suddenly

118

above: Itinerant lama on the Barkor

above right: Prostrating round the Barkor

right: PLA lorry and the Potala

far left: Pilgrims in the
Jokhang

below left: Young monk
in the Jokhang

left: On the road towards
Namtso Lake

below: Nomads at
Namtso Lake

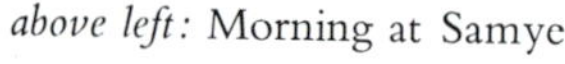

above left: Morning at Samye

above: Dancers waiting their turn, Sera

right: Outside the Jokhang, Mönlam Chenmo

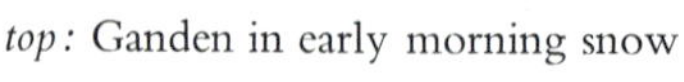

top: Ganden in early morning snow

above: Prayer wheels at Gyantse

right: Buddha by the road on the way to Drölma Lakhang

far right: Rebuilding Ramoche temple, Lhasa

above: Full moon rising over the Jokhang butter sculptures

left: Alms givers at the Jokhang during Mönlam Chenmo

picked up and set down in the middle of another century or another planet. He also looked older than anyone we have ever seen in our lives, so we asked his age. Very slowly, he counted on his fingers up to forty, stopped, considered, and indicated 'and then a bit more . . .'.

This time the journey passed without incident, except that the road was broken in one place so we had to drive for a while down the middle of a river. In our sophisticated Japanese vehicle this caused no problem, but the public bus next day had more trouble negotiating this stretch of water.

Shigatse, Tibet's second city, is today a jumble of featureless concrete blocks engulfing the original town with its solid white houses and covered marketplace. The town always seems to me to have a numb and shell-shocked feel, like someone after an accident or a patient convalescing after surgery, functioning, but not quite in control of his own identity. It has neither the important feel of a metropolis like Lhasa, nor an intimate village atmosphere like Gyantse. An occasional truck roars down the bleak main avenue in a cloud of dust. Streets too wide for the few cyclists that wobble down them open up dreary vistas of grey concrete, with the sad ruins of the fortress looking down from the hill. Dogs lope hungrily along the pavements looking for scraps. In the noodle shops a few bored-looking Chinese soldiers stare vacantly out on to the streets. Nearer to the market things are livelier: cobblers and bicycle repairers spread their tools on the pavement, an old woman sells *momos* from a covered basin, traders and customers haggle over eggs, but there is no comparison with the colour and dynamism of the Barkor in Lhasa.

Shigatse's great glory is Tashilhunpo monastery. Its name means 'Heap of Glory' and it does spill down the mountain in a glorious heap of red and white walls, golden roofs and flapping awnings. It used to rival Drepung in size and importance and in the old days had about 4,000 monks. Now there are about 600. Tashilhunpo was not as badly treated in the Cultural Revolution as many other monasteries and rebuilding there is going well. Buildings which last year consisted of foundations and low walls are this year complete with gold roofs shining in the sun, and the whole monastery looks freshly painted in a dazzle of white and gold.

Our favourite temple there is now complete: a strange looking building, an elongated trapezoid in shape, it looks like two temples, one on top of the other, and you wonder why it is so tall until you enter it and find yourself at the gilded feet of an enormous Maitreya Buddha and stretch your eyes up through the gloom to where his face smiles down at you from a great height.

Maybe Tashilhunpo's good state of repair is due to its association with the Panchen Lama. The present Panchen Lama, the tenth, was brought up in China, and lives in Peking, where he holds a senior government position. He returns to Tibet for special religious occasions such as *Mönlam* and for political occasions such as the 25th anniversary, in 1985, of the founding of the Autonomous Region. Panchen, which means 'Great Scholar', was a title bestowed by the fifth Dalai Lama on his tutor, who was subsequently recognized as a reincarnation of Amitabha, the Buddha of Infinite Light. The teacher-student relationship continued through the centuries with the elder of the two acting as the tutor of the other, and the Panchen Lamas becoming the abbots of Tashilhunpo. China has a long history of trying to exploit the differences between the two divine leaders for its own advantage. The ninth Panchen Lama ran into serious conflict with the thirteenth Dalai Lama over his support for China and had to flee the country, and the present Panchen Lama is regarded by some, probably unfairly, as a puppet. He was in fact imprisoned and probably tortured during the Cultural Revolution, and the fact that he is kept in Peking is probably an indication of his spiritual power and the reverence in which Tibetans hold him.

Above the monastery is a huge *tangka* wall many metres high, where banners are displayed on ceremonial occasions. On our last visit in 1985, a huge *tangka* was about to be unfurled for the first time for twenty-five years to commemorate the visit of the Panchen Lama.

Straying around the monastery this time we ran into a disconsolate tour group. They had had a walk of several hours to reach their tour bus from the Nepalese border over a road made impassable by landslides, and at one point had had to run for their lives to avoid falling rocks. Their tour leader had been buried alive, but fortunately had also been dug out alive. They were gloomily contemplating the prospect of their return by the same route. Among them was an old man who had accompanied Spencer Chapman on some of his climbing expeditions in the thirties. Now he was stomping around the temples with his walking stick, fuming away. What was upsetting him most was not the landslide, but the way they had been treated by their tour guide. 'You mean they were rude to you?' I shouted into his good (right) ear. 'No, I mean the lies they tell!' On the road from the border to Shigatse, their guide had pointed out ruined temples and forts, and blamed their destruction on these British tourists and Younghusband. The trouble with this piece of historical rewriting is that Younghusband went nowhere near the Nepal border, coming up to Gyantse, not Shigatse, via Sikkim and Yadong, a few hundred miles to the east! It makes one wonder what other 'inaccuracies' are told by guides around the country, with what aim and with what effect. In mainland China we never heard anyone try to blame the Cultural Revolution destruction on anything other than the Cultural Revolution: why pretend it didn't happen in Tibet? The net effect must be to make tourists sceptical about *any* information they are offered.

We left the irate tourists stumping irritably back to their minibus and returned to the hotel for a farewell dinner with our friends. The next morning, in the freezing dark, we got up and said goodbye: they were dashing to the border, as they had a plane to catch from Kathmandu. The world of international jets and deadlines seemed a long way off to us: the pace of life is pretty slow here. But we had our own Monday morning deadline to meet and as they sped off in one direction, we boarded a creakingly slow Chinese bus in the other. Last year we had continued the journey all the way to the border, so for much of our trip back to Lhasa we were with our friends in spirit, wondering where they had got to, and one journey became superimposed on the other.

We settled into the bus, trying to scrape a clear patch in the layer of ice on the inside of the window so that we could see out. The bus contained an assortment of traders, peasants and workers; our travelling companions on the bumpy back seat were a weatherbeaten Tibetan trader and three dead wildcats in a yak-hair sack, eyes glazed and teeth bared in stiff grins. Their whiskered faces bobbed alongside ours for most of the journey. As the bus lurched along, spinning up clouds of choking dust, grinding to a halt in a *ssshh* of escaping air as a tyre punctured, or fighting its way through the middle of the river with water lapping in at the doors and seeping up through the floorboards, we imagined the faster progress of the landcruiser in the other direction.

We headed north, passing villages on the plain where women were threshing with flails in courtyards or winnowing the grain in large flat baskets, and imagined our friends climbing southwards out of the plain into a different landscape of barren mountains and contorted rock in swirling colours: brown and yellow valleys giving way as the road swings up and round a corner to purple, gold and black rockscapes. As we laboured painfully up the Karo La, we travelled in our minds towards the border across high thinly-grassed plateaux with the snowy Himalayan chain as a backdrop, past villages painted like the French flag in red, white and blue, looking as if a conquering army led by Napoleon had passed that way. Lumbering along the lakeshore, we followed our friends across a grassy plain strewn with ruins: a Dali-esque landscape of soft outlines, vast spaces and the melted remains of mud forts. As we wheezed and groaned up to the Kamba La, we imagined them descending off the Tibetan tableland down the steep staircase of hairpin bends that leads into a different world of damp rhododendron forests and luxuriant undergrowth.

At the top of the Kamba La, everyone yelled '*Lha . . . Gye!*' (the gods are victorious), much to the surprise of the few Chinese on the bus. The driver stopped because he had a string of prayer flags that he wanted to add to the flapping lines already decorating the pass, and everyone except the wildcats got out to admire the view or circumambulate the shrine.

We had cause later to be grateful that the driver had had the forethought to propitiate the mountain gods before descending the pass. The few moments we spent at the top of the pass were the last minutes of peace before a nightmare helter-skelter freewheel in neutral down the other side with the Yarlung river swaying ever closer through alternate windows as we lurched round the curves. We prayed that a tyre wouldn't blow or the brakes fail. In between the alarming swings as the driver wrenched the vehicle round the bends, we tried to distract ourselves by getting the camera out of the window for shots of the glorious golden light on the valley and mountains. We hurtled out of the last hairpin, hit the tar-macked road, and there was a sudden explosion followed by a hiss of expelled air and the smell of burning rubber. A tyre had blown.

Back at Gyantse we had had a puncture and stopped to change the wheel. At the time we had been rather curious as to why the driver had exchanged the flat tyre for an equally flat tyre from another bus, but it now occurred to us that we had no spare. We all clambered out while he took off the wheel and mended both it and the spare. The process took a couple of hours, but it was a tranquil, beautiful spot. We walked along the river feeling privi-leged to be alive, as we surely would not have been if the accident had happened a few minutes earlier.

We finally arrived in Lhasa at about nine o'clock, very tired and dusty after a bone-shaking thirteen hours. We ate quickly, then mounted our bikes for the forty-minute ride through the freezing dark along the river to the campus. Stumbling up the stairs with one thought (bed) in mind, we were astonished and, I will confess, not exactly overjoyed, to find one of our more earnest and deter-mined students sitting encamped on the landing outside our door clutching an English book and cassette. He was not in the least disconcerted by our dusty, tired and grumpy arrival. 'I wait for you return,' he announced, a little unnecessarily. 'Oh, Norbu,' we groaned, 'can't it wait till Monday?' It appeared that it could not. Marching into the flat ahead of us, he explained what he wanted:

the entire contents of the book (an English–Tibetan dictionary) recorded onto the tape with enough space, please, between the words for him to repeat. Delighted as we were that he was taking his studies so seriously, we were a little less hospitable than we usually are on such occasions: promising that it would be done, though not, perhaps, in time for Monday morning and managing to evade further discussion on such burning issues as whether the verb 'like' is followed by a gerund, we manoeuvred him to the door and stumbled, glassy-eyed and zombie-like, to bed.

Letter thirteen:
The Gesar Storyteller and an Ancient Abbot

The other day, while walking across the dusty campus through the trees which are all that remain of the former *lingka* or park, I was surprised to see a sort of track, about ten feet wide, traced on the ground, winding from a gateway, through trees, round the houses and on to the main avenue. Each side of this track was marked with a continuous white line of what looked like chalk or flour. I asked the cheerful lady who operates the photocopier what it was all about – was it part of a children's game, or was there going to be a festival of some kind? 'Someone has died,' she said. The white lines of *tsampa* flour are traced on both sides of the route the dead body follows when it is taken from the house, to protect it from bad spirits.

Later we heard that the dead man had been a very famous figure in Tibet. He was one of the last old storytellers to know the complete Gesar epic. For some years he had been working with the help of the University, recording on tape all the famous stories, which are a major part of the oral tradition of Tibetan culture. While feeling regret that his passing meant the disappearance of yet another part of Tibetan culture, we were thankful that at least the authorities had seen fit to record his stories before he died, and relieved that the years of repression and destruction, when such stories would have been forbidden as 'nationalistic', did not last longer. At least there are still people alive today who were brought up before 1959 and who can transmit their culture to today's young Tibetans. Craftsmen, musicians, dancers, painters, builders, storytellers: their knowledge is still there, just, alive and at present being actively encouraged by the authorities. If the repression had lasted another generation, there would be no one left to pass this knowledge on. Even now, there is not much time left!

Gesar, the warrior king, is a national hero. He probably existed as a real historical figure in Ling, in eastern Tibet, but, rather like Arthur or St George, his stature has grown far greater in the popular imagination than it ever could have been in historical reality. He personifies justice, protects the poor and the humble, and defends Buddhism. His name may be related to Caesar, whose reputation probably travelled eastwards along the Silk Road and thence down into Tibet.

A full recitation of the epic can take several weeks to complete, the story being danced and sung as well as recited. The tales are full of fantastic supernatural happenings: Gesar is born after a sort of 'immaculate conception', from a magic sphere of light, and comes into the world not as a baby, but as a fully-formed young boy, able to speak and possessed of magic powers. The ruler of Ling is worried that Gesar has come in fulfilment of an old prophecy, to take the throne. He employs a sorcerer to kill the boy, but Gesar always escapes and eventually entombs the sorcerer in his meditation cave, by using a piece of *torma* (a *tsampa* cake), which he turns into a huge boulder. Later, Gesar wins a long horse race, thereby fulfilling the prophecy and becoming King of Ling. On the way he acquires a magic whip, hat and arrow quiver, which once belonged to Padmasambhava. These three relics help him through countless other exploits. Although the Gesar story takes place a thousand years or more ago, there are several prophecies contained within it, which say he will one day return to rule once more as a just king over his country.

In the Arts Department, there hangs a portrait of the old story-teller: his wrinkled leathery face and piercing dark eyes look so alive you almost expect him to start telling the epic over again.

Last weekend we had another trip to a monastery: our Chinese colleagues quite obviously think we're crazy to get up early, on our one precious day off, to travel miles along dusty, bone-shaking tracks that resemble rocky riverbeds more than roads just to see some old ruin! Often the end-point is really just an excuse for the journey itself. This time our driver was not Tsering, but the cheerful young man who had taken us for butter tea on the way to Samye – Tenzing. Unfortunately he did not have an aunt in the direction of Drigung, but we still had a good time together – and more than enough butter tea.

We were up early on the Saturday morning, for this was to be a whole weekend trip. We crossed the bridge that leads out of Lhasa in the half-dark and drove beside the 'Waters of Pleasure' on the southern bank, black mountains etched on a yellow sky forming the backdrop to our journey. We raised clouds of dust as we went and we rattled around in the empty jeep like peas in a pod: on several occasions our heads hit the roof as we bounced along. The traffic along this road, which is one of the two routes to Chengdu, the nearest large Chinese city, was mainly coming towards us: donkey carts, tractors with trailers, army-green 'Liberation' trucks, all carrying the same cargo – wood.

A day's journey east of here, the barren, sparsely grassed mountains give way to an alpine scenery of meadows and evergreen forests. The entire Arts Department recently went on a pilgrimage from Lhasa to Nyingchi expressly to paint trees – not much scope for that around Lhasa! But mostly the area has a less aesthetic, more mundane use as a source of wood for fuel, furniture and building. A friend who recently acted as cook for a Swiss trekking expedition in that area (now why do Swiss people want to pay upwards of four thousand dollars apiece to fly halfway round the world just to go trekking in a region that looks almost exactly like Switzerland?) said that people there are very worried about the rate at which trees are being cut down without replanting. Certainly, if the number of lorryloads of firewood we saw in the first couple of hours is anything to go by, the forests must be disappearing at an alarming rate.

The sun was well up by the time we turned off the main road at a village called Medrogungkar. There is a small temple here built by Songtsen Gampo in order, as the legend goes, to subdue a demoness who was threatening Tibet. Four such temples were built at places said to correspond to the demoness's hips and shoulders, to keep her firmly pinned down in place. We headed north-east from here, still following the Kyichu river, a brilliant turquoise blue in a valley of olives and browns. Ours was the only vehicle on this road, but there was plenty of traffic: yak train after yak train, all going in our direction up the valley. The yaks each carried two heavy sacks of coarsely woven woollen cloth, one on each side. We found out just how heavy they were as we tried to lift one back on to a yak, when, as often happened, we frightened the yaks into prancing skittishly up the mountainside, leaving the man cursing. The sacks all contained *tsampa*: this autumn's harvest of barley was being carried up from the cultivated Lhasa valley to isolated settlements higher up in the mountains. One panic-stricken yak managed to drop his load into an icy mountain stream. We stopped, guiltily, to help. The herdsman simply peeled off his curly-toed felt boots and waded barefoot into the glacial water. We discovered, to our relief, as we helped haul the drenched sack out of the river, that it contained butter, not barley flour, which would have been ruined by the soaking.

We continued on up the valley, which gets narrower and steeper as the river flows through a gorge, and our conversation, out of tune with the peace of the valley and the cloudless blue sky, was about the tension on the Indian border. We first heard about this in November when it was reported that there had been fighting near Shannan. A couple of days later we were startled to hear jets screaming overhead. At first we couldn't work out why we were so astonished by the sound, and then gradually realized that it is a sound that we ordinarily never hear at all. There are one or two planes a day in and out of Lhasa, but the airport is a couple of hours away from the city, and Lhasa is not on the flight path to anywhere. Lhasa residents were just as surprised as we were, and everyone came pouring out of offices and homes to stare up at the sky, and again it seemed there was fighting with the Indians near the border.

The Chinese dispute the McMahon line, the border between the two countries laid down by the British, since they claim it is a colonial legacy and as such is invalid. There are two places where the border is hotly disputed: one in western Tibet, a desolate region called the Aksai Chin which is claimed by both countries, but which to all intents and purposes seems to be under Chinese control – if an area so remote and desolate can be said to be controlled by anyone. The Indians did not in fact discover that the Chinese had built a road through the area until some time after its construction. The other disputed area, Arunachal Pradesh, is to the south-east of Tibet and is under Indian control; in fact it was India's decision to confer statehood on this area that aroused Chinese anger and led to the present state of tension. No one knows how serious the fighting is, though rumours are flying. It is a strange, uneasy feeling being in a country where an unacknowledged conflict is going on. I would have thought that India, if not China, would have reported it, and that we would have heard something through the Western media, but they seem silent. It is so remote a corner of the world that no one is going to notice: perhaps these border conflicts are such routine occurrences that neither side bothers to report them.

From the Kyichu valley, and talk of war, we turned into the Drigung valley and less disturbing, if less topical, talk about the history of Drigung. Tenzing had never been there before (our journey was punctuated by turns, double-backs and pauses to ask the way from passing nomads – no road signs here!), but he knew it used to be a big and very important monastery. He also knew the Drigung lama had fled to India, and had heard that there is now a very old abbot there, who can or used to be able to do lamaistic feats of the kind reported by Alexandra David-Neel in *Magic and Mystery in Tibet*, such as keeping warm though naked in the snow and trance-walking.

Drigung is, like Talung, one of the Kagyu monasteries, founded in the twelfth century by the disciples of Milarepa. The monastery stands in a very dramatic situation, hanging onto and spilling down the sides of a nearly vertical cliff, overlooking a dry valley, which at this time of year is a study in different shades of brown: grey-brown of the few bare trees, velvety khaki-brown of the mountains, dusty brown of the bare earth, which turns to a richer reddish brown where it has been ploughed up ready for planting. The fields are long and narrow here, some straight, some gently curving. The land is shared out among the different families who farm the valley: some good fields, some bad, so the pattern of fields looks like a medieval strip-farming system. There is a small creamy-beige mud-brick village among the swirly irregular fields at the base of the cliff. The monastery is very spread out: unlike the other monasteries we have visited, which tend to be close-packed collections of massive, solid, fortress-like buildings, with narrow alleys running between the temples and living quarters. Drigung consists of a main temple and a smaller one, with a large number of dwellings scattered across or sometimes built into, the mountainside. Steps and switchback paths lead from one house to another.

The monks, who had rarely seen a foreign visitor, gave us a very warm welcome with tea and *tsampa* in their best reception room. We shared out biscuits and chocolate: they had never tasted either before. Afterwards a young novice monk led us on a long walk across the mountain, through the monastery buildings and out on to the open mountainside, then climbing up and doubling back to re-enter the monastery at a higher level. At some distance from the monastery, the steep hill opened out into a broad meadow or alp. There was a sky burial site here, a large one, fenced round with fluttering prayer flags. Shards of white bone littered the site. Looking at it, Tenzing became very sombre. 'How many people have the birds eaten here?' he wondered aloud, and continued to mutter 'many people, many people,' as we walked round the large flat central stone where the bodies are cut up, and peered into a small building on the far side. On one wall was a mural of Buddha, and the floor was piled high with what looked like old pieces of black cloth, dark and dusty. As our eyes became accustomed to the dark interior, we realized suddenly that the place was piled from floor to ceiling with hundreds and hundreds of circular human scalps. We stared, fascinated, trying in vain to calculate how many deaths were represented by these gruesome piles of hair and skin, and how many scores of years they had been accumulating there. Tibet is full of sudden images that bring you up against your own mortality with a shock. As we walked back down the hill in silence, a pair of vultures wheeled above us, outstretched wings bigger than a man.

Back in the monastery, we were taken to see the abbot. Eighty-eight years old, very frail, he was half-sitting, half-reclining on a bed in a tiny dark room, wrapped up in sheepskin blankets. His days of magic and mystery are nearly over, but two bright alert black eyes twinkled at us from a deeply wrinkled face. He blessed us all and gave us two balls of *tsampa* and a handful of yoghurt and honey, which flowed stickily through our fingers as we slurped it up. To the Tibetans he also gave two threads, one red and one yellow: a kind of charm against sickness or bad luck.

From Drigung we retraced our way a few miles and took a side road up a very narrow valley to the north. This road leads to a small nunnery where we planned to spend the night. The valley was spectacular, overhung by craggy limestone peaks with a bright blue stream pouring down, and high waterfalls, which had turned to ice, on each side. The scenery was quite unlike any we had seen in Tibet so far, both sombre and romantic, like an illustration from a fairytale. Keats would have loved its gloomy grandeur!

The little *ani gompa*, or nunnery, is at the head of the valley in a narrow gorge, under the shadow of a huge jagged limestone mountain: one temple surrounded by a clutch of small whitewashed houses which straggle up the gorge along the banks of the torrent. At the lower end is a guesthouse, a long narrow earth-floored building containing nothing but a stone shelf at one end. This is the bed. Muffled up to the eyes in our down sleeping bags we were, surprisingly, not too cold, and almost comfortable. Outside the door was a hot bath! A hot spring bubbles up just there and has been channelled to form a little bathing pool in a circular enclosure of stones. It was wonderful to soak in the bubbling hot water, sitting on the algae-green stones, gazing up through the sulphurous steam at the clear sky and mountain peaks. We had almost forgotten what hot water felt like! The rocks are all covered in slimy green weed and the gases bubbling up made us quite drowsy: when we emerged we felt faint and weak from the combined effects of heat and gas, and we literally collapsed into bed.

The next morning we went for a long walk along the stream, where there was a wooden water wheel, turning at quite a rate, but serving only to spin a frilled and decorated prayer wheel. We ate a breakfast of tinned apples and Nepalese biscuits on the shoulder of a hill overlooking the village, then began to climb the mountain. I don't know exactly how high we were, but judging from shortness of breath, we were higher than we have been before: maybe about 17,000–18,000 feet. We climbed into the sun, while the village below was still in shadow, remaining so until midday. We could see steam rising from the hot spring pools, hear monks and nuns chanting, and the sound of horns being blown. Postman birds, ice-cream birds, sparrobins, something like a thrush – a very dapper dark coat with lighter patterns, and red-beaked choughs flying overhead. We clambered up a steep, sharply twisting path that led up through a thicket of short reddish bushes to a sunlit alpine meadow. As we climbed we could see the village and a scattering of temples on the opposite hillside. These eventually disappeared into the cleft between the mountains, and the view from the meadow was of a different valley, running at right angles to the main one, flanked by much higher snow peaks. We had lunch at the top of the mountain, then walked back down again to rejoin Tenzing, who had spent the morning relaxing by the spring. The sun's rays had just reached the village and the yak tethered in the courtyard, whose long black coat that morning had turned into a thick layer of woollen icicles, was beginning to thaw out.

We drove back through golden afternoon light – much faster than we had driven up. On the way we passed crowds of pilgrims, some walking, some slowly and painfully measuring their length in caterpillar prostrations all the way to Lhasa. Some people come all the way from Chamdo that way, Tenzing said. Lhasa is full of pilgrims at present, and has been since the harvest ended and work in the fields finished for the winter. They are a distinctive sight: women and men in great sheepskin coats, grimy and smelly, but warm! Some of these coats are trimmed with fur: fox, leopard or wildcat; some have broad stripes of multicoloured cloth sewn onto the skirt as decoration. A number of the women have peasant scarves in red or green tied around their heads in a sort of turban, while others have their long black hair braided into 108 narrow plaits, brightly coloured silken tassels braided into the plaits with elaborate hair ornaments of silver and turquoise. Many of the men wear beautifully embroidered brocade hats with fur earflaps, or round and fluffy fox-fur caps, rather Russian in appearance.

Wild-looking men with matted hair – distant cousins of Indian sadhus in appearance – mumble mantras and twirl prayer wheels as they stumble round the holy circuit. The wildest of these are still, in this sharp wintry weather, bare-chested as they prostrate themselves round the Barkor. The holiest of them are doing this breadthways instead of lengthways, an interminable process. The courtyard in front of the Jokhang is packed now with prostrating bodies, and the murmur of *Om Mani Padme Hum* repeated again and again under countless breaths sounds like the moaning of a flock of doves. The wildest holy man of all – a daily sight in the Barkor – bare to the waist, covered in dust, crazy staring eyes, has Dalai Lama badges pinned through the flesh on his shoulder.

These pilgrims in some ways seem to treat the town as if it were no different from the countryside they have just come from: their tents are pitched all along the riverside and along the highways leading out of town; and anywhere, everywhere in the centre of town, you come across groups of them squatting on the pavements or at the side of the road, cooking up stew or soup, picnicking as if they were in a field or on a mountainside.

For us, all this colourful winter clothing and crowds spells a Christmas atmosphere. It wouldn't surprise us at all to find that Father Christmas actually lives here, in some forgotten room of the Potala, dressed in a sheepskin coat, embroidered brocade fox-fur hat and highly coloured felt boots with curly toes. In fact we hear that this year's 'Lamp Festival', which follows hard on Whitewashing of Houses, falls on 26th December, so we will have a doubly festive day then!

Letter fourteen: **Christmas in Lhasa**

It is Spring Festival Eve: an overcast day, the dull light makes the mountains – khaki-brown with a light sprinkling of snow – look like an old sepia-tinted photograph. From the street outside comes the sound of children's voices and the intermittent explosion of firecrackers, a noise we have heard every day, with increasing frequency, since the first New Year, the international one on 1st January. I wonder if it will continue till the next New Year, the Tibetan one, on 28th February. This must be the only place in the world where you can celebrate three New Years in quick succession. Outside, the streets are crammed with people making last-minute purchases of beer, wine, meat, vegetables and, of course, firecrackers for the festival tomorrow, or cycling home with their newly-acquired chicken or Lhasa river fish tied to the handlebars of their bike.

A Christmas feeling is in the air, although the shops are just as drab and dreary as usual, and the assistants just as surly. (When I did a shopping role-play with our Second-Year class, two of the girls playing shop assistants just sat behind the 'counter' of their 'shop', reading books and turning all the 'customers' away with the same answer: 'Don't have.' When I asked them what they were doing, they replied, giggling, 'Oh, we're Chinese shop assistants.')

Yesterday afternoon, the University put on a surprise party to celebrate the festival – rather too much of a surprise for us, since, when two students came to collect us, Charlie was elbow-deep in water trying to unblock the sink, and I had just washed my hair, which was soaking wet. The evening was a blend of Chinese and

Tibetan party styles: speeches, sunflower seeds and star turns gradually gave way to *chang*, chat and dancing. There was a very friendly atmosphere, and the evening was full of Tibetan verve and jollity: some very good Tibetan dancing and songs, with everyone joining in lustily for the choruses. This was the latest in what has in fact been a whole series of parties from Christmas Eve onwards; perhaps the Eve of the Year of the Rabbit, and the most important festival in the Chinese year, is a good time to recap on our rather unusual Christmas.

The University were terribly worried about getting things right for us, and pre-Christmas fever started nearly as early here as back in England – except that in our case, this took the form of a visitation from our *Waiban* (Foreign Affairs Bureau) officials. Beaming all over their faces and bearing an enormous checklist, they settled themselves down in our armchairs and, helping themselves to tea and mandarin oranges, they began: 'Your Christmas Day is coming soon.' 'Yes,' I confirmed. 'We would like to check some detail.' 'Okay,' I said, wondering nervously how accurate my memories of the Christmas story were. They then began to tick off the items on their list.

'We have order two Christmas cake. Will be enough?'

'Also, we have Christmas tree. It is about this high,' (measuring about four feet from the ground) 'we would like to know, is this right height for Christmas tree?'

'And about candle. Red is the right colour, I think?'

'The Party . . . ,' what has the Party to do with religious celebrations, I wondered, and then he went on . . . 'Would you like Christmas Day Party in your home or other place? Is evening or afternoon the correct time?'

'Christmas song is important, I think. Have you tape or shall we obtain?'

'Invite any Foreign Friend. We will send car pick up.'

'The University want to decorate your flat, is okay?'

'The Jesus was born in a . . .' 'Manger,' I supplied. 'Yes, manger. Would you like a manger?' I said I didn't think that would be necessary. Then concluding, 'The University want to make you very happy. You can ask for anything you want,' they left.

Fired by their enthusiasm for our festival, we flung ourselves into it and determined that a Tibetan Christmas should lose nothing by being 5,000 miles from and two miles above a traditional English one. Christmas shopping taxed our ingenuity as we struggled to find where you could buy such things as crepe paper and gold paper to make decorations. It took me about a week of intensive shopping to assemble the ingredients for a mincepie. Shopping in Lhasa is always a rather random activity and depends a lot on chance and which lorries bearing what cargoes have arrived from China that week. One week there will be no toilet paper, another no apples or candles. Christmas shopping had one bright spot, when the normally grumpy and taciturn assistants in the Friendship Store took a sudden interest in my need for gold paper and decorations. 'Is it your Spring Festival?' they asked, and soon I had half the assistants in the shop, jolted out of their normal torpor, crowding around me eagerly to ask questions about Christmas traditions, which made me think that the reason for their habitual surliness is probably simply excruciating boredom.

We went to six parties in the seven days between Christmas and New Year, and finished up in a state of collapse from so much high-altitude festivity. Dancing at two miles above sea-level can make you quite puffed! On Christmas Eve, we had a little foreigners' get-together at the Lhasa Hotel, where we indulged in ex-Everest expedition fruitcake and mincepie concocted by me out of an unlikely assortment of ingredients and cooked in the vast kitchens of the Lhasa Hotel. The evening was well lubricated with a sort of mulled wine, or rather mulled brandy cooked up by the manager. Feeling and reeling very much the worse for wear, we somehow wove our way back home through the night on our bikes, the Potala swaying drunkenly above us, and then we filled *forty* stockings at about one o'clock in the morning! . . . walnuts, sweets, tangerines, necklaces for the girls and keyrings for the boys. (The whole enterprise came to a grand total of something like £8!) The students had all brought one sock (clean) to class that morning, rather puzzled as to why. We lurched from classroom to classroom in the early hours of Christmas morning, pinning up stockings above the blackboards. It was amazing to see the students' faces the next morning: very curious, rather baffled, politely unsure whether to take them down and open them or not (in China, it seems, you don't open gifts in public, but take them home and unwrap them in secret). When they did finally open them, they were delighted, but still, I think, rather puzzled: it *is* an extraordinary custom, seen from this distance/height! Christmas was a working day, but punctuated by visitors bearing gifts and stopping in for coffee and mincepie or lunch. Our Christmas lunch consisted of a tin of Budgen's ham, some Bonbel cheese, and mincepie, all washed down with a bottle of wine purchased at outrageous expense at the Lhasa Hotel and saved for Christmas. (The other ingredients, lest you should think that a British super-market chain has opened a branch in Lhasa, were gifts sent by thoughtful friends.)

In the afternoon, we rehearsed the Second-Year students for a couple of funny sketches they were putting on. Our First Years, meanwhile, since it was Thursday, had Political Study, and were sitting in small groups reading one of Chairman Mao's essays to each other. When they had finished, we taught them to make stars out of gold paper and, wondering what the Chairman would have thought, decorated the famous tree with these and small parcels wrapped in coloured paper, which again caused the students some puzzlement. ('This is all terribly complicated,' I heard one mutter as he tied the parcels to the tree.) The parcels were actually matchboxes containing stamps off all our friends' letters, which we had saved up for the students. We had wrapped the matchboxes in crepe paper and tied them up with red and green cords – threads from Khampas' hair-tassels which we had bought in the market.

In the evening was The Party, attended by a potentially uncomfortable but surprisingly harmonious mixture of students, staff and top admin people. It went very well – and I am pleased to report that the candles were indeed red, that two cakes were enough, not only for us, but also for all our students and colleagues, that the Christmas tree did not exceed the regulation height, and that a manger did not form part of the festive proceedings. We started off with some carols we had taught the students. Imagine a roomful of Tibetans all lustily singing 'We wish you a Merry Christmas' and 'A Partridge in a Pear Tree'. I wonder what Buddha would make of that?

Then the Second-Year students put on their performance of mimes and sketches. Some of them are quite talented, and one mime in particular, about an old tramp on a park bench, had everyone in stitches: the President nearly fell off his seat with laughter and even the dour party secretary and political people were helpless with giggles!

While everyone was singing another selection of carols, I raced upstairs with one of our colleagues and helped him dress up in what must be the world's strangest-ever Father Christmas outfit: a red hood decorated with tinsel, a red silk fur-trimmed Tibetan *chuba*, knee length with wide sleeves, big black Tibetan riding boots, and a beard made of cotton wool and yak hair. He looked pretty convincing actually – but then the Lhasa streets look as if they are full of Father Christmases anyway! This Chinese one was rotund and jolly and did the '*Ho Ho Ho*' bit very well while distributing presents to all and sundry.

Then we did a round of silly party games, in English style. They had never before played Pass the Parcel or Musical Chairs (which we have rechristened Chinese Bus). It was chaos! Everyone cheated like mad, picking up their stools and running round with them. Again we were all paralysed with laughter.

Order was restored with a more Chinese part of the evening, where everyone had to do a turn. The President and his cousin, the Vice-President, did a display of Tibetan dancing, and the head of our department did a Mongolian song. Can you imagine the Vice-Chancellor of an English university doing a folk dance for the students? Then Western culture took over in the shape of disco – but even then it was a strange mixture of Western pop, Hong Kong pop, Indian pop and traditional Tibetan music. The

Tibetans are all natural dancers. Their dances are often a rhythmic tap and shuffle to plonky banjo type music, often performed on a plank or board to give a better sound. (We have christened it 'bent plank music', because the first dancer we ever saw in this style performed on a warped plank.) It is actually as difficult as it looks simple: the steps are delicate and surprisingly complicated and our efforts to learn them ended in stumbling failure. Anyway, it seems to convert naturally to disco, and disco seems to lend itself to Tibetan dances, so the dancing was a real mix of styles too. The whole evening was a lovely zany meeting of cultures. The President summed it up when he said to our Father Christmas: 'This is wonderful – a Chinese man, wearing Tibetan dress to play an English Father Christmas.'

On the 29th there was another university party – I have never taught in an institution which enjoyed them quite so much! When ordinary daily life is in general drab and comfortless, festivals take on a heightened meaning and greater importance, and people really fling themselves into the celebrations. This party was held outdoors (an outdoor party in the middle of a Tibetan winter is something of an act of faith), attended by the whole of the University. Following an old Chamdo tradition, an enormous bonfire was lit in the middle of the basketball pitch (although I suspect the tradition just specifies a bonfire, not a basketball pitch). Everyone stood round in a huge circle and a few speeches were made, then each department offered a display of that by now typically Chinese art form – formation disco. The formal part of the evening over, the dancing then began. To our embarrassment, we had to start this off under the critical eyes of about 1,000 students. Very soon everyone was dancing round the bonfire, and this went on until about midnight. Again, what a mixture! Disco to Indian pop, traditional Tibetan circle dances to Western pop, and disco to Tibetan tunes.

This was a party entirely without refreshment, and the other university parties we went to ran on nothing stronger than sweet tea and sunflower seeds, in sharp contrast to the official New Year party for foreigners at the *Waiban* headquarters in town, which we attended on the following evening and for which we received gold-embossed invitations in Tibetan and Chinese. We went with two people from the Lhasa Hotel. The only other foreigners were the staff of the Nepalese Consulate and their wives, referred to in the opening speech as the 'Nepalese Consul, the Vice-Consuls, and all the madams from the Nepalese Embassy'. We were dubbed 'Mr Charlie from Tibet University and his madam', which did not please me greatly.

This was also a riotous occasion, though less because of an overflow of spontaneity and goodwill than the free-flowing drink. Speech followed speech and we toasted dignitary after dignitary and economic achievement after economic achievement, not forgetting of course our comrades the herdsmen and armed police. All televised for the edification of the masses watching Tibet TV. Small wonder that when the dancing started, no one wanted to begin! Actually, the music was quite good, and we had by now become so immune to dancing badly in front of large numbers of people, that we began – and of course were recorded for posterity by the TV cameras.

Charlie had another moment of fame later, when the time came for doing turns and he was pushed in front of the TV cameras to give a rendition of Auld Lang Syne. (By the way, the film *Lhasa*, made by the Beijing film crew, and including shots of Charlie in the language lab with our shell-shocked First Years, most of whom had never seen a real live English person before, let alone had one talking to them through an array of complicated equipment, is now on general release and playing to packed houses in Lhasa – which means that every time we go into the post office or the bank, someone says: 'Oh, I saw you in the cinema last night . . . .')

Several of the Nepalese Consulate got quite merry on the *maotai* (through their madams remained demurely sober). Two of them got up in front of the microphones and cameras, and launched into a tuneless wailing that was apparently a Nepalese folksong. Their madams doubled up with laughter and tried to boo them off, but they were undaunted and even gave an unsolicited encore.

Another lurched around the dance floor grabbing every available female. We decided he was more Vice than Consul, or perhaps an Attaché – he was certainly quite difficult to detach!

We had assumed that that was the last of the New Year festivities, but the next day, New Year's Eve, we were presented with two invitations to parties, one from our First-Year class, one from our Second-Year class. So we spent the evening party-hopping between the Second Years upstairs, and the First Years downstairs. The whole campus was full of parties in different classrooms all over the University, and after a while was full of nomadic party-goers, visiting one party after another. Our First Years are all Tibetan, the Second Years mostly Chinese, and the two parties were very different in character, as we found when we left the Second Years demurely seated in a ring cracking sun-flower seeds, sipping tea and watching each other perform songs or dances, and descended to the First-Year classroom to find it full of firecracker smoke and loud music, with their Chinese teacher looking rather out of control.

By midnight the two parties had merged and we celebrated New Year with a great burst of firecrackers and a chaotic but enthusiastic rendering of Auld Lang Syne. We had told the students about kissing at New Year and the suggestion pleased them greatly, but girls and boys don't touch in public here, so when New Year struck, they honoured the English tradition in a novel way: a group of girls descended on me like a flock of doves to kiss my cheek, while all the boys embraced each other.

We rounded off the New Year celebrations with a trip to Mindroling monastery, where we went on National Day, a few hours' drive away down the Yarlung Tsangpo valley, a lovely ride and a peaceful spot. We ate a freezing picnic of bread and ex-Everest expedition corned beef and cheese spread, and then wandered around the monastery, watching the monks – no New Year holiday for them – making *tangkas*, beating copper to make bowls and copying ancient engravings onto new silver and brass horns. What a lot of love and devotion is going into the restoration of these old monasteries: a re-creation of the past, exactly as it was in every detail. Wandering around the village, we met a small group of ragged children, who immediately lined up in front of us and sang 'Frère Jacques' in perfect French accents. I wonder where they learnt it?

The landscape on the way to Mindroling looked like a Breughel painting: bare brown frost-encrusted fields, winter trees and various medieval-looking people in the background. We stopped for a while in a small village to watch a scene that came straight from Breughel: the village pond had frozen solid and all the children were skating on it. They had home-made skates, simply thin blocks of wood with a metal wire tied round to give a cutting edge. Some were performing quite sophisticated feats on these primitive skates.

Amidst all these Tibetanized 'Western' festivals, there was one which was wholly Tibetan. This was 'Lamp Festival', which fell this year on our Boxing Day and which marks the day of Tsongkhapa's death. All the festivals are rather later than usual – Tibetan New Year usually coincides more or less with Chinese New Year, and Lamp Festival is usually in November – apparently because 1986 had 'two Julys'! August, or the eighth month, had been declared inauspicious, so they postponed it by creating two seventh months. It has been a hopeless task trying to teach our students the names of the English months – they are confused enough trying to correlate the Chinese and Tibetan calendars and the addition of a third source of confusion was more than they could cope with.

Lamp Festival takes place one month after the Whitewashing of Houses, which in turn takes place one month after Washing Festival. Whitewashing of Houses has its origin in the belief that at a certain time (15th day of the ninth month) a rather awesome goddess called Pelden Lhamo, who is the patroness of Lhasa, makes an annual outing from her home in the Jokhang for a tour around Lhasa, and all houses must then be freshly whitewashed for her inspection. Everywhere we went, we could see people refurbishing the outside of their houses by the simple expedient of hurling buckets of whitewash at the walls.

Lamp Festival was lovely. I went down into town at about eight o'clock with a group of friends and students and the Barkor was a beautiful sight: every house had a row of butter-lamps burning on each window ledge, and the Jokhang was practically aflame with lamps in a long row across the rooftop and a ledge across the centre of the building.

I have never seen the Barkor so crowded: from one side of the street to the other, in front and behind, as far as the eye could see, was a solid mass of people all moving slowly clockwise round the holy way. It was a good thing that everyone was moving in the same direction – otherwise it would have been impossible to move at all. The only illumination was from the flickering butter-lamps and the glow of the juniper fires lit in hearths and incense burners all along the way. And the people, for such a large crowd, were very subdued: the only sounds were the shuffle of countless feet, the crackling of the juniper twigs in the prayer kilns, and the low murmuring of *Om Mani Padme Hum* from countless voices.

My students were very strict with me and made me do all sorts of things I have never done before, such as walking *in between* a certain telegraph pole and the wall of a house, and passing one side of a prayer kiln but not the other. I asked why. They didn't know, but said: 'If we don't do these things, the old women will be angry with us.' We walked round three times, to complete the *kora*.

In the main square in front of the Jokhang temple, a huge juniper fire was roaring and the area in front of the temple was packed with prostrating bodies rising and falling in dark waves. The temple doors were, however, locked fast. I asked why it was closed; on such a holy occasion surely it should be open. My friends just looked at each other. 'Yes,' was all they said.

Letter fifteen: **A Trip to East Tibet**

At the end of our original contract we were offered a free trip by
the University, perhaps as a special treat or perhaps as a reward
for six months' 'good behaviour'. In fact the State Education
Commission in Peking had sent down a letter, instructing the
University to take us on a ten-day trip, visiting 'three cities'.
This caused the literal-minded bureaucrat from the Foreign Affairs
Bureau (who, in the words of one of our colleagues, 'thinks he's
a big shop, but is really a small potato') some perplexity, as he
tried to work out where in Tibet could possibly be described as
a city. Lhasa, the capital, is the size of a small market town; the
other towns are really just large villages. We put in several requests
for places to visit, ranging from the just-about-practicable to the
outrageous, but it was clear really, right from the start, that we
would be taken to the area the University had in mind as 'suitable
and convenient': that is, Shannan, the Tsetang area, south-east of
Lhasa, often described as 'the birthplace of Tibetan civilization'.

We had planned a big loop, south to Tsetang, then north
to Nyingchi in east Tibet, then back to Lhasa; but here another
bureaucracy, the Public Security Bureau, intervened. We were
told that the road from Tsetang to Nyingchi was impassable at
that season. This of course was nonsense – when in Tsetang we
saw plenty of trucks laden with wood from Nyingchi. The real
reason was military: that road runs very close to the Indian border,
in the very area where the dispute we described earlier took place.
Things seemed to have cooled off a bit during the winter. According to a newspaper report, China did not want to make trouble
during 1986, the international Year of Peace (although that did not

145

stop the skirmishes on the Vietnam border), but was preparing for an assault once the Year of Peace was over! Hu Mu, the timid little soldier who attends our First-Year classes, has mysteriously vanished, we assume to the border.

So, one bright blue morning at the beginning of February, we all set off southwards in a battered old Beijing jeep. 'We all' included, besides ourselves and the driver, a cadre's daughter who had cashed in on a free trip to Tsetang to visit her family with a huge carton of noodles (unobtainable in Tsetang?) and a brand-new thermos which she clutched nervously to her chest all the journey, particularly when we spoke to her, which seemed to cause her uncontrollable panic. The other member of the expedition was, of course, our minder. Used to our Sunday expeditions, accompanied only by the driver and his extended family, we had forgotten that as this was an official trip, we would have to have a 'guide'. It would have been nice to go with one of the real friends we have made, Chinese or Tibetan, who are genuinely interested in Tibetan culture, even if they don't always know a great deal. Our 'minder', a stranger to us, was neither interested nor informative. He smoked and chatted to the driver and largely ignored us. One of the hardest things about living in China, and one we will never get used to, is the patronizing attitude of bureaucrats who will never let you do things the way you would like – the only thing is to switch off and repeat to yourself 'Mother(land) knows best', like a mantra, over and over again.

Enough griping. Early on this Sunday morning we set off at a bumpy 25 mph, first westwards towards Drepung and then south to the Yarlung Tsangpo valley. The Lhasa river was still frozen at the edges in lacework patterns, beautiful in the early light. Herds of cattle were being moved along the road. There were young lambs in the fields, and ravens were carrying nesting material into the treetops. The air was mild after the bitter cold of Christmas, and whenever we stopped we could hear the spring-like sound of birdsong all around. We passed a medieval-looking group of horsemen, who appeared to be carrying lances with coloured pennants – in fact, they were trotting towards the riverbank to

146

renew the prayer flags on poles in the middle of the river. In a nearby village, the inhabitants were also putting new prayer flags up on the rooftops, ready for New Year, and all the houses had bright new pelmets and door hangings. Stopping to photograph the magnificent ruined silhouette of a *dzong* (hilltop fortress) on the south side of the Yarlung Tsangpo (site of the ambush of a PLA convoy by Khampa guerillas in 1959), we disturbed a huge flock of wild geese. They swirled up and round overhead, black and white patterns against the reddish tints of the trees. Then east, through the sand-dune desert of the Yarlung Tsangpo valley – the only colours the brown of the mountains and the blue of the sky and river. A minor breakdown and puncture later, we snorted into Tsetang in the early afternoon.

Tsetang is where Tibetan culture, and the Tibetans themselves, began. According to legend, in a cave high up in the mountains to the east, an ogress coupled with a monkey. The monkey was the incarnation of Chenrezi, the Lord of Compassion, and the ogress was the incarnation of Drölma, a female goddess. The monkey heard the ogress crying with loneliness in her cave in the mountains and hurried to see what was the matter. She begged him to stay with her. Overcome with pity, he went to Chenrezi to ask for advice. Chenrezi told him that the time had come for Tibet to have children, and that he was to take the ogress as his wife. The pair had six children, representing both the six kinds of beings (gods, demigods, humans, ghosts, animals and hell-beings) and the six kinds of people in Tibet. These six children multiplied until there was not enough fruit on the trees to feed them all. Their monkey father went back to Chenrezi to seek advice once more, and was given different kinds of seeds to take back and plant. So agriculture, too, had its beginnings in Tsetang.

Now Tsetang is a largely Chinesified town, with the usual regimented concrete block architecture, but all around it are reminders of its ancient history. The Valley of the Kings, a bumpy 20-mile drive south, is where most of the ancient kings of Tibet were buried in the seventh and eighth centuries, under great tumuli which have been eroded over the centuries to become a natural part of the landscape again. The tumuli are spread over the hillside and valley floor – just one of them, the supposed tomb of Songtsen Gampo, has a small temple on top (rebuilt in 1983). No actual excavations have been carried out, and some authorities believe this king is in fact buried in Lhasa. We stumbled up and down the tumuli and across the dry ploughed earth of the barley fields, looking for a sculptured stone lion, which is on top of one of the tumuli furthest up the hill. Richardson has a photograph of it in *A Cultural History of Tibet*, and it is still there today, undisturbed by war and revolution.

Above the village of Chonggye is a partially rebuilt temple, Riwo Dechen, on Tiger Hill. As we climbed up the track, we had a free view of a Tibetan dance performance – or more probably the rehearsal for some New Year festivities. In a farm courtyard far below, a group of young men and girls were rehearsing an elaborate dance routine to a loud drummed accompaniment, and it was a delight to watch these swirling dance patterns from an aerial viewpoint. The monastery ruins stretched along the hillside above Chonggye, looking very different from the magnificent buildings in Richardson's photographs. Huge Cultural Revolution slogans were fading on the broken walls, only a couple of decades after they had been painted, in the same way that the enormous slogans made out of white pebbles on many mountainsides have now been eroded by rain and wind and rolled downhill so they are only just recognizable. It is a pity the result of all the violence and destruction will last much longer than the slogans and political rhetoric which inspired it.

When we got to Yumbulagang, down another fork of the valley south of Tsetang, we were pleased to see the reconstruction of the temple was almost complete. It is known as the 'first building in Tibet', and was probably a king's palace. It looks rather like a cross between an English parish church and a Spanish castle, with a tall tower, set on a magnificent rock promontory above the valley. On our last visit we had been completely taken in by the reconstruction – the monks had said 'there was just a little damage' – until we saw photographs of the ruins taken in the early 1980s and accompanying a magazine article by Heinrich Harrer after his return to Tibet in 1983.

The second time around, there was still the same shock of surprise as we rounded a bend in the road and saw Yumbulagang perched on its high rock. As we walked up the path towards it, prayer-flags flapped in the breeze above our heads and wind chimes tinkled around the eaves. Inside, it is bright and cheerful – swirling murals in gleaming new paint decorate the walls, and it is lighter and less gloomy than most Tibetan temples. Downstairs was a room we remembered well, with eight serene Buddhas painted on the wall.

This time, we climbed right up inside the tower, almost expecting to find bells as in an English church, but there were only rafters festooned with *katag* and prayer-flags, with wind chimes ringing outside in the cold air. At the foot of the promontory was a small village. It is always interesting to look *down* on a Tibetan village from a mountainside. When you wander around the streets, there is a strangely empty feeling, as all the houses are enclosed in courtyards with high mud walls and the narrow streets are practically deserted, with just the occasional glimpse of life through a courtyard gate here and there. From above, in contrast, the whole village is milling with activity: the village is a pattern of squares, and squares within squares: houses within courtyards. Inside these squares, people are moving about their daily business: women cooking and feeding chickens, old men snoozing, children playing. This village had hay piled up on all the rooftops. The colours, as always in Tibet, were simple and strong: whitewashed houses, golden hay, bare brown ploughed earth, all shining under the bright high blue and sunlight.

That evening, we stumbled around Tsetang, looking for the 'first field in Tibet' which is supposed to be behind the People's Hospital. We found plenty of fields of course, but nothing to distinguish the 'first field' from any of the others. I don't know what we were expecting: a neat little blue and white plaque maybe! Peasants make pilgrimages here at planting time to take a handful of earth from the field, which they then scatter on their own fields to ensure a healthy crop and a good harvest.

We had a very positive experience when we visited another small temple just south of Tsetang called Trandruk. We had also visited it in 1985. Then, it was a complete wreck: the temples and outbuildings were being used as storehouses, the courtyard was full of broken images, a chaos of severed limbs and shattered heads. Now the temple was cheerfully painted, the courtyard neatly swept and, displayed in pride of place inside the temple, was a magnificent *tangka* unlike any other we have seen in Tibet, depicting Chenrezi sewn with thousands of tiny pearls on a black background: the design looked very Indian.

Our visit to Samye the next morning was also a very positive experience, for the same reasons. We took the ferry across the river in the freezing early morning, starting out before dawn from Tsetang, the gold sunrise behind us as we walked down to the river's edge, the river a cold, dark blue in the thin morning light. As the sun came up, the mountains across the river turned to rose and gold in the reflected light, and the river to mingled rose and bright blue. Clear lines in the sharp light, which later melted into a mid-morning blur of haze and dust. The river was very low, and it took nearly two hours to cross, the boatman negotiating the swirling currents and weaving his way between sandbanks. Sandbanks! They were more like great slices of desert in the middle of the river. It was bitterly cold. Even when the sun came up over the mountain, there was no warmth in it. A group of pilgrims huddled up in their sheepskin coats in the middle of the boat, passing round a blackened old kettle full of *chang*, singing loudly to ward off the cold.

At Samye, we warmed up with glass after glass of hot sweet tea in a sunlit courtyard that contained, beside ourselves, five hairy black pigs and two calves feeding at a trough. Our minder and the driver then went off: they had a busy morning ahead of them, for they had brought a large tin of butter to make offerings in all the temple butter-lamps. These huge drums of butter are on sale everywhere round the Barkor in Lhasa, labelled 'EDIBLE FAT: FROM

 I wonder if Norway knows what happens to its gift – most of it ends up in temple butter-lamps being burnt for Buddha! Our driver pointed to the tin and said 'from India' with a grin. 'No,' we replied, 'from Norway.' What he meant was that the tins come into Tibet from India, and are sold at some border town to the Barkor traders together with all the bangles, lipstick, face cream, brilliantine hair oil, perfume, pirated disco tapes and glossy posters of Indian film stars that also find their way into Tibet. I wonder through what nefarious channels the tins get diverted from the Indian aid pro-gramme to the border, and what enterprising trader first spotted a lucrative market for Western butter in Tibet. Perhaps there is a solution to the EEC butter mountain here?

Well, they both went off with their tin of Burnable/Edible Fat, and we followed them towards the temple to see what was new. What was new, was that they were beginning to construct the third storey: the one that was originally built in the Indian style, with three roofs. This was a pleasant surprise for us, as we had somehow assumed that work would stop at two storeys. On the second storey, the faded murals we had seen on our previous visit were now freshly painted in gleaming colours, and one, not yet repainted, had outlines drawn in on the damaged and obliterated sections, ready to be filled in. All along the upper cloister, monks were sitting in the sun, each in his own patch of sunlight, each engrossed in his own private activity, chanting, copying prayers, reading. Two monks were rinsing out a robe and spreading the enormous length of purplish cloth out to dry in the sun on the temple roof. Sounds drifted up from the village and fields around: donkey bells, children calling, a tractor chugging past. And all around, beyond the temple and village, the vast unreal distances of Tibet, like scenery from a dream.

Because of the 'impassable road', we had to return to Lhasa and set out again along the northern route to Nyingchi. This is a long drive, so we started out at 6 a.m. in a thick black night studded with brilliant stars – Tibetan nights have more stars than I ever dreamt existed. Is it because the air is so clear, or because you are two miles closer to them? The road follows the Lhasa river as far as Medrogungkar, a route we had travelled before when we went to Drigung. This part of the journey was in darkness and we were beyond Medrogungkar by the time the thick black began to thin to pale blue. As we wound up and over the pass, through scenery like the Scottish Highlands, the sun rose over the mountains ahead of us. There was thick ice over the road at the top of the pass, and we crawled over it in four-wheel drive. Our hearts stopped as, ahead of us, a lorry heavily overladen with a high swaying load of logs rocked on the ice and nearly overturned. At one point part of the road had fallen away, and we had to get out and rebuild it with rocks and stones before we could get across.

As we left the pass, the scenery began to change. The craggy mountains were thinly grassed with scrubby olive-green-gold, and there were small bushes and dwarf conifers – we realized where our Christmas tree had come from! The style of architecture changed too, as we came down off the pass, almost as if we were crossing the border into a different country. At first, the houses were built of mud brick, though in a very different way from the solid trapezoid mud castles in the Lhasa valley. These were made of irregular roughly cut cubes of mud all heaped crazily on top of one another. They looked like piles of peat sods, or, from a distance, like dry stone walling. Windows were simply a square hole framed by four planks, with no glass. These were succeeded by stone houses which looked very solid, with very steep roofs of slate and tiny windows. Then, as the hillsides became more and more densely wooded, wooden towns and villages started to appear; not, as you might imagine, in alpine chalet style, but rather more like Wild West log cabins in appearance. Mixed in with these traditional Tibetan buildings, of whatever construction, were the usual modern buildings, all alike, long, low, one-storey barrack-like constructions with cement walls and glaring tin roofs, easily recognizable because they are so out of tune with their surroundings. The traditional Tibetan buildings of wood and stone and mud look as if they have grown out of the landscape; these look as if they have been crudely dumped on to it.

The scenery became gradually more and more alpine as we drove further eastwards, with conifer forests on the lower slopes and snow peaks towering behind. Some mountains were bare and craggy, with small bushes growing among the slabs of rock; some were grassy and studded with small conifers. We followed a bright blue river, rushing along on a stony bed. The cliffs were fantastic rock formations in diagonal stripes, huge slabs pushing out of the ground. At lunchtime we stopped for tea and noodles in a small one-street town – just a line of shacks straggling along the main road: the town had a pioneer feel to it, like an American town must have felt one hundred years ago. As we drove on eastwards, the vegetation continued to change; there were more trees, larger ones, mostly pines and firs, with some holly bushes in between. There were no temples in this region, but many small shrines on the hilltops, built of wood and surrounded by prayer flags on tall flagstaffs. The prayer flags were very different from the small rectangles of white, blue, red, yellow and green, that flutter over Lhasa. These were long vertical strips of white cloth, printed in black; seen from a distance, flapping in the breeze, they look like ship sails. Driving along the road, we got the strange impression that many-masted schooners were sailing in and out among the hills!

In the middle of the afternoon we arrived at our destination, a small army town called, curiously, Bayi, or '8/1 Town', in memory of the founding of the PLA on 1st August 1927. We stayed in the town's only guesthouse, a Chinese building with a bare dusty compound, where nomads were encamped around cooking fires. They stared at us curiously as we emerged from the jeep. Pigs snorted around the doorway to the hostel and a few scrawny chickens pecked around in the dust. The creaking of the water pump in the yard made an incongruous duet with the strains of Western disco music coming down the corridor from an enormous cassette player.

Bayi is very spread out and monumentally ugly. The Army garrison, an agricultural college, a woollen mill and the logging industry are its *raisons d'être*. In the middle of nowhere, with fantastic scenery all around, is this muddle of quickly built barracks of concrete with tin roofs, crude wooden shacks and the worst in grotesque modern architecture: concrete block low-rise in garish colours. One building façade was studded with pieces of bright green glass, from broken beer bottles! The main street was lined with very rough plank houses, one-storey dwellings or little shops with sloping roofs, some with doors, some with small hatches through which you could buy sweets, cigarettes and alcohol.

The initial Wild West aspect of the place was tempered by a feeling of profound lethargy which grew deeper the closer we looked: bored shopkeepers lolled in doorways, eyeing the passers-by. There were small booths, watchmakers, cobblers, bicycle repair men, at intervals along the sidewalk, and a succession of photographers' stalls with gaudy painted backdrops depicting various Chinese urban scenes – Beijing, Shanghai, Suzhou, Guilin – against which you could pose, and this in a town set amid the most dramatic mountain scenery! At the end of the main street was an open market square, filled with pool tables and shooting ranges where you could fire airguns at balloons. All the young men in town were here, hunched over the pool tables, looking cool in blue jeans and mao caps, cigarette in mouth. We walked down a side street lined with wooden shacks: some open, selling beer, cigarettes and sweets, and some boarded up. Women were gossiping, men lounging in doorways, and everyone turned to stare as we walked past.

We were looking for matches, but couldn't find a box any-where: eventually one shopkeeper told us there hadn't been any matches in Bayi for four days – all used up on Spring Festival firecrackers, I suppose, and now the whole town was waiting for a lorry from Chengdu. It made us realize how isolated the place is, and now dependent on supplies from China, which must all be brought in by truck, four or five days from Chengdu.

The fixed population seemed to be mostly Sichuan Chinese, although there was a floating population of Tibetan nomads, traders and herdsmen who come in from the backwoods and camp around town. There is not much to do in Bayi after the pool tables and airguns have been packed away, as we found out when we took an evening stroll in search of a noodle shop for supper. The entire young male population seemed to be lined up along the bridge over the muddy river that flows through the middle of the town, lolling against the parapet, smoking and chatting, but really eyeing the pretty girls who, dolled up for the evening in jewellery and make-up, even high heels, minced along arm-in-arm rather self-consciously, looking straight ahead and avoiding the men's stares.

Next day, our minder arranged to show us the sights of Bayi. This was easily done, there not being much to see. We went first to the woollen mill, a collection of big dreary draughty sheds, full of the clatter of ancient machinery and wool dust. I remember it best for its enormous and anachronistic portrait of a youthful Mao Zedong in flowing blue robes and heroic stance, looking more like the Good Shepherd than the Great Helmsman. The bored-looking loom operators, deafened by their tyrannical machines, seemed unimpressed by the propaganda slogans and pictures stuck all over the walls, and the 'safety at work' posters had obviously never been read.

From the mill, we went out of town, to see what was described to us simply as 'a big tree'. Big, it certainly was, a 1,000-year-old giant conifer, three trunks growing and intertwining from one root. It would have taken about ten men to encircle it with arms outstretched. The hillside behind the tree was covered with graves: many people had obviously decided this was an auspicious place to be buried. The gravestones were inscribed mostly to dead PLA or Public Security men, born far away somewhere in central China, now reposing under strange cement tombs, sealed at one end with rocks. They looked like an array of eerily silent beehives in the gloom beneath the conifers, with ravens croaking above and snow gleaming on the mountains opposite. In a strange way these graves reminded me of the old cemetery in Macao, full of Europeans who died in the service of their country, or on business, or simply because their family had taken them far, far away from home.

In the afternoon we visited the Agricultural College, on the other side of the river. Given the limited extent of higher education in Tibet, and as we had worked in an agricultural college in Wuhan for two years, we were very keen to see it. We were given tea and melon seeds, enormous local apples and a statistic-packed introductory talk by one of the college leaders. He seemed at first rather perplexed as to why we had come, or maybe it was just his shy, gentle manner. We were especially grateful to him as the very next day he would be leaving Bayi, which he clearly loved, for Lhasa, to take up a senior post in Tibet University, which he was not looking forward to. Instead of doing his last-minute packing or spending the day with his family, here he was addressing two unknown foreigners and guiding us around the college campus. It is much more attractive than that of Tibet University, perhaps because it is an agricultural college and they are better at growing trees and flowers. There are 833 students, of whom seventy per cent are Tibetan, the other thirty per cent being the children of Chinese settlers. As it is the only agricultural college in Tibet, the students come from all over the country, but the brightest ones are sent to institutions in China so that those who come here are of rather a low level, and are also quite young (sixteen or seventeen on entry). The generally very low level of Tibetan education is a big problem. Most students have a basic one-year course, after which they specialize in Veterinary Medicine, Timber, Animal Husbandry, Agricultural Engineering; but many students require three years' basic courses on entry, followed by three years' specialization.

After two hours, full to the brim with giant local apples and statistics, we left the college and went out to tea with some friends of our minder's . . . and were pleasantly surprised to find that we knew them already. On our trip to Talung, we had been in the company of a very pretty, apple-cheeked, long-haired Tibetan girl, whom we would often see near the campus gates. There she would be with her friends in make-up, earrings, and latest clothes, or sometimes demurely walking out with a boy, a discreet two feet apart. What a shock to find her here, with cropped hair and a crumpled, baggy PLA uniform! She and a friend had been billeted on a family in the Bayi middle school, and were training to be PLA nurses.

Of course, we made no mention of the rumoured impending war with India, not wishing to alarm her mother, who was on a two-day visit to see her. But Bayi is uncomfortably close to the border, and presumably nurses might be badly needed if anything does start there. At sixteen, she had actually volunteered to join the PLA as a nurse, and would now spend two or more years based in Bayi for training. She and her friend sat holding hands and giggling over a comic book, and occasionally being sent into peals of laughter at some joke by our minder (who was being quite flirtatious). The girls seemed far too young to be in uniform, but were also strangely touching – I suppose the dangerously senti-mental side of army life, young girls in uniform etc, is partly what patriotic propaganda is made of. I can just imagine those two girls in some soul-stirring TV documentary about PLA life. Their parents looked so proud of them. I wonder what our friend's mother really thought about next morning when she set off with us in the predawn starlight. She said goodbye to her daughter without so much as a peck on the cheek. Just a sheepish smile and a wave of the hand.

On our last evening in Bayi, full to bursting with butter tea, we said goodbye to the family, and walked in the slanting light up a mountainside to the east of town. From a path through the woods, we had seen a very interesting wooden temple structure, like a ghostly square-rigger shipwrecked on the mountainside, and we wanted to investigate it more closely. We clambered up a path beside a rushing stream, through woods whose trees were draped with offerings of prayer flags or wool. In the half-dark we finally reached the temple, which seemed to be a local shrine on the edge of a ploughed field. It was of very simple construction, consisting of a big central stupa enclosed in a wooden framework. But all around were huge masts, hung with vertical sail-like prayer flags. Indeed the whole framework was covered in flags, and they all fluttered and rustled like sails in the evening breeze. From a distance, the shrine seemed to be a ghost-ship sailing through the forest. Standing inside it, we could have been on board. It was a very moving, eerie place.

Before dawn next morning we were off on the twelve-hour ride home. A slow dawn behind us, reflecting rose and crimson off the snowy peaks ahead, was gradually turning to gold. From the still dark valley where we were, it looked as if the tops of the peaks were coated in honey, which was slowly dripping down. The golden light stayed on the peaks for a long time, gradually turning to a clearer, harder, blue light. Halfway home, we stopped for a dip in a hot spring on the other side of the river. Our minder and the others, the driver and the army nurse's mother, declined to come with us. 'Why?' we asked. 'It's too early in the year,' they said, 'you shouldn't bathe until the spring, you'll catch cold.' They were right. We did. But it was worth it!

We crossed on a creaking, swaying plank suspension bridge and made our way to the two deep pools, enclosed by circular walls and steaming in the cold air. There was no one around, and we quickly stripped off and plunged in. I can't tell you how good hot water feels, when you haven't had a bath for months! We splashed around happily for a while, and then were surprised by some giggling – a group of ragged children had come to watch the fun. Before long, one or two disappeared to fetch their mothers, who in turn dragged along their husbands, to gape at the astonishing spectacle of two completely naked foreigners splashing around in their hot spring! Soon we had an entire village as our audience – children, men, women, dogs, goats . . . probably the most exciting event for months in that mountain hamlet.

We crossed the pass again, and went down into the Lhasa river valley. By now, there were no more trees or even shrubs to be seen, and we had returned to the stark landscape of bare gold-brown mountains and brilliant blue rivers: the two colours we will always associate with Tibet. We felt again that sense of vast distances that we missed in Bayi. There was a clear golden evening light as we drove past Ganden. Herds of sheep were being driven home; there were pigeons, ravens and flocks of gulls over the river. Finally, the distinctive shape of the Potala on its hill in the misty distance, and we were back home in time to see a bright red sunset over our own mountains, from our living room window.

Letter sixteen: **A Colder Climate**

The longer we stay here, the more attracted we are to Tibetan culture and to the Tibetans. Things that at first seemed strange and exotic now seem normal and comfortably familiar. We are no longer struck by the sight of people prostrating in the Barkor, and we don't even notice the smell of yak butter. We have even learned to like butter tea! And Tibetans are so easy to be with: we love their gentleness, warmth and good humour, and their hospitality: all the little courtesies that go with paying a visit or receiving friends.

It is lovely to receive or to present a *katag* – you feel really honoured when someone puts the white scarf round your neck. It is obviously, a very old custom in Tibet and legend says it was introduced by Padmasambhava, who brought so many other things to the country. The king of the time, a very proud man, was waiting to receive the famous sage from India. As Padmasambhava came forward, he held his arms up in greeting and the king delightedly assumed he was about to prostrate himself before him in a gesture of humility. Not a bit of it! Flames darted from Padmasambhava's hands, setting light to the king's clothes and burning all but the cloth around his neck and shoulders. The king meekly approached the holy man and offered this remnant of cloth as a sign of respect and humility.

At a dinner last week we were introduced to another lovely Tibetan custom: singing you to drink! Our friend's sister offered each of us in turn a glass of *chang*, singing as she did so. She would not stop until the glass was drained. Then she refilled the glass and offered it to the next person, singing a new song for them. Often, the old songs were specially chosen to suit the person she was singing to. She sang one for Charlie and a bearded friend, about men with beards coming from the West, and one for her brother, who lives in Nepal, about how much a sister misses her favourite brother when he leaves home.

Every time we have been to a Tibetan family, we have come away with mixed feelings of happiness and sadness: happiness at the warmth and hospitality we have been shown, and the general gaiety of the occasion, and sadness at the suffering that often seems to underlie the gaiety. The wounds of the past two decades are still open and every family seems to have a private sorrow: a son who died, a daughter in exile, a father who was imprisoned. It was not until recently that we learnt that one of our colleagues, who has always impressed us with his energy and joviality had spent twenty years in prison. Faced with the courage and resilience and irrepressible good humour of these people, we can only feel humble.

Of course, we have Chinese as well as Tibetan friends, some of whom we love very much, and one of the saddest things about living here is to see how racial tensions can affect individual relationships and turn human beings into abstractions. I went for what turned out to be a horrible picnic with three Chinese friends, who wanted to show me a little temple to the north of the city. A friend teaching in Lhasa came with us, and three of her Tibetan students decided to come too. What a tense afternoon! The Tibetans would not go round the temples with the Chinese and, when the time came to eat, they virtually turned their backs on the Chinese and refused to eat their food. Sitting between the two camps, making uncomfortably polite conversation, I said to my friend, 'I feel like a buffer zone.' I wanted to say, 'Look, these individuals aren't personally responsible for the Cultural Revolution – they suffered too. Why can't people look at each other as individuals, and not as ideas or symbols?' I felt so powerless to interfere, caught up in cross-currents of feeling which are not mine and which I can only begin to try to understand. I kept my tears back till I got home, then poured myself a stiff drink and cried into it for most of the evening.

The Tibetans have suffered so badly, and many of the Chinese in Tibet behave with such a lack of understanding and respect, that such attitudes aren't surprising. I recently saw Chinese tourists in a monastery, the new breed of young city slickers, cynical sophisticates from Shanghai, mocking an old man with a prayer wheel and then pretending to prostrate in front of the Buddha, laughing all the time. I was so incensed that I went up to them and tried to explain exactly what I found so repulsive about their behaviour. They just stared, and when I walked away, I of course heard them laughing at me too. These two incidents seem to me in a way to typify the sad state of Chinese–Tibetan relations in this city. If you are treated with contempt, you respond with anger: hence the whole unhappy cycle of fear and mistrust from which it is so hard to escape and which turns the individual human being into a representative of politics or race.

There are pockets of harmony though. The University in general seems quite a positive place, perhaps because a university is, by definition, concerned with the future and with development. Our students live together quite amicably at very close quarters, although other less privileged young people, particularly those who are unemployed or in menial jobs, seem angry and alienated. The Arts Department in particular seems a harmonious and happy place, and we often go there to cheer ourselves up. I suppose the people who teach and learn there have a common language in art or music that unites them beyond racial differences, and this leads them to explore and learn from each others' cultures, to accept and to rejoice in the differences.

We had a much happier visit to Pabongka a month or so later with our students. We all cycled out to Sera and, leaving our bikes in a farm courtyard at the bottom of the hill, trekked up the bare stony brown mountainside to the temple. This temple used to be the oldest in Lhasa, and was built on a rock over a cave where Songtsen Gampo, the eighth-century king who brought Buddhism to Tibet, came to meditate. The temple had been nine storeys high, but like almost everything else of this nature in Tibet, was destroyed. The rebuilt temple is two storeys high, and perched on a huge rock overlooking a parched brown treeless valley. From below, it looks like a huge ship. Carved in stone, and painted on one of its rock walls, is what is said to be the first *Om Mani Padme Hum* in Tibet.

The little temple is full of paintings; one in a narrow corridor leading into the main temple downstairs depicts the Allegory of Co-operation: a bird, a rabbit, an elephant and a monkey under a big fruit tree. The bird brings a seed and plants it, the monkey waters it, the rabbit manures it and the elephant comes to enjoy its shade and protect it. This, the Tibetans say, is how the earth was prepared for mankind. The best mural is a relief painted over in bright colours in a little chapel at the back of the main temple hall. It is carved into the rock that forms the temple, and the monks say that 'nobody made it – it grew out of the rock by itself.'

There are also many rock paintings on the boulders around the temple, and some of these have been enclosed and made into little shrines. We had a picnic in the courtyard: the monks brought us cushions and carpets to sit on, low elaborately painted Tibetan tables, and large thermoses of butter tea, turning our simple meal of bread and eggs and yoghurt into quite a banquet!

We had another class outing to a little temple called Drölma Lakhang, about two hours' cycle ride out along the airport road. This temple is historically very interesting and was left unscathed during the Cultural Revolution. This surprised us because it is quite close to Lhasa, and beside the road, whereas we have seen temples in far more remote locations that have been razed to the ground. The monks told us that the 'Indians' asked for it to be spared, rather as Zhou Enlai ordered the Potala to be preserved. That there was enough rationality around in those violent times to hear and obey these requests almost seems to make the violence more chilling.

The temple is associated with Atisha, a great Indian Buddhist teacher, who came to Tibet in the eleventh century, and who lived, taught and eventually died at Drölma Lakhang. He is a venerated figure in Bengal, and for that reason the Bengali government asked for the temple to be preserved. The statues are old and Indian in style and are quite different from any others we have seen in Tibet: less elaborate, more primitive, with the simplicity and directness of an earlier age. The monks showed us round, explaining the meaning of various statues and murals and recounting legends associated with them. I particularly liked one story they told about a mural on the front porch, which seemed to be an interesting combination of spiritual devotion and hard-headed practicality: the monks, praying for the safety of a sick friend, were instructed to repeat a prayer several hundred times. Worried that they could not accomplish the task in time, they asked Atisha for help. He taught them the Sanskrit version, which is much shorter, and in this way they were able to perform the task and the friend recovered.

After Christmas, the weather got much colder. We have no heating, and for a few weeks it was between five and ten degrees below freezing inside our flat in the morning when we got up. Struggling out of multiple layers of pyjama and tracksuit into multiple layers of thermal underwear, jeans, pullovers and down jackets, via a very quick splosh in the sink, was something of an act of heroism. Some days, we confess, the quick splosh was omitted. Thick ice in beautiful frost flowers used to remain inside the windows till midday or later. Once, when I washed my hair, it froze and handfuls of 'snow' fell out when I brushed it! Washing hung out on the line used to freeze instantly and, blowing in the wind, jeans and shirts would bang icily on the cracked windows. Our toothbrushes were frozen solid, and so were our towels.

After New Year, things went from basic to primitive, as all the pipes and drains froze up. (Now, what architect was responsible for putting all the pipes on the north side of the building, which never gets any sun?) We have had no running water now for about two months, so fetching water means taking your pail to the pump, and obeying calls of nature means a trip to the three-holer in the yard. But most of our colleagues and all our students live like this all the time. It is amazing how long all the ordinary chores around the house take in such conditions. I am beginning to realize why our colleagues teach only six hours a week – the rest of the time is taken up with queuing for vegetables in the market, fetching water, heating water, waiting for the electricity to come on so you can cook, or patiently cooking on the petrol stove (boiling a kettle of water takes about one hour), boiling water to wash clothes, taking them to the pump to rinse. We are also beginning to see why the advertisement specified a hardy married couple! We have both lost quite a lot of weight in our seven months here – about two stone apiece – whether because of the monotonous diet or because the altitude affects metabolism, I don't know. But the sunshine is Lhasa's great saving grace: it is impossible to get depressed when every day dawns blue and cloudless. By midday, the sun is strong enough for you to shed quite a few layers of down jacket and pullover and you can get quite badly burnt on a cycling trip, or even shopping in the market. It is already much warmer now and getting perceptibly warmer every day, although still quite bitter in the mornings and after the sun goes down.

The big news in all the papers has of course been the student demonstrations in Peking, Hefei and Shanghai, followed by Hu Yaobang's dismissal and the subsequent crackdown on 'bourgeois liberalization' and 'Western-style thinking'. I keep getting flashbacks to the 'Campaign against Spiritual Pollution' of 1983–4 when we first came to China. The student demonstrations, with their somewhat naive and vaguely formulated demands for 'freedom' and 'democracy' were not reported for about three weeks in the Chinese media, although we were getting daily reports on the BBC World Service. Not a whisper of a demonstration among our students here, who did not even know what was happening in faraway China until it was all over. Official reaction seemed at first to waver between condemning the demonstrations and glossing over them, but the crackdown came with the news of Hu Yaobang's 'resignation'. We heard about this on the BBC World Service, just before we were due to go out to (yet another) university party. The head of our department was with us as the special newsflash was broadcast. At the party, he told the dean what had happened. She just shook her head. 'It's not true,' she said, and refused to believe it. 'Your BBC is wrong.' But later on during the party, some of the leaders were summoned out to listen to the news on Chinese radio, and when they came back we saw them in a little huddle earnestly analyzing the news.

From 'inside the whale' it all looks very confusing. There have been quite a few arrests and expulsions from the Party: six student representatives have been arrested on charges of spreading social unrest; the head of Hefei University, where much of the trouble was, has got the sack; three prominent intellecutals noted for their radical views, Wang Ruowang, a writer, Liu Binyan, a journalist, and Fang Lizhi, a physicist have all been expelled from the Party; and the 'progressive' propaganda chief has been replaced by a hard-line Marxist. Maoist slogans have reappeared in the papers, which have been exhorting people to 'take grain as the key link' and to engage in 'production for production's sake' instead of producing cash crops for profit, together with several references to 'self-reliance', one of Mao's favourite concepts and directly at odds with Deng's policy of opening up to the West.

There has been a call for a tightening up of censorship in literature and a return to the socialist ideal that literature should never forget its primary aim of serving the people and socialism. Papers have been full of 'model worker' stories – people working selflessly for the good of the country – rather than stories of enterprises making record profits. There has even been an attempt to resuscitate Lei Feng, a socialist hero of the Mao era: a PLA soldier about whom any number of parables were told, recounting his heroic and selfless actions – sharing his lunchbox with old peasant women, spending his free time washing his comrades' socks, etc, etc. I should think the new generation of Chinese youth is far too cynical and streetwise to go for that old stuff any more. That is probably what the hardliners in the Party are worried about. 'A return to socialist morals and the collective spirit' is how they phrase it. Disco out, Lei Feng in.

Signals are pretty confused though. At the same time as all the above, the papers are reiterating that there will be no change in the economic reforms, and no return to 'leftist errors'; that the door to the West will stay open. Around the last week or so, a 'line' seems to have emerged: the 'Campaign against Bourgeois Liberalization' will be confined to the Party, there will not be a mass movement in Cultural Revolution or Spiritual Pollution style. Expulsion from the Party, rather than imprisonment, seems to be a favoured punishment. And the economic reforms will go on. Zhao has even mentioned political reform and the need for greater democracy – exactly what the students were protesting about.

It is difficult to know what *is* happening! And here, so far away from the centre of the action, it is doubly difficult. Most people seem to think that the campaign won't affect Tibet very much, and that it will be confined mainly to a clean-up within the Party, although Tibetans must be anxious about the removal of Hu Yaobang, the leader who initiated the present reforms in Tibet. It makes you realize, with a shock, how unpredictable things are in China, and what insecurity must underlie the apparent normality of everyday life. Will what is officially approved today suddenly be forbidden tomorrow? Fear is a constant background to life here.

The 'Crackdown on Crime' which started in 1983 is still going on, and on Valentine's Day we had another unpleasant shock: cycling back to the University along the river road, we suddenly ran into hordes and hordes of people streaming along the road in the opposite direction. The road was completely blocked with people walking or pushing bicycles. We had to dismount, and we struggled with our bikes against the flow of the crowd. Further along, squads of soldiers were marching in columns, each soldier carrying a stool. Police were ineffectually trying to control the traffic and clear a way for a cadre's curtained limousine. Beijing jeeps tried unsuccessfully to force a way through the massed bodies. Our first thought was that this was all some kind of pre-New Year festivity, and that as the river road forms part of the Lingkor, everyone was making a ritual circuit of the city. But there were so many Chinese amongst the Tibetans – surely they wouldn't be celebrating a Tibetan religious festival? Then we became aware that people were not heading towards anywhere, but in fact were all coming away from the same place – the Sports Ground. A gradual realization took hold of us – we had seen the same thing before in Wuhan. When we asked a group of people what was happening, and they all made the same gesture – holding a gun to the head – we realized with dawning horror what had been happening. All these swarms and swarms of people had walked in, cycled in, been bussed in, transported in, piled into the backs of trucks, to witness the public sentencing of eight criminals. Four had been sentenced to death for robbery. The head of our department looked at us with blank incomprehension when we expressed our indignation: 'But they took a lot of money,' he said. The whole affair was somehow especially horrible because we had at first mistaken it for a religious celebration.

Letter seventeen:
A Tibetan Hospital and some Small Temples

Although Lhasa is really quite a small town, after eight months there were still a number of places we had visited only fleetingly, or not at all, and first on our list was the Hospital of Traditional Tibetan Medicine. One of our friends, who knows a lot about medicine, accompanied us to the new, concrete-block-style four-storey building which lies just to the west of the main plaza, the Jokhang square. In fact we had already visited it as patients, when we first came to Lhasa in summer 1985, but we were then so blocked up with 'nostril clog and snivel' (as the cold medicine packet puts it) that we had not taken much in — except to note that the Tibetan medicines we were prescribed after a lengthy and complicated pulse reading actually worked and cured both clog and snivel.

This time we were more alert and could take great interest in what our guide, a fluent English speaker educated in India, had to say. Downstairs there was a sort of chapel, dedicated to the founders of Tibetan medicine with gold statues of each of them: Yutok Yönten, who founded the first medicine temple in the eighth century; Desi Sanggye Gyatso, who established Chakpori; and Khyenrab Norbu, a famous early twentieth-century physician. The hospital itself, Mentsikhang, was founded by the thirteenth Dalai Lama in 1916.

Upstairs, on the top floor, was a large room hung with *tangkas*. These did not depict deities or scenes from Buddha's life, like those in temples, but were teaching aids, rather like wallcharts. The largest was a schematic outline of Tibetan medicine as a tree with three roots, nine trunks, forty-two branches and two hundred and twenty four leaves. The first root, Anatomy, was divided into two trunks – pathology and physiology. The second root, Diagnosis, had three trunks – observation, touching and investigation. The third root, Treatment, had four trunks, which were nutrition, lifestyle, medicine and massage. Surgery was banned in Tibet during the ninth century, after the king's mother died during an operation. Another *tangka* showed a chart of medicines and the sources from which they were obtained: metals, minerals, stones, trees, fruits, flowers, oils, vegetables and animals. Complex and beautiful herb charts followed. Other *tangkas* showed diagrams of circulatory and respiratory systems, and of cauterization points. One, rather like a strip cartoon, depicted the stages in pulse diagnosis. Small pictures showed what the patient must refrain from doing before a pulse examination (drinking tea or alcohol, eating too much, sex, or violent exercise), then a series of pictures showed various aspects of pulse diagnosis. In many of the pictures there were what I took to be flowers blooming from the patient's wrist, until I looked more closely and saw that they were little balloons like thought bubbles, containing the picture of an organ, showing graphically what the doctor could read from the patient's pulsebeat.

Pulse diagnosis is a vital element of Tibetan medicine, and during his training the doctor has to develop the ability to use two points on each of the three middle fingers of each hand to gather different information about the patient's disease from his pulse. Detailed descriptions in the medical tantras link different diseases to pulses that 'flutter like a flag in the wind', move like a 'vulture attacking a bird', a 'hen pecking grain' or a 'fish leaping out of water to catch a fly'.

Downstairs again was a room where various pills and the raw ingredients to make them were displayed: shells, pearls, antlers, horns, tiger's teeth, together with a bewildering variety of herbs. In the small treatment room next door there was a display of silver instruments for cauterization, moxibustion and bloodletting, all beautifully engraved, and gold needles for acupuncture. Three patients, an old lady and two young men, sat chatting in this communal treatment room, all bristling with needles like hedgehogs. In the pharmacy on the ground floor two old women were wrapping powders in little squares of paper. The walls were lined with small drawers, beautifully painted with flowers in bright colours, containing different pills and powders.

We were struck by how decorative an art this science seemed: the intricately painted *tangkas*, the engraved instruments, the bright furniture, all seemed incongruous in these shabby and functional surroundings of dusty concrete walls and floors, reminders of an age that had more time for detail and a greater eye for beauty. Modernization has brought greater efficiency though, if greater ugliness. The powders that once had to be painstakingly crushed by hand using a pestle and mortar are now ground by machine and many of the herbs are specially cultivated. Previously, medical students would have had to spend months in wild areas identifying and collecting the medicinal herbs. Tibetan medicine is based, like medieval European medicine, on 'humours': wind, bile and phlegm, which move in the skeleton, blood and flesh. Good health depends on keeping a stable balance between the three humours. Tibetan medicine is also intimately bound up with astrology, and we visited a fascinating room full of astrological charts, calendars and star maps. Tibetan calendars for next year, the Year of the Fire Rabbit, are already on sale in the market place. They contain weather forecasts for the coming year, prophecies of forthcoming events and complicated tables for determining which days will be auspicious or inauspicious for you personally. We asked our guide and the friend who came with us whether nowadays people prefer Tibetan medicine or the Western medicine available at the People's Hospital. 'It depends,' they said, 'for acute cases people generally go to the People's Hospital, but for chronic conditions most people prefer Tibetan medicine.' 'If you were ill which would you choose?' we asked. There was no doubt about it. 'Oh, Tibetan medicine, of course!' they said.

Lhasa is full of small and large temples, some in good condition, some ruined, some converted into apartment houses or stores. It is lovely to be able, after shopping for yak meat or buying your potatoes in the market, to climb up on to the flat roof of one of these smaller temples and look at the Lhasa roofscape. One of our favourites is a little temple down an alley to the north of the Jokhang. This temple, Nechung, is connected with the temple to the State Oracle, near Drepung, also called Nechung. From its roof you can see down into the Jokhang cloisters and have a fine view of the gold temple roofs as well as the roofs of the neighbouring houses, cluttered with flowerpots, tools, old bikes, chairs. One roof even has a tent pitched on it, presumably for visiting relatives. A large incense burner stands in a courtyard below where women are pounding reddish clay with sticks. An old lady dozes in the sun, sleepily turning her prayer wheel; chickens peck around on the flagstones. A line of bright new golden prayer wheels are spun by pilgrims.

Passing the Jokhang one day, we saw a truck unloading crate after crate of these prayer wheels. 'Where do they come from?' we asked the driver. 'Chengdu!' was the answer. Now what is a Tibetan prayer wheel factory doing there, we asked ourselves. The low muttering of prayers and the whirring creak of the prayer wheels as they spin on their axles are a constant *basso continuo* to the afternoon's other noises. Of all the sounds rising up to us on the rooftop in the clear blue afternoon, those and the flapping of prayer flags in the breeze are the most distinctively Tibetan.

Inside the temple, all is busy renovation. Three boys are making clay images. One oils the moulds. Another thumps the clay into the moulds and carefully separates the two halves. A third sets the statues to dry and uses an old hacksaw blade to cut away the surplus clay. Each time we visit, the same loving process is going on, and racks of images are stacked to one side of the temple, some painted in reds, greens and gold, some still the bare reddish clay.

The interior has all been redecorated since our first visit in 1985, when it was nothing more than a (re)building site. One of the many images in the glass-enclosed cases at the front is of the State Oracle in full regalia. These glass cases full of images make the place, more than any other we have visited, look like a huge doll museum.

Another temple we visited with two friends was a nunnery called Ani Sangkhung, tucked away in the Barkor backstreets near the mosque. The nunnery was built on the site where the seventh-century king Songtsen Gampo meditated to turn the floodwater back when the Lhasa river burst its banks and threatened to flood the city – like King Canute, but with rather more success. There is a small cave below the temple with a shrine where he meditated. This was a well-kept little temple, sunny, neat and colourful – the feminine touch maybe. The nuns were all busy cleaning it ready for New Year and decorating the altar with *torma*, red *tsampa* cakes, butter sculptures, butter flags, and offerings of fruit, barley and many different-shaped loaves of bread. Perhaps because of these preparations and the Christmas Eve atmosphere of anticipatory festivity, the little temple seemed to me to have a joyful atmosphere quite different from the cavernous darkness of many of the larger temples.

Ramoche, sometimes called 'Little Jokhang', is in the north of Lhasa and its rebuilding is now almost complete. We spent a very pleasant afternoon there, joking with the carpenters who were making the timber framework for the golden roof which will complete the building. Only eighteen months before, in 1985, we had spent a morning watching the floor of Ramoche being stamp-danced into concrete by teams of women using thin poles with circular flat stones at the end. They sang and danced rhythmically backwards and forwards for hours, tamping the pebbly mud mixture into concrete. Some of the songs required the women to form two lines facing each other, which then stamped forwards and backwards in turn singing a dialogue to each other as they did. These alternated with others where they formed a procession which spiralled its way from the perimeter into the centre. The melodies, sometimes cheerful and march-like, sometimes sad and haunting, would echo around the dusty gloom of the half-built temple. Young craftsmen were building the wooden frames, later to be covered with mud and straw, of huge Buddha images.

Now the interior of Ramoche looks well-worn and greasy with butter and it would take a practised eye to tell exactly what has been remade and what, if anything, is original. There must be very little of the latter, as Ramoche was very badly treated during the Cultural Revolution.

Chakpori, the 'Iron Mountain' facing the Potala, is not what it used to be. Like a Swiss cheese, it is now bored through with tunnels of a secret nature, and on top, where the Medicine Temple used to stand, there is now the huge TV mast, monument to a different set of values, and which, like Blackpool Tower, is all lit up at night. However, at its foot is the beautiful little cave temple of Palhalupuk. This temple has more than its fair share of young monks, nine- or ten-year-olds with shaved heads and red robes, who are looked after by some elderly monks and who take it in turns to pester visitors for 'Pen! Pen!' or 'Dalai-Lama-picture!' But their greetings are friendly enough, and the old monks work away peacefully at their sewing or manufacture of intricate butter carvings and *tsampa* cakes. There is always a happy atmosphere at Palhalupuk and its small dimensions and unique structure give it an intimacy all of its own. The main temple is really just a small cave looping round a central rock pillar. Fantastic grinning faces sway and dance in the light of the butter-lamps, their bright colours daubed on the grease-impregnated rock. There is a famous carving of Songtsen Gampo and his two wives and a dark grimacing figure of Pelden Lhamo. Below this, a larger cave is lined with glass-fronted cupboards contained posters of *tangkas* and a pile of battered scriptures.

It is much quieter here; just one figure is working at the back by the light of a single electric bulb. But he spots me and hisses: 'Come here! Come here! Quick, picture, quick!' But I do not want to take any flash photos here. 'Come!' he grabs me by the arm and hustles me over to his workplace. I try to pull away. But then he presses something into my palm. 'Quick!' He puts his finger to his lips, 'Ssh!' as another, older monk comes in. Later, I go outside and look at the object he has given me. It is a little clay image of the Buddha, one of many that he has been moulding in the dark corner of his cave. I keep this secret, unexpected gift for several months, until it finally crumbles into broken pieces of red clay.

A week or so before New Year we had a class cycle trip with our students to Ganden. This was quite an expedition and seemed to require about as much organization and advance planning as an attempt on Everest. First, I went to some friends to borrow sleeping bags and down jackets for the students (we have our own) and a camping gaz stove to cook on. The acquisition of all this Western paraphenalia delighted the boys, who were fascinated by the idea of sleeping bags. ('It will be my first time for Sleeping in a Bag,' said one.) They were intrigued with the little camping stove and thrilled with the trendy down jackets which they immediately put on, despite the burning afternoon sunshine. When we cycled back to the boys' dorm to leave the stuff, they swaggered into the room, calling to their room-mates, 'Look at us! We've just come back from Hong Kong!' Then we chased around trying to borrow a bike for one of the girls who didn't have her own (and who, by the end of the gruelling first day, probably wished we hadn't been able to find her one!). Finally, we organized provisions for the trip. We cooked up an enormous yak stew with potatoes; the students brought eggs, bread, fruit and a big rucksack full of beer, which they seemed to think was indispensable.

In the end we set out at about eleven (we had agreed 9.30, but this was 'Tibetan time', which seems to run an hour or two later than clock time) on a bright blue cloudless morning, all of us on bikes with far too much luggage: bags, water bottles, yak stew and, of course, all the beer. The first stretch of road to Ganden is tarred, but the last twenty-five miles or so is unmade, and cycling is very difficult. There was a glorious feeling of freedom as we swept out of the gates, swooped over the bridge and away off down the road.

For the first couple of hours the road is as smooth as glass and we spun along merrily past bare ploughed fields and groves of willows along the river, through villages with bright new prayer flags and door hangings fluttering in the breeze, overtaking the occasional donkey cart or tractor. One of the carts we passed was piled high with young saplings, stripped of leaves, a few branches at the top of their thin trunks. 'Look!' said the students, 'New Year trees, like your Christmas trees.' The trees were prayer flagpoles, being taken to Lhasa for people to set up on their rooftops and decorate with brand-new flags ready for the New Year.

We stopped for tea at the halfway point, an old teahouse at Taktse Dzong, a little village clustered beneath the ruins of a fortress perched on its craggy outcrop of rock. From there it was a short way to the big suspension bridge across the Lhasa river that we had crossed on our way to Yerpa and Talung – and it was there that our troubles began! We swished under the wires of the huge bridge, which were creaking and whistling in the wind, building up in preparation for the afternoon dust-storm, and on to the rocky unmade road that leads east to Chamdo. This was difficult cycling! Gravelly bumps alternated with stretches of sand-drift and you would plough into these on your bike and come to a dead stop. Lorries would occasionally roar past and when that happened, the only thing to do was to get off the bike and turn your face aside, away from the choking dust they churned up. Clouds began to gather and by mid-afternoon one of the daily winter dust-storms had started.

The whole journey was very slightly uphill; no steep gradients, but even so, on a 'Magpie' or 'Flying Flower' with no gears, this was hard work! Still, with a long break for a picnic of eggs, bread, curried potatoes, fruit and dried persimmons, and several beer stops, we survived – though when we arrived, five hours later, at the foot of the Ganden mountain, we were both exhausted and the girl students looked half-dead. The boys, however, were still bright and chirpy, and still resolutely wearing their down jackets – we had taken ours off long before Taktse and had shed several more layers since then.

We thankfully dismounted and left the bikes in a farmyard at the foot of the mountain, and started off on the long climb up. We took the old pilgrim path which winds up the mountain behind the monastery. The path followed a dried up river for some way, then led along one side of a steep gorge and finally started to twist up the mountainside – a two-hour climb with increasingly expansive views behind us of the Lhasa river valley, and of side valleys branching off to the north: the immense lonely distances of Tibet. Ahead and above us was the jagged broken silhouette of Ganden on the skyline. All along the way were prayer cairns, doing double duty as route markers and acts of devotion. At the top we arrived at a narrow pass hung with cheerful prayer flags: it felt like a welcome.

From there we dropped down to the monastery and found the monk in charge of the guest room, a grey-haired old man, who at first seemed rather bemused by our late arrival and all our luggage. But once he had established control over the situation, he turned out to have a twinkle in his eye and a nice sense of humour. The guest room led off a courtyard on the second storey of one of the monastery buildings, colourful with painted pillars and roof beams. It was furnished with a number of benches covered with carpets and cushions placed against the walls, and a collection of brightly painted tables in the centre. It was occupied when we arrived by two monks with sewing-machines and a Chinese electrician who was installing a generator. The monks soon packed up and went off to supper, and the Chinese electrician moved into an adjoining room with a group of noisy monk-electricians, who chattered and sang and clattered in and out of the room all night. We took possession of our territory, and then began to cook up the yak on the camping gaz in the courtyard, much to the amazement of all the monks who came to inspect and to marvel at this extraordinary gadget. Dinner was rather late as the cooking process was subject to frequent interruptions, while the students proudly demonstrated to successive groups of observers how this miracle of Western high technology worked. Finally, we sat down to a candlelit supper in the courtyard, sitting on cushions around one of the little painted tables. However, the cold drove us inside before long (despite down jackets) and even then threatened to put an early stop to conversation and beer drinking. 'Never mind,' said our cheerful students, 'we can have Chatting in the Sleeping Bags.'

The next morning after an Anglo-Tibetan breakfast of butter tea and bread and jam (bread and jam seemed as strange an idea to them as butter tea did to us), we set off round the temples. I always find Ganden a very emotional experience: the ruins seem so stark and so cruel, such a terrible symbol of hatred and destruction. None of the romance you associate with ruins in England (Fountains, Tintern . . .), though I suppose those English abbeys were annihilated in something of the same spirit of reformist zeal as their Tibetan counterparts. The difference is partly because these ruins aren't softened by nature – no surrounding trees or clinging ivy – they just stand against the skyline like a bald statement of sorrow. But mostly the difference is because the destruction and the suffering were so recent – these ruins haven't been softened by time either. I tried to imagine a Ganden ten, twenty years from now, to create in my mind a new Ganden reborn from the ruins, golden roofs instead of broken walls silhouetted against the blue.

In the afternoon, armed with a picnic, we went for a long walk along the ridge behind the monastery. It is an old pilgrim route that leads ultimately to Samye, three or four days' walk away, and marked by prayer cairns on every crest. From the ridge there were splendid views on both sides, of range after range of snowy mountains rippling into the distance. The ruins of Ganden, which dominate the skyline when you stand below them, fade into insignificance, dwarfed by the huge peaks around them. Eagles flew overhead, their shadows rushing over the ground, so close you could hear the swish of air through their wings.

But the students didn't really see the sense of going for a walk just to get to a place to have lunch, when we could do this much more conveniently exactly where we were, without making an effort. Why rhapsodize over the mountains? Still worse, why invent an imaginary place for lunch if you don't *really* have to get there? This was one of those situations that make you reconsider your own implicitly held assumptions in the light of other, perhaps more commonsensical beliefs. Is love of landscape the product of a society that doesn't equate countryside with hard work? And is the notion of a 'country walk' as a leisure activity the product of a society that has come to equate hard work with mental rather than physical activity? Anyway, we went for the walk, and the picnic, though we had another culture shock later, when one of the students raised his arm and flung his beer bottle far down the mountainside, where it bounced off the slope and shattered onto a rock. Another student raised his arm to do the same, but we stopped him, and this led to a long discussion about rubbish and pollution. In the end they saw our point, and agreed never to throw bottles down mountainsides again. But one of them, from east Tibet, kept on saying, 'I don't like these mountains. No trees. Just rock and stone.' 'And green!' his friend replied. 'Green?' we echoed. 'Yes, green broken beer bottle,' he teased.

We returned to the monastery down a steep tussocky hillside in the late afternoon to have 'Chatting in the Courtyard', followed by 'Cooking on the Camping Gaz' and 'Eating in the Room'. Our girl student decided she couldn't face the long ride home and left on a truck with the electricians (who had successfully installed the generator, with the result that lights kept flashing on and off erratically all through the night).

This second night was even colder than the first; we slept with all our clothes and down jackets on, inside our sleeping bags, and were still frozen. In the morning we woke to the glow of pink dawn light on SNOW! Everywhere was covered with a light dusting of white, and the pink early glow was followed by a beautiful gold light which moved slowly down the mountain till the whole monastery was bathed in it. The snow on the other side of the mountain was thicker and we had an exhilarating walk down, snow crunching under our feet, our footsteps the first to mark out the path that morning, the thin air so fresh and crisp you could almost taste it. The cycle ride back was much easier than the outward journey, partly because

it was downhill all the way, but mostly because we had eaten
and drunk our way through a whole rucksackful of provisions.
We blew into Lhasa in a dust-storm in the early evening, hot
tired and dirty, and after a last beer went our separate ways,
the boys regretfully and unwillingly surrendering the down
jackets.

Letter eighteen: **A Tibetan New Year**

On our return from Ganden, Lhasa was in a ferment of New Year preparations. For several days there had been a steady flow of pilgrims into the city, in readiness for the *Mönlam*, or Great Prayer ceremonies, and many of these colourfully-dressed people were camped out along the Lhasa river, or out on the way to Sera: nomads from Nagchu in long sheepskin coats decorated with *appliqué* strips of brightly coloured cloth, peasants from Nyingchi in medieval-looking tunics of black wool decorated at the corners with triangles of rich brocade, tall Khampas from Chamdo.

For many of these pilgrims, used to life in a small mountain village or herding yaks and sheep in the lonely wastes of the Jangtang plateau, Lhasa must have seemed a huge metropolis. Traffic terrified them, and they would scuttle across the road in a panic, holding on to each other's skirts or coats, colliding with unwary cyclists and causing cars to brake and swerve. The Barkor was fuller than ever with prostrating bodies, but that is at least a pedestrian street – on the Lingkor they were a real traffic hazard – and we decided that Lhasa should have a special traffic sign all its own: a red triangle enclosing the symbol of a prostrating body. The Barkor was full of people selling prayer flags and *katag* for New Year and, about a week before the festival, the three huge prayer flagpoles on the Barkor were uprooted from their bases of cement and rubble and redecorated with new prayer flags. Two of these were replaced before New Year, but one, an enormous pole wound round with strips of yak skin, lay like a felled tree at one corner of the Barkor.

Stallholders were selling brightly painted wooden boxes, shaped rather like miniature cradles with a partition down the middle, ears of wheat dyed in gaudy colours of red and blue and purple, and butter flags. These are small spatula-shaped pieces of plywood, the broad flat end of which is decorated with intricate flowers and whorls of coloured butter. These items are all for the New Year custom of *Tashi Delek*: the wooden box is filled with barley – one side with barley grains, the other side with *tsampa* flour – and decorated with the ears of wheat and the butter flags. This is then placed on the family altar inside the house. When a guest visits during the New Year period, he is offered the box and must take four symbolic pinches of the barley, three of which are thrown in the air as an offering and one of which is eaten for *Tashi Delek* or good luck.

The day before New Year, we noticed that many of the stallholders were selling an assortment of pickled vegetables cut into strips, grated cheese, and what looked like miniature dumplings. Shoppers would come along with their plastic or paper bags, and a handful of each of these things would be put into the bag. We asked the students if this was some special food for New Year, and they told us about the New Year's Eve meal of *gu-du*, or nine bowls. As usual there was a heated discussion between those from Lhasa, those from Shigatse and those from Chamdo, as to the exact nature and meaning of the custom, but the basic custom seemed to be the same, with regional variations.

On New Year's Eve you must eat nine bowls of noodles, after which the devil will 'weigh you'. Presumably after the nine bowls of noodles, you will be too heavy to drag down to hell! In the bowls of noodles, concealed in dumplings, are various different objects, all of which have a meaning – a bit like the lucky charms in a Christmas pudding. If you find salt in your bowl, it means you are lazy, cotton means you have a good heart, but charcoal means you are hard-hearted, as does gravel. Wheat means you will have good luck all year, and small symbols of the sun, moon and stars, made of flour and water, also mean good luck. A 'piece of noodle as long as a finger' means you always tell the truth. There was some disagreement about paper: if you find it in your bowl, said one, it means you are a thief. No, said the others, it symbolizes money – meaning you will get rich. 'What do you do when you find them?' I wanted to know. 'If it's something good, then you tell everyone "Look what I've found", but if it's bad, then keep silence.' In Lhasa, before you eat the evening meal, you must take some food from the bowls and put it in a tin at the crossroads – this means, 'Don't let the devil come to my house.' In Shigatse, the same custom existed, but the food was taken from the bowls after the meal was over.

New Year's Eve was traditionally the time for 'devil dances', performed at the Potala and the big monasteries, to ward off evil for the coming year. There didn't seem to be any of these taking place this year, but all the rituals we did observe seemed designed to scare off devils. The whole evening, indeed the whole night, was punctuated by noisy explosions of firecrackers: these were at their height shortly after dark – I have never seen or heard so many firecrackers. In the centre of town, it sounded as if there was a war going on, and people were throwing them around everywhere.

We had a long cycle ride home through the centre of town, and it was an eerie experience. Fires were burning in the centre of every crossroads, where there was a jumble of old tins and the remains of bowls of noodles, together with small crosses made of two bundles of straw tied together. It felt like witchcraft to us, perhaps because the crosses unexpectedly reminded us of Christianity. We wheeled our bikes through the dimly lit and half-deserted Barkor. A few people were still letting off firecrackers and making fires.

Householders were marking out the areas in front of their doorways with complicated patterns in white flour sprinkled on the earth. Some of these patterns took the form of criss-cross lines, or swastikas, others were extremely elaborate: lotuses, conches, endless knots, dharma wheels, sun and moon, fish, and kalachakra symbols – all auspicious symbols, placed in front of the doorway for good luck and to prevent evil spirits from entering the house. On the Barkor square, some old women with huge basins of noodles were dishing out food for the beggars and, later, we saw a man distributing two-*mao* notes to an eager group of beggars.

We didn't get much sleep that night: the fireworks didn't stop till past midnight. They started again at abour four in the morning – everyone gets up early on New Year's Day, for if you are the first person to enter the Jokhang on that morning, you have good luck all year. Even those families who don't go to the Jokhang get up early to pray at the family altar. The mother gets up first, at about four o'clock, and makes hot *chang* with brown sugar and *tsampa* and brings it to the family in bed, and fills the bowls at the family altar. Then the family eats a special New Year breakfast of barley porridge with meat and ginseng root.

It is the custom on the first day to go round to friends' and neighbours' houses with a kettle of *chang* and the wooden *Tashi Delek* box to wish them Happy New Year and good luck. Everywhere we went on New Year's Day, we saw people with kettle in one hand, box in the other, on their way to pay social calls, and we would be called over to take a symbolic pinch of *tsampa* and sip of *chang* (you must flick three drops into the air with the fourth finger of your right hand before drinking, as a libation to the gods).

We got up early too, to go to the Jokhang with some friends. At six o'clock the streets were still dark, a few fires were still smouldering at the crossroads, the feeling of black magic and superstition, so powerful the night before, was still in the air. Along the Barkor, shadowy figures were prostrating, there was the sound of mumbled prayers, pilgrims were lighting juniper fires in the prayer kilns. We went into the Jokhang, slipping on the buttery flagstones, and joined the long queue of pilgrims with their offerings of scarves, fruit, barley, *tsampa*, *chang* and butter-lamps, snaking round the inner courtyard of the temple and winding in and out of all the tiny side chapels. The pilgrims are patient and smiling as they shuffle slowly round the temple: a great feeling of quiet happiness.

Inside the temple it is dark and mysterious, lit by rows of flickering butter-lamps. Massive ancient wooden pillars stretch up into the darkness – it's like wandering round an enchanted forest. Rich colours glow dully through the gloom. In one corner a monk is singing in front of a row of lamps; in another there is a blue statue with staring red eyes, pointed teeth and tongue and fierce gold eyebrows. *Tangkas* and banners hang down from the ceiling. Pilgrims in filthy sheepskins with wild matted hair shuffle in and out of the chapels bowing their heads in front of the images. A monk dispenses holy water from an old kettle. Overhead is a row of lions: paws outstretched, ready to pounce. Gold gongs hang between their paws. Near them are shelves with rows of what look like small dolls in rich brocade costumes in small glass cases, gathering dust. Look up, and row on row of carved faces stare down at you from the roofbeams. There is a smell of incense and, more overpoweringly, of yak butter. A row of old women, white hair braided into 108 narrow plaits, are sitting cross-legged in front of the golden jewel-encrusted statue of Shakyamuni, telling their rosaries. One old man is polishing a silver bowl with handfuls of barley. After every circular sweep of his hand, he tells off a bead on his rosary.

We go up a narrow staircase to an upper temple where monks are chanting, beating a big drum, blowing huge horns of engraved silver, and then finally out onto the roof to watch the dawn, which is stormy: shadowy mountains surfacing through pink and grey cloud, a watery sun touching the gold roofs and dragons' heads on the temple tops, the Potala on its rock in the distance. Lhasa roof-life is always interesting – a strange roofscape of many different levels and tiers, the rooftop courtyards adorned with prayer flags, prayer kilns, and often with small shacks or even tents. In the old days it was forbidden to build houses more than two storeys high, as no one should be able to look down on the Dalai Lama when he was carried round the town in a procession. Lhasa citizens created extra living space in the form of small shacks on top of their houses, which could be taken down hastily at the time of a procession. The Dalai Lama has gone, but the shacks remain.

In the dawn light, the roofs were alive with activity: people getting up, fetching water, preparing meals, washing. Smoke was rising from juniper fires on all the rooftops as people lit their prayer kilns to offer up prayers to greet the new day. Down below, the Barkor square was beginning to fill up, people parading round in their New Year finery: splendid costumes of silk and brocade. Brocade and fur hats for men and women. Long silk *chubas*, sheepskin-lined in bright colours of red and green and purple. Elaborate turquoise jewellery and headdresses. New aprons in gaudy striped cloth. New suits, new boots, new dresses – even the Khampas had bright new red tassels in their hair.

The first day of New Year is strictly for close family, but invitations for the second day onwards had been coming in thick and fast, and our engagement diary was really full: it felt rather like being in the middle of a Victorian novel, hobnobbing with old Lhasa families, meeting all the old aunts and cousins. As Lhasa is so small, and most of the families seem to be interconnected, we could not really begin to work out how people were exactly related to each other, but we met just about everybody it seemed! For a while it was as if things were not *so* different now from the endless round of parties and picnics that Harrer describes.

On the second day, we were invited for lunch with the family of the friend who had taken us to the Tibetan hospital. They actually live on campus, but when he invited us, he said: 'Oh, we won't live there next week. New Year isn't the same on campus – the people there are all Chinese, and it's very dull. We're moving back to our old house in Lhasa.' Here he gave us complicated directions about how to find the gate up a back street behind a temple in Old Lhasa. Then he thought better of it and said he would take us there himself: 'It's much nicer in the old house, and all the family will be together.' Evidently the old house was used by the relatives most of the year, but for the festival period they all moved in together.

It was a very cold day with flurries of snow and dust-storms. We managed to find the gateway and, as we entered the house, all had to do *Tashi Delek*. Then we were given some *chang*, and also some really good butter tea. By now, we really like that, and can tell better butter tea, as served in people's homes, which is thicker and more buttery, from worse, which is thinner (meaner on the butter). Special New Year pastries were pressed on us – delicious crisp flaky pastry, tasting something like shortbread with yakbutter. Some were in the shape of long flat folded pancakes, like *millefeuille* pastry, others were more like tangled balls of noodle, and all dusted with icing sugar. There was also hard sweet cheese or curd to nibble on (it looks amazingly like cauliflower heads), and of course sweets and fruit. We sat and chatted, and had more tea, and more *chang*, pressed on us. Relations came in and sat, and time, as always in Tibet, did not seem to matter very much, everyone enjoying doing nothing very much.

We began to wonder whether the invitation really had meant 'lunch', and maybe we ought to be leaving . . . and just then the meal started. It was a lovely sight. All the family were in their best new Tibetan dress: long skirts and aprons for the women and smart new *chubas* and black riding boots for the men, both sexes wearing fur-lined brocade hats. We sat on benches covered in colourful Tibetan carpets, around a box-like, highly decorated table, and feasted on *momos* (or politely, *shemo*) and mutton and yak and curried potatoes and stews and dried meat and *chang* and more *chang* until we're all quite bloated and can't eat any more. But no, we must have *tsampa*, rolled into balls for us by the head of the family. After lunch, the men settled down round the same table and played a form of dominoes, betting with buttons, not money! We chatted and had yet more tea, until it got dark, when we made our way home in another snowstorm.

Our next 'engagement' was even more splendid, as it was with one of the old noble families. The food was really superb (as it should have been – it was prepared by one of the Dalai Lama's former cooks, specially brought in for the evening). Four rooms of the rambling courtyard house were taken up by this feast, to which all sorts of different people had been invited, including, we were glad to see, some Chinese (which at first surprised us!) colleagues of the head of the family. We sat and had tea and *chang*, and pastries, and made polite conversation.

Then suddenly our friend reminded us: 'Did you bring the picture-book?' Of course! A few weeks ago, two American friends had sent, and miraculously it had actually reached us, a 1955 *National Geographic* which they had found in an old bookstore. It was full of colour photographs, taken by Harrer in the late 1940s of Lhasa as it was then, and of the people he knew. This 'picture-book' was the sensation of the evening! The old ladies, sitting cross-legged on the carpeted benches making polite and sleepy elderly conversation, suddenly burst into life and grabbed each other like schoolgirls: 'That's Tashi! Ooh, and look, isn't that Norbu's sister?!' 'Let's see, let's see! No, I don't believe it! That's my old teacher!' The magazine was practically ripped to shreds as they crowded round to look. Their faces were wonderful to watch: here were long-lost friends and relations, and they were rediscovering a long-lost family photo album – but in a foreign magazine over thirty years old!

The great names of Tibetan society flew around the room, Dele Rabden, Tsarong, Norbu, Taring, Rashagar . . . everyone wanted a look. Suddenly someone said: 'This is you!' and sure enough there was a photograph of a teenager in full court dress, and a stout man in his sixties was gazing at himself in the photo. 'Yes, that's me, and that's my father . . .' The excitement was such that until now everyone had forgotten they were hungry. Now there were a few anxious looks at watches and clocks . . . the cook hadn't yet arrived. Evidently the Dalai Lama's ex-cook was in great demand for feasts all over town, and had been held up at his luncheon appointment.

At times like this we realize with a shock how recently the changes in Tibetan society have come about, that a short time ago Tibet was still a medieval society. I had a similar realization in the incongruous context of a grammar lesson. I was teaching 'If . . .' and, to practise it, was asking the students, 'If you had lived fifty years ago, what would your life have been like?' One of the students said casually, 'Oh, I would have been a nobleman.' His friend, sitting beside him, said, 'I would have been a serf.' I looked at these two young men, sitting together, one with his arm thrown affectionately round his friend's shoulders, and tried to imagine the one labouring on the other's country estate. Interested, I pursued the grammatical exercise with more questions: what would they have worn, what would they have done during the day? When I asked, 'What would you have eaten?' they both gave the same answer: '*Tsampa*.' 'Just *tsampa*? Surely not!' I said to my 'nobleman'. He considered for a moment. 'Well, the *best* tsampa,' he conceded with a grin!

But we didn't just have *tsampa* that night! We had twenty-one courses, finishing up with a delicious *huoguo* (hot pot) containing beancurd, fish, squid, meat and vegetables. We then sang to each other (even we had to, in reply to some lovely, quavering songs from the old ladies) and ended up dancing between the wooden pillars of the huge living room to a random mix of Tibetan, Indian, Chinese and disco music! The old ladies seemed to like the disco best, but couldn't be persuaded to abandon their cross-legged contemplation of the 'picture-book' to come and dance.

Cycling in through the university gates one afternoon after yet another luncheon engagement, we bumped into the President, who said, 'You must come round to our house and have *Tashi Delek* . . ..' He looked a bit worried, and then went on, 'The trouble is, I'm very busy, but how about tomorrow?' 'Yes, that would be lovely,' we replied, and he continued, 'Tomorrow breakfast?' 'Tomorrow *breakfast*?' we echoed, rather surprised, wondering if perhaps Tibetan time had got completely confused over the New Year period or whether meanings had slipped through somewhere between Tibetan and Chinese and English. 'Yes, breakfast, how about nine o'clock?' 'Breakfast with the President' sounds like something aides have to do in the White House, or the title of a novel, but not something we had expected in Lhasa! The reason for this early invitation was that he had a meeting to go to (presidents don't get much holiday) and we shared this presidential breakfast with the Vice-President too.

The meal was very filling, a good warming start to a cold winter's day – more of the sweet pastries, thick butter tea of course with *tukpa* (thick Tibetan noodles) and yak meat, followed by a sort of barley porridge which also had meat in. We topped this off with a big bowl of sweet rice pudding containing sultanas and ginseng root – rather like the Chinese *ba bao fan* (eight treasure rice) but with two, not eight treasures. More tea, more chat, more pastries, and suddenly it was time for his meeting. He hurriedly put *katag* scarves round our necks as we climbed heavily onto our bikes, and he got into a curtained black 'Shanghai' sedan.

It was only when he had gone that we realized he had given back to us the *katag* we had presented to him on arrival. We had never been quite sure about *katag*-etiquette, but thought we had got the hang of it after a few days of New Year. Some recipients seemed to keep them on for a decent time, others immediately took them off and put them down. But we were confused by getting back the same *katag*!

That evening we went to perhaps the most memorable of all our parties. Originally our students had planned to invite us to their party. ('We should all wear our native dress,' they said, to which we replied, looking down at our blue jeans and sweaters, 'Will it be okay to come like this? This *is* our native dress!' feeling rather ashamed that we didn't have Morris dancing kit, or kilts, or at least something to surprise them with.) But unfortunately it had to be called off because of illness in the family in whose house it had been planned.

Feeling rather sad about this, we weren't sure about the alternative: a departmental do organized by the Arts Department for the staff. We feared it might turn out to be a formal stuffy 'official' evening. Ha! How wrong we were! It was the most spontaneous, let-your-hair-down occasion we have been to here, and perhaps the best thing about it was that it was a mixture of Chinese and Tibetan colleagues. It was hosted by the gentle, sad-looking head of the Arts Department – who turned out to be the most jovial and uninhibited person after a few glasses of *chang*. We ate a superb delicate meal, the spicing of which seemed almost Indian, and were amazed to find that this meal too had been prepared by the Dalai Lama's ex-cook, obviously much in demand all over Lhasa in the festive season!

After this, we drank more *chang* or Chinese wine, and danced and drank and danced, and then our host did some solo dances to Tibetan music, and then he made one of his young Chinese female staff dance Tibetan dances with him, and then everyone had to do a turn. Since this was a Music Department party, the Tibetan dancing and singing were wonderful. We danced and drank, and before we knew it, it was 2 a.m. 'Perhaps we'd better go . . .' but he caught our glances, and was pouring out more *chang*, and getting everyone in the household, servants, old aunts, children and all to dance. It wasn't till much later that we finally tottered off to bed, having spent almost eight hours dancing at high altitude!

The disco craze has reached Lhasa, and all the places we were invited to in our last months involved dancing . . . two miles above sea level. At first we found dancing and singing quite exhausting, but we must have been pretty fit by the end! Certainly, despite all the eating, we lost weight – as a result of being so high up for several months, or from too much dancing, we'll never know.

The 'secular' part of New Year was now over, and we had a few days of normality to get over these wonderful social occasions, which the Tibetans themselves really threw themselves into – perhaps because for so long they were not allowed to celebrate New Year at all. The host of our last party had, as a young man, been part of the Dalai Lama's music ensemble – and subsequently had spent twenty years in jail for this 'crime'. It is almost too painful to describe how one old lady we know went through a long, horribly moving mime for us in her living room, to show us just how families would have been treated by Red Guards during the Cultural Revolution at New Year time: people hardly dared wish each other '*Tashi Delek*' for fear of being overheard: gangs of soldiers and youths would come in and brutally search the house for traces of traditional Tibetan activity. But now 'things are much better' she said with tears in her eyes, as she calmed down and pressed another sweet pastry on us: 'Before, I couldn't even have offered you these.'

The religious part of New Year was only just beginning though: *Mönlam Chenmo* or the 'Great Prayer', had been banned completely for over twenty years before 1986, when it was reinstituted with great celebrations and a visit by the Panchen Lama. We were very interested to see how this second year of the new *Mönlam* would compare with reports we had had of 1986. Would the Panchen be coming down from Peking? Would the crowds be as big? Would the police have to use their infamous 'electric sticks' to control them? In 1986, *Mönlam* was a fortnight of what one might sceptically call propaganda-hype – except of course for Tibetans it was more a welcome chance to celebrate New Year in its full, traditional manner. We were rather worried about this: would it be 'genuine' or not? First reports, indicating that the Panchen would not be coming, and that *Mönlam* this year would only last for seven days, seemed to justify our reservations. However, our general conclusion is that 'things are indeed much better' and we only hope that they continue that way. Although the Chinese authorities exploit the ceremonies to the full for propaganda purposes, the celebrations meant so much to our Tibetan friends, and you cannot fake that kind of sentiment, even for propaganda purposes!

Mönlam did not start very auspiciously for us, partly through a confusion of dates, and partly through the 'assistance' of our Foreign Affairs official (Mr Ye or 'Big-Shop-Small-Potato', whom you have met before). The first day of Tibetan New Year fell this year on 28th February, so 2nd January, according to some of our English-speaking friends, was actually going to be 1st March (if you see what I mean), or alternatively the third day would be the second of the third month or . . .. At this point we usually tried to find out if they were using English, Chinese or Tibetan January, February or March, or Month One, Month Two, Month Three. Matters were usually made worse the more 'sophisticated' the person was (i.e. less inclined to admit that he, too, was hopelessly confused by the total muddle of a triple calendar). Anyway, we believed we were on safe ground when we met Big-Shop, and were told that the University had tickets for us to visit the

Jokhang on the first morning of *Mönlam*, which would be on the eighth day, i.e. 'Week Sky', which is Sunday in Chinese, i.e. the seventh day of the week, which would be the eighth day of January (Month One), or alternatively Sunday 7th March. He said he had the tickets ready and that he would come and collect us at 8 a.m., and we reconfirmed he meant on Sunday morning. 'Yes,' nodded Big-Shop, and bustled off like the small potato he really is. I suppose it was inevitable that on Friday night we got to bed late after too much beer with some friends, and so the *Rat-a-Tat-Tat* of Mr Big-Shop on our bedroom door at 6.30 on Saturday morning was not such a pleasant surprise as he intended! 'Hurry up, we're late!' he announced as we groaned and scratched our heads. 'Late for what?' 'To go to the Jokhang.' 'But I thought you said . . .' and gave up. Obviously *Mönlam*, with no one in the whole of Lhasa knowing exactly when anything was planned to happen, or even what was planned, was going to be fun.

It wasn't Big Shop's fault, really. We couldn't expect a small potato like him to understand, or even be much interested in, the activities of the monks of Lhasa. He was just as confused about dates as we were. But as we marched through the dark streets towards the Jokhang, even we could tell that the bugle blast through the cold morning was a military bugle *reveille* from the nearby PLA camp, not, as he officiously informed us, 'the monks calling the people to prayer'. He hadn't a clue what was going on, and he was quite probably nervous!

We'll never know what he meant by his 'Yes, I have the tickets' to us a few days before. We thought it meant someone had pulled a few strings for us with some cadre friends in the local government, or perhaps with one of the monks . . . but whatever, it did not mean that Big-Shop actually had tickets!

We arrived in front of the Jokhang, breathless from our walk ('Hurry, we'll be late!'). And then Big-Shop discovered just how small a potato he really was, much to his embarrassment, in front of us. 'We are from Tibet University,' he began. The young, tough-looking monks on the gate did not so much as look at him. 'We are from Tibet University,' he continued, 'and these foreign guests want to visit the Jokhang.' One of the monks turned his head and glowered at us. 'The University says we can go in to see the Great Prayer,' he went on, while we just wished we had nothing to do with it at all. There were two major obstacles to us getting in. The first was: We Didn't Have a Ticket! The second was: Big-Shop was trying to get us one! The more he insisted, and the more he spoke in urgent, officious Chinese, the less the guard-monks took any notice. At one ghastly moment, Big-Shop actually tried to push himself through – he is not very big, and the monks were tall, strong-looking youths who would not have looked out of place as bouncers at a London night club. I feared it might turn ugly (it was dark, cold, and everyone was tired and breakfastless) and said to the by now trembling Mr Ye, 'Look, it doesn't matter, let's forget about it, we'll come back tomorrow.' But he was determined, and his jaw jutted out as he strode off and started talking frantically to . . . a policeman! 'Oh, no, now we're really going to cause trouble,' I thought, and prayed that there wouldn't be a confrontation. Luckily the policeman simply said, 'You'll have to get tickets,' and turned away on his heel. Then Mr Ye uttered those ominous three words, which, to anyone who's spent any time at all in China, spell doom: '*Deng yi xia*,' he said, meaning, 'Wait a moment.' We waited, and waited, and got colder and colder . . . and finally, an hour later, he did come back, beaming all over his face and waving the tickets!

Someone, somehow, had obtained for us an official pass into the Jokhang, which meant that from the afternoon of the First Day of the Great Prayer, we were at liberty to walk in and out as we pleased. We felt so glad we had decided to stay on just to see it, as it formed a climax to the whole period we spent in Lhasa (and, of course, it was the high point of our Tibetan friends' year too).

We could wander in and out of the Jokhang at different times of day during the week-long Prayer Festival, and have been left with a composite blur of impressions – rather as if we had spent one whole long day in the temple rather than several scattered visits. Sometimes we would go upstairs, through the entrance guarded by the bouncer-monks, to a balcony which surrounds the inner courtyard of the Jokhang on four sides, and look down on the ceremonies from there; at other times we would join the long queue of pilgrims and move with them in a slow shuffle through the main entrance and round the perimeter of the courtyard, where the ceremonies were taking place.

The policemen down in the courtyard were pretty rough on those loitering with intent to take photos, and a few times we were pushed so hard that we nearly fell over. The Chinese police seemed rather jittery throughout the whole occasion. Perhaps the sight of so many massed Tibetans made them anxious. Perhaps it was the enforced exposure to a culture they find alien and make no attempt to understand. Maybe the long hours of mumbled prayers, the gloom, the smell of yak butter, got on their nerves and they vented their frustration by snapping out orders and shoving the pilgrims around.

Through various visits at different times of the day, we got a sense of the rhythm of a day in the Jokhang. Most days seemed to follow the same pattern, and after a while we could predict what would be happening at a particular time. Most of the day was spent in chanting prayers. The monks all sat cross-legged on the flagstones in the courtyard, their maroon and purple robes spread out around them. The pleated cloaks, gathered at the neck, fell around their hunched shoulders. From above it made a pattern like hundreds of red cockleshells on a grey beach. One of the abbots of Sera or Drepung or Ganden, gorgeous in rich brocade robes, was seated on a throne at the front to lead the chanting, which would at times rise to a crescendo, then fade away again, or at other times drop to a husky growl.

Downstairs in the courtyard, an endless stream of pilgrims mumbled their way around the edge of the ceremony: old men and women in long sheepskin coats, tall Khampas, families, young girls in giggling groups, toothless old grannies (who were the most persistent and successful queue-jumpers), trendy young guys in imported blue jeans and leather jackets, nomads from the Jangtang, pilgrims from Nyingchi in black tunics and flat caps, mothers with fat bundles of babies strapped to their backs – the whole of Lhasa, it seemed, with many thousands more from all over Tibet, was filing through the Jokhang.

Upstairs, there were more pilgrims, in their best clothes: elegant grey *chubas* for the men, with white silk *katag* around their necks, and brocade and fur-flapped hats; fine long pinafore dresses and brightly striped aprons for the women. No grubby sheepskins up here! We later learned that these were pilgrims who had given substantial donations to the temple as New Year alms. They all carried *katag* and incense sticks, and a rolled-up scroll, and stood in a long queue, filing down the stairs to present the *katag*, incense and scroll to the abbot. In the afternoon, two monks unrolled the scrolls and passed them to one of the high lamas, who read them out in a singsong chant, passing them on to another monk on the other side, who gathered them all into a heap, tying them into a bundle with the *katag*. The lama never paused for a second in his singsong reading: the rhythm was never broken. Other pilgrims threw scarves wrapped around prayer scrolls down from the balcony: these were then thrown from one monk to another, until they reached a pile at the foot of the abbot's throne.

Mid-morning, the ceremony was broken up by an interlude, when everyone filed out of the Jokhang to another courtyard at the side to hear a sermon given by one of the abbots seated on a splendid throne of carved and lacquered wood covered in brocade cloth. The throne was on a dais, where the senior monks sat. The junior monks squatted on the stone courtyard. They must get very cold and stiff sitting on stone flagstones for hours at a time, even with their robes bunched up underneath them!

The sermon was sometimes preceded by handclapping debates. These are lively and great fun to watch. An older monk will fire questions at a group of younger ones. As he poses each question, he claps his hand loudly and points at the examinees. The traditional method of passing examinations was by such oral debates: the Dalai Lama took his *geshe* or 'doctoral exams' in this way at Sera, Drepung and Ganden.

Sometimes we arrived at the Jokhang in time for the monks' breakfast or lunch. The first day the monks fast, but thereafter the chanting was punctuated by meals. These took place at high speed, in contrast to the slow monotonous rhythm of chanting. A group of monks would suddenly jump up and run out, returning still at a run with huge pails and wooden ladles. They scampered along with these between the rows of seated monks, dishing out tea and *tsampa* at breakfast, or at lunchtime a kind of sweet rice porridge with sultanas and dried fruit, rather like what we had eaten at the presidential breakfast. Each monk had a small wooden bowl, and ate with his fingers. I wondered if so much frantic activity was part of the ritual, or simply a reaction from sitting still for so long. After lunch, there was a kind of monks' recess for an hour or so, when the red-robed figures streamed out of the temple into the square, to loaf around and chat in the sunshine, or sit on the wall in maroon rows. It was rather like schoolboys at break.

The climax of all this religious activity came on the night of the full moon (15th March, or 16th January, or third month, fifteenth day, or . . .). This was Butter Sculpture night. All day, there were crowds and crowds of people on the Barkor and the Lingkor. We went to the Potala that morning and, looking down from there, we could see wave after wave of prostrating bodies on the Lingkor, a steady rhythm of rise and fall. The monks were busy all day in the Jokhang, sculpting the butter on huge wooden frames, and putting up scaffolding at four points around the Barkor. At about seven o'clock that night, the police threw a cordon round the centre of Lhasa, and proceeded systematically to clear people off the plaza and the Barkor. The side streets leading on to the square were all completely filled with people – a solid mass of bodies stretching from wall to wall and from one end of each street to the other. Outside the Jokhang, the monks began to put the butter sculptures up. Finally, as the full moon rose above the gold roofs of the temple, the police allowed us on to the square.

In front of the Jokhang were five huge wooden boards covered with the most intricate designs of leaf tendrils and flowers, swirls and whorls and intertwined dragons. In the centre of each of the boards was a row of 'pictures', as if in a gallery, of deities or lucky symbols of endless knots or conch shells. All made out of butter! On the temple roof were monks blowing horns – a haunting wailing sound, and seated on the ground in front of the sculpture was another row of monks, chanting.

There were four sets of sculptures on the four sides of the Barkor, one from each of the great monasteries of Sera, Ganden, Drepung and the Jokhang. But we didn't get to see the others until past one o'clock in the morning – the crowds were so dense! Apparently in the old days the sculptures ran the whole way round, and there was a grand competition between the four monasteries, to see which could produce the most beautiful display.

We stood around in the square for a long time, until one of our friends, whose family has a house near the square, found us and invited us in. We had butter tea and New Year pastries, and then spent a long time on the roof of their house, watching the crowds, crowds, crowds of people milling around on the square below. Just as we were about to leave, one of his cousins came in with a huge steaming pot, so we were all served a midnight bowl of noodles!

When we went back down into the square, the crowds had thinned out, so we went round the Barkor. The most delightful thing was the mood of the crowd. The streets were as packed as they had been at Lamp Festival, but now the mood was one of exuberance! People were laughing and singing. Everyone would grab our hands and shake them, wishing us 'Tashi Delek!' or, pointing proudly at the sculptures, ask 'Good?' Some people were drunk, but most just seemed high on Happiness.

It was past two o'clock when we got to bed, and we were up again at half past six, because we wanted to see the procession which marks the end of *Mönlam*. The statue of Jampa, the future Buddha, is taken out of the Jokhang and paraded round the Barkor. We walked through deserted streets to a Barkor full of mumbling pilgrims – and got a surprise: all the sculptures had disappeared! It was as if the previous night had been a hallucination, a strange highly coloured dream.

The square in front of the Jokhang was already full of people when we arrived, but we managed to squirm through to the front. Outside the temple was a lorry covered with orange cloth, with a throne on the back – a bit like a float for a carnival procession. Two or three monks on the temple roof were making clashing, wailing music with horns, cymbals, trumpets and drums. As we watched, other monks joined them, their heads bobbing up over the parapet, looking comically like seals. Then the gilded Jampa was brought out of the Jokhang, and arranged on the throne, with an orange umbrella over his head.

The area in front of the temple was by now packed with people, and police and monks had to move everyone back as the procession began. We were literally lifted off our feet in the press of people. Monks in their yellow hats, with horns and trumpets, led the procession. Then followed men in brocade gowns with gold designs on yellow, blue and red backgrounds. The gold and blue men had big drums tied to their back, and these were beaten by the men behind, dressed in red and gold. Then followed a troop of monks with banners made of silken patchwork, and bundles of incense sticks. Finally came the Jampa-lorry; people surging forward as it passed, to throw *katag* or to press their heads against the orange cloth. As the lorry moved off, the crowd closed in behind it and followed. We went up on to a nearby rooftop, and waited for the return of the procession: it took about an hour for them to complete the half-mile circuit (which on normal days takes about fifteen minutes to stroll round).

When the procession returned, the lorry was completely covered by piles and piles of white *katag*, Jampa swaying on his throne above the heads of the crowd, which would open up for him to pass, then immediately close up again. When the lorry drew up once more at the front of the Jokhang, Jampa – the Buddha of the Future – was returned inside, there to remain until the same occasion next year.

Our last week in Lhasa was an exhausting one – physically, because of all the late nights and early mornings; and emotionally, because we had to say goodbye to so many dear friends. We seemed to end up having little farewell parties most evenings, which were happy-sad occasions. I wonder when we will see all these lovely people again?

On our last day, we were rather torn as to what we should do; we wanted to visit all our favourite places in Lhasa, but obviously didn't have time. In the end we made a last visit to the Jokhang, still thronged with pilgrims after *Mönlam*.

In contrast, the Potala was practically deserted, which reinforced our impressions that it is now in most senses a museum. But how many times have we contemplated it, from how many different angles, and how many photographs have we taken of it at how many different times of day under different weather conditions! How quiet the palace is now: a show-piece for pilgrims and tourists and kept in beautiful condition certainly, but now an empty house. It used to be the seat of a 'God King', the centre of important affairs and intrigues of religion and government at the highest level, and must have been full of colourful comings and goings and the chatter and gossip of hundreds of people. I wonder how the Dalai Lama would feel about his old home if he ever visited it again? Certainly, he would hardly recognize the view of Lhasa. There is a photograph, taken by Heinrich Harrer from the Potala roof, published in that 1955 *National Geographic*. It shows the track, lined with trees on both sides, leading from Shöl to the Jokhang. On either side of the track, for almost a mile, stretch fields, parks and water meadows, and the only building visible is the tiny 'Turquoise Bridge'. Lhasa itself, surrounding the Jokhang, is like a small village in the distance. Today you can just make out the line of that track: some of the old trees still stand between the concrete blocks and the walls of different 'units'. Just discernible, behind the Friendship Store, are the blue roof tiles of the covered bridge, miraculously still standing, but tucked away in the Customs Unit, boarded up and filled with rubbish. The incessant rattle and honking of trucks and buses rises up to the Potala roof, blending in with the slushy pop music or military marches from a hundred tannoy loudspeakers scattered among the units. What a contrast! And barely thirty-five years have passed since Harrer took that photograph.

Appendix 1: **Tibetan History**

For the sake of clarity, we have organized this brief outline of Tibetan history into nine periods. However, history is rarely as neat as this and some of the periods overlap, as you will see.

1. The early *Bön* period

pre 7th century — Tibet ruled by line of kings beginning with the magical descent from heaven of the first king, Nyatri Tsenpo. Early indigenous animistic religion called *Bön*.

2. The Yarlung kings

617–649 — First religious king, Songtsen Ganpo, introduces Buddhism to Tibet through influence of his Nepalese and Chinese wives. Builds up Tibetan empire, builds Jokhang and introduces first Tibetan script.

649–742 — *Bön* regains influence. Tibet expands into central Asia.

742–797 — Second religious king, Trisong Detsen, restores Buddhism and invites Padmasambhava, the Indian Buddhist master, to Tibet.

763 — Tibet invades Chang'an, the capital of China.

779 — Samye founded. Great debate between Indian and Chinese Buddhism. Indian Buddhism dominant and Buddhism established as state religion.

783 — Peace treaty with China.

797–815 — Sons of Trisong Detsen continue war with China, and dissemination of Buddhism.

815–836 — King Ralpachen establishes peaceful relations with Chinese and initiates translations of Buddhist texts.

836–842 — Under King Langdarma, Buddhism is persecuted. He is assassinated in 842.

3. The Dark Ages

842–1244   Power struggle between various small factions and principalities. Buddhism in decline until 11th century.

4. Buddhist Renaissance

978 onwards   Influential teacher, Rinchen Tsangpo, invites Indian teachers, and revival of Buddhism begins.

1012   The Indian translator, Marpa, is born. He establishes the Kagyu order. Dies 1097.

1040   Birth of Milarepa, Marpa's disciple and great poet-mystic of Tibet. Dies 1123.

1042   The great Indian teacher, Atisha, arrives in Tibet. His disciples found the Kadam order. Dies 1055.

1057   Reting monastery (Kadam) founded.

1073   Sakya monastery and Sakya order founded.

1179   Tsurpu monastery (Karmapa) founded.

1180   Talung monastery (Kagyu) founded.

1182   Sakya Pandita born.

1189   Drigung monastery (Kagyu) founded.

5. The Sakya Dynasty and Mongol Overlordship

1207   Tibetan delegation sent to Genghis Khan, relations established and tribute paid.

1227   Death of Genghis Khan.

1244   Sakya Pandita invited to meet the Mongol Khan. He cedes Tibet to the Mongols in return for a guarantee of no further invasions.

1254   Kublai Khan gives the Sakya Pandita authority over Tibet. Politico–religious patron and priest relationship develops between Mongols and Tibetans, and Sakya hierarchs rule Tibet for a century under Mongol patronage.

1354–1642   Sakya overthrown and religious rule under the Kagyu order replaced by secular rule by kings.

6. The establishment of the Geluk order and rise of the Dalai Lamas

1357   Birth of Tsongkhapa, the great reformer who founded the Geluk order. Dies 1419.

1391   Birth of first Dalai Lama (recognized posthumously).

1409   Ganden (first Geluk monastery) founded.

1416   Drepung founded.

1419	Sera founded.
1434–1534	Power struggles between U and Tsang (backed by Geluk and Karmapa influence respectively). Tsang ruler emerges, but conflict continues.
1447	Tashilunpo founded.
1475	Birth of second Dalai Lama.
1543	Birth of third Dalai Lama. Mongols notice growing importance of Geluk leaders. Altan Khan invites the third Dalai Lama to Mongolia, where he is given the title of Dalai Lama (Great Ocean).
1558	Birth of fourth Dalai Lama.
1617	Birth of fifth Dalai Lama (The Great Fifth).
1641–1642	Gushri Khan invades Tibet, deposes Tsang ruler and Karmapas and enthrones fifth Dalai Lama as ruler of Tibet.

7. The Dalai Lamas and Manchu Overlordship

1642–1682	Consolidation of Geluk power under Dalai Lama with Mongol backing. Country becomes unified and Dalai Lama unites religious and temporal rule. Potala built. Tashilunpo abbot given title of Panchen Lama.
1682	Death of fifth Dalai Lama. Kept secret by Regent.
1683	Birth of sixth Dalai Lama, the Merry One, poet and libertine.
1697	Sixth Dalai Lama enthroned.
1706	The Mongolian prince, Lhabzhang Khan, invades Tibet with support from the new Manchu dynasty in China, and deposes sixth Dalai Lama. He offers Tibet as tribute to the Manchu emperor, Kang Hsi, and is given the post of governor. The sixth Dalai Lama is sent to China and dies on the way.
1717–1720	Dzungar Mongols invade Tibet and murder Lhabzhang. Kang Hsi sends troops to Lhasa and defeats Dzungars. The Chinese troops bring with them the seventh Dalai Lama and he is enthroned in 1720.
1721	Tibet decreed a protectorate of China and two Ambans or Chinese officials left in Lhasa to supervize relations.
1720-1757	The seventh Dalai Lama plays little part in affairs of state. Tibet ruled by lay administrations with Chinese support.
1757	Seventh Dalai Lama dies.

1758	Eighth Dalai Lama born. During his reign, government of the country conducted by a council of four ministers (three laymen and one monk).
1792	Gurkhas invade and reach Shigatse. Driven out by Chinese troops.
1806–1815, 1816–1837, 1838–1856, 1856–1875	Ninth, tenth, eleventh and twelfth Dalai Lamas. None reaches majority and Tibet governed by Regents.
1876	Thirteenth Dalai Lama born. Under his reign, religious and secular power once again united.

8. Tibet and the Great Powers

late 19th century	Russia and Britain conflict over trade interests in Tibet.
1904	Younghusband expedition. British Army under Younghusband sent to force trade agreement with Tibet. Dalai Lama flees to Mongolia.
1909	Dalai Lama returns.
1910	Chinese establish control over east Tibet and send troops to Lhasa. Dalai Lama flees to India.
1911	Revolution in China. Republic declared. Tibetans expel Chinese from Lhasa.
1913	Dalai Lama returns. Declares Tibet free of Chinese overlordship.
1913–1914	Simla Conference between Britain, Tibet and China to establish exact nature of relations between them. Tibet defined as an autonomous state under Chinese suzerainty. China refuses to ratify agreement, declaring Tibet to be an integral part of China.
1933	Thirteenth Dalai Lama dies. Appointment of Regent. Chaos, instability and infighting follow.
1935	Birth of fourteenth Dalai Lama.
1947	Indian Independence and end of British involvement in Tibet.

9. Chinese Rule

1949	Victory to Communist forces in China. Declaration of People's Republic.
1950	Chinese troops advance into east Tibet.
1951	Seventeen Point Agreement signed between China and Tibet, under which Tibet is promised that her political and religious systems will remain intact, but that the Tibetan army will be incorporated into the PLA and

that China will govern Tibet's foreign affairs. Chinese troops arrive in Lhasa.

1959 Rebellion in Kham and uprising in Lhasa. Dalai Lama flees to India. China repudiates Seventeen Point Agreement and begins to dismantle social, political and religious structures in Tibet.

1964 Tibet declared an 'Autonomous Region of the People's Republic of China'.

1966–1976 Cultural Revolution.

1976 Death of Mao Zedong.

1979 Beginning of liberalization policy and economic reforms in Tibet. Delegations from the Dalai Lama allowed to visit Tibet.

1980 Hu Yaobang visits Tibet and is horrified. Further reforms introduced, including dismissal of many Chinese leaders and greater religious freedom.

1983 Campaign against Spiritual Pollution and beginning of Crackdown on Crime.

1984 Tibet opened to tourists for the first time.

1986–1987 Campaign against Bourgeois Liberalization.

1987 Party Congress in Peking. Deng Xiaoping and many hardline leftists retire to be replaced by younger reformists.

1987–1988 Pro-independence riots in Lhasa and other places in Tibet.

Appendix 2: **Tibetan Buddhism**

Tibetan Buddhism is a unique form of Buddhism, influenced both by the indigenous *Bön* religion and by the Indian tantric tradition, both of which it has absorbed and transformed. It is impossible to summarize this highly complex belief in a few pages. What follows is the briefest outline of some of the main features.

1. The Development of Buddhism in Tibet

The original religion in Tibet was an animistic faith called *Bön*. Buddhism was introduced initially under Songtsen Ganpo, who was influenced by the faith of both his Chinese wife, Wen Cheng, and his Nepalese wife, Trisun. Trisong Detsun, one of his successors, continued to promote Buddhism, inviting the great Indian sage Padmasambhava to visit Tibet to 'subdue the demons' and establish Buddhism. After his death its influence began to decline, until an eleventh-century renaissance when great Indian teachers such as Marpa and Atisha came to Tibet. The Sakya and Kagyu orders were founded at this time. In the fifteenth century the great reformer, Tsongkhapa, founded the Geluk sect, which gradually assumed pre-eminence. Under the Chinese, from 1959–1979, and particularly during the Cultural Revolution 1966–76, Buddhism was suppressed, but since the early 1980s there has been a policy of 'religious freedom'.

2. Buddhist traditions

There are three great traditions in Buddhist faith: the Hinayana tradition, dominant in Sri Lanka and south-east Asia; the Mahayana tradition, dominant in China and Japan; and the Vajrayana or tantric tradition which developed in India.

Hinayana

This is the basic tradition of Buddhism, based most closely on the sutras or teachings of Buddha. Hinayana Buddhism lays stress on three main aspects of existence: suffering, transience and the insubstantiality of what we call reality. The goal of the Hinayana Buddhist is to achieve liberation from this unsatisfactory existence and attain Nirvana, which essentially means extinction or cessation. The individual who does not reach Nirvana is trapped in an endless cycle of death and rebirth. If one's actions are meritorious, one can be reborn into a better existence; if they have been evil, one will be reborn into a lower form of existence. To achieve enlightenment and liberation involves recognition of the 'four noble truths' and following of the 'eightfold path'. These are, respectively:

1. Existence is suffering;
2. Suffering is caused by desire;
3. Eliminate the cause of suffering and suffering will cease to arise;
4. The eightfold path is the way to eliminate desire and extinguish suffering.

1. Right understanding;
2. Right thought;
3. Right speech;
4. Right bodily contact;
5. Right livelihood;
6. Right effort;
7. Right attentiveness;
8. Right concentration.

To become a Buddhist involves 'taking refuge' in or committing oneself to the 'Three Gems': the Buddha and the enlightenment he represented; the Dharma (the path to enlightenment revealed by Buddha); and the Sangha (the Buddhist community).

Mahayana
This is a later development of Buddhism which lays less stress on personal salvation and more on the relation to others through compassion and love. The tendency in Hinayana to renounce the world and work for one's own enlightenment is replaced in Mahayana by the compassionate ideal of the bodhisattva, the being who works selflessly for the enlightenment of all living things, perhaps renouncing his own attainment of Nirvana to be reborn again in order to help others to achieve enlightenment.

Vajrayana
This tradition lays stress on the tantric discipline, a form of esoteric instruction which aims to provide a direct route to enlightenment through practices involving identification with a personal or tutelary deity.

Tibetan Buddhism contains strands of all three great traditions woven into a complex and unique whole.

3. The Tibetan pantheon

The plethora of Buddhas, deities, bodhisattvas and other figures in the Tibetan pantheon is one of the most confusing aspects of Tibetan Buddhism for the non–Buddhist, or even for a Buddhist from another tradition. The pantheon consists of:

Buddhas
These include: Shakyamuni, the historical Buddha; Jampa, the Buddha of the future; the Medicine Buddha; and the five Buddhas representing aspects of energy.

Bodhisattvas
These are associated with various qualities and include Chenrezi, the bodhisattva of compassion, and Manjushri, the bodhisattva of wisdom.

Tantric deities
These represent various aspects of enlightenment. Each deity may be found in wrathful or compassionate aspect. The wrathful deities urge the overcoming of obstacles and the liberation of energy; the compassionate deities represent the path of love and compassion. In addition, many deities are portrayed in sexual embrace with a consort, symbolizing the union of the male and female aspects of the path to enlightenment: compassion and active engagement united with wisdom and depth of understanding.

Protectors
These are guardians and patron gods and goddesses, such as the Temple Guardians, protectors of the four compass points, or Pelden Lhamo, patron goddess of Lhasa.

Historical figures
These may be past Dalai Lamas, kings of Tibet, Indian masters such as Padmasambhava, or other lamas connected with a particular temple or monastery.

Bön deities
Many of these have been absorbed into the Buddhist pantheon and transformed in the process, but any number of local gods (connected with a particular mountain or lake, for example), household gods and evil spirits still remain.

4. Monasteries and the monastic tradition

There are four main orders of Tibetan Buddhism. In order of founding, these are: Nyingma, Sakya, Kagyu and Geluk. There was an early order called Kadam, but this has largely been absorbed into the Geluk order.

There are some differences of doctrine and practice, but analysis and explanation of these differences would require a highly detailed and specialist knowledge of Buddhism. It is estimated that there were about 6,500 monasteries in Tibet and that between a quarter and a third of the male population were monks. Not all monks would study Buddhism, however: some were assigned to duties such as administration, gardening or cooking. For those who did study, the course was long and exacting, taking, in some cases, fifteen to twenty years, and consisting of courses in basic philosophy and logic, Buddhist philosophy and doctrine and monastic discipline. Monks who completed the course were awarded the degree of *geshe*, or Doctor of Divinity, by public examination. They could then pursue tantric techniques under the guidance of a personal teacher or guru. Monastic discipline was strict, and monks would pass their day in attending services, chanting prayers, listening to teachings, memorizing the scriptures, and testing their knowledge through debate.

5. Popular religious practice

The study of Buddhism was restricted to the monkhood. There are no 'services' in Buddhism as there are in Christianity or Islam. The study of Buddhism by laymen is a modern Western development. For the layman in Tibet, religious practice consisted – as it still does – of the repetition of prayers and mantras, by recitation or with a prayer wheel, the performance of acts of devotion such as prostration, circumambulation or pilgrimage, and the giving of offerings.

6. Art and literature

All Tibetan art and virtually all its literature, except for some folk tales and songs and the love poems of the sixth Dalai Lama, is religious. Tibetan art is to be found in temples and monasteries and takes three forms: statues, *tangka* and murals. These may depict various deities or scenes from the life of Buddha, or the life of a bodhisattva or historical figure. Tibetan literature consists of the 108 volumes of the Kangur, the Buddhist scriptures, and the 227 volumes of the Tengyur, the Indian commentaries on those scriptures, together with a vast number of commentaries by Tibetan lamas.

7. Religion and politics

From early times, religion and politics have been inextricably mixed in Tibet, and Tibetan history has been characterized by rivalry and feuding between the different orders with one or another being dominant politically at various periods. In addition, the different orders have at times allied themselves with different factions of the lay nobility. At other times there has been hostility between clergy and the lay government. In the thirteenth century, for example, it was the Sakya order that was dominant. This period of Sakya rule was succeeded by secular rule and then a period of feuding between the lay rulers of Tsang, backed by the Karmapas and the rulers of U backed by the Geluk, with first the Karmapa/Tsang alliance and then the Geluk/U alliance triumphing. Although the emergence of the Dalai Lamas for the first time united religious and secular rule, there continued to be considerable infighting and rivalry between the various sects, particularly in the periods before the maturity of each new Dalai Lama when the country was governed by a regent. The last years of the thirteenth Dalai Lama, for example, were characterized by tension between the lay administration, which wanted various changes, and the clergy, who resolutely opposed all change; while the period of regency during the childhood of the fourteenth Dalai Lama was beset by dissent and factionalism among the ruling clergy.

Appendix 3:
Social and Political Organization in Tibet
prior to 1959

1. Social organization

Society in Tibet was very highly stratified, with a clear division into upper and lower: the nobles and the common people. Within the nobility there was a very strict hierarchy, with a system of gradation according to rank. In theory all land belonged to the state, and nobles and monks were granted their large estates in return for taxes, in the form of produce and government service in the case of the nobles, and prayers and rituals in the case of the monks. In practice, though, the noble families and the monasteries had a hereditary right to their estates. The estates were farmed by peasants, tenant farmers who held land from the landlord in return for provision of services on the land and to the family. Besides nobility, monks and peasants, Tibetan society included nomads, traders and beggars, together with a class of outcast or 'untouchable' occupations such as butchers and disposers of the dead.

2. Political organization

The Dalai Lama was the head of both Church and State, uniting in his person religious and secular authority. He, or the Regent who ruled for him until he came of age, headed two administrations: one secular, composed of monk and lay officials, and one religious, composed of monks. The chief officer in the secular administration was the Prime Minister, a lay official who formed a liaison between the Dalai Lama and the highest administrative body, the *Kashag*, or Cabinet. This body was composed of four officials: three laymen and one monk, and was the main decision-making machine on all governmental and legal issues. Below the *Kashag* was the Executive Council: a kind of civil service of lay administrative officers such as tax officials, treasurers, military officials. At regional level, there were four Provincial Governors who supervised 100 administrative districts, each governed by two officials, a monk and a layman.

The head of the religious administration was the Lord Chamberlain who was the chief of the Dalai Lama's household and the overseer of the treasury. Below him was a monk council composed of four monks, parallel to, though less important than, the *Kashag*. Its function was to oversee the monasteries and to supervize the monastic 'civil service'. This consisted of four treasurers and a body of monk officials.

In addition to these two administrations, there was a consultative body called the National Assembly, which was called together, particularly in times of national crisis, to give advice. It was composed mainly of high lay officials and the abbots of the great monasteries, but could be expanded to include representatives from all walks of Tibetan life.

Reading List

Allen, Charles, *A Mountain in Tibet*. London, André Deutsch, 1982.

Avedon, John F, *In Exile from the Land of Snows*. London, Wisdom Publications, 1985.

Batchelor, Stephen, *The Tibet Guide*. London, Wisdom Publications, 1987.

Bell, Sir Charles, *Portrait of a Dalai Lama*. London, Collins, 1946.

Booz, Elizabeth D, *A Guide to Tibet*. London, Collins, 1986.

Buckley, Michael, and Strauss, Robert, *Tibet: a Travel Survival Kit*. Berkeley, Lonely Planet Publications, 1986.

Byron, Robert, *First Russia, Then Tibet*. London, Macmillan, 1933. (Penguin, 1985).

David-Neel, Alexandra, *Magic and Mystery in Tibet*. London, Unwin, 1984.

David-Neel, Alexandra, *My Journey to Lhasa*. London, Heinemann, 1927. (Virago, 1983).

Dowman, Keith, *The Power-Places of Central Tibet: The Pilgrim's Guide*. London, Routledge, 1988.

Epstein, Israel, *Tibet Transformed*. Peking, New World Press, 1983.

Fleming, Peter, *Bayonets to Lhasa*. Hong Kong, Oxford University Press, 1984.

Govinda, Lama Anagarika, *The Way of the White Clouds*. London, Rider and Co, 1960.

Grunfeld, A. Tom, *The Making of Modern Tibet*. London, Zed Books, 1987.

Gyatso, Geshe Kelsang, *Buddhism in the Tibetan Tradition: A Guide*. London, Routledge, 1984.

Gyatso, Tenzin (His Holiness the Dalai Lama), *Kindness, Clarity and Insight*. Ithaca, Snow Lion, 1984.

Gyatso, Tenzin (His Holiness the Dalai Lama), *My Land and My People*. New York, McGraw Hill, 1962. (Potala Corporation, 1977).

Harrer, Heinrich, *Return to Tibet*. London, Weidenfeld and Nicholson, 1984. (Penguin, 1985).

Harrer, Heinrich, *Seven Years in Tibet*. London, Rupert Hart Davis, 1953. (Granada, 1976).

Hedin, Sven, *To the Forbidden Land: Discoveries and Adventures in Tibet*. Delhi, Asian Publications, 1986 (selections from *Trans-Himalaya*).

Hopkirk, Peter, *Trespassers on the Roof of the World*. London, John Murray, 1982.

Huc, R-E, *Souvenirs d'un voyage dans la Tartarie*. (Livre de Poche, 1962).

Hyde-Chambers, Fredrick and Audrey, *Tibetan Folk Tales*. London, Shambhala, 1981.

Landon, Perceval, *Lhasa the Mysterious City*. London, 1905. (Kailash Publishers, Delhi, 1978).

Norbu, Jamyang, *Horseman in the Snow: The story of Aten, an old Khampa Warrior*. Dharamsala, Central Tibetan Secretariat, 1979.

Norbu, Jigme Thubten, *Tibet, patrie perdu*. Paris, Albin Michel, 1963.

Norbu, Thubten and Turnbull, Colin, *Tibet, its History, Religion and People*. London, Chatto and Windus, 1969. (Penguin, 1976).

Richardson, Hugh M, *Tibet and its History*. London, Shambhala, 1984.

Seth, Vikram, *From Heaven Lake: Travels through Sinkiang and Tibet*. London, Chatto and Windus, 1983.

Shen, T L, and Liu, S C, *Tibet and the Tibetans*. Stanford University Press, 1983.

Snellgrove, David, and Richardson, Hugh M, *A Cultural History of Tibet*. London, Shambhala, 1986.

Snelling, John, *The Sacred Mountain*. London, East-West Publications, 1983.

Spencer Chapman, F, *Lhasa the Holy City*. London, Hogarth Press, 1938. (Alan Sutton, 1984).

Stein, R A, *Tibetan Civilization*. London, Faber, 1972.

Taring, Rinchen Dolma, *Daughter of Tibet*. London, John Murray, 1970.

Tucci, Guiseppe, *To Lhasa and Beyond*. London, East-West Publications, 1985.

Waddell, L Austine, *Tibetan Buddhism*. New York, Dover Publications Inc, 1972. (Reprint of *The Buddhism of Tibet*. London, W H Allen and Co, 1895).

Wang Furen and Suo Wenqing, *Highlights of Tibetan History*. Peking, New World Press, 1984.

Glossary

Ali: the Chinese name for Ngari, the area of western Tibet around Mount Kailash.

Amdo: region of north-east Tibet, now within the Chinese provinces of Qinghai, Gansu and Sichuan.

Amitabha: the Buddha of Infinite (or Boundless) Light, one of the five Buddha types recognized by Tibetans. The Panchen Lama is believed to be an incarnation of Amitabha.

Ani gompa: a nunnery, from *ani* (woman) and *gompa* (monastery).

Ani Sangkung: a small nunnery in central Lhasa.

Atisha: an Indian Buddhist teacher who came to Tibet in the eleventh century to assist in the advancement of Buddhism and died at Drölma Lakhang. His Tibetan name is *Jowoje*.

Aufschnaiter: Peter Aufschnaiter, contemporary of Harrer in Lhasa.

Baijiu: white spirit made from grain.

Barkor: octagonal street encircling the Jokhang, a holy pilgrim-circuit.

Bodhisattva: a being who has attained enlightenment, but who compassionately refrains from entering Nirvana in order to teach and save others.

Bön: the indigenous Tibetan animist religion, which existed there before the arrival of Buddhism.

Cadre: usual English term for the Chinese *ganbu*, an official, bureaucrat or other responsible person within the Chinese administration.

Campaigns: Against Spiritual Pollution; For Spiritual Civilization; Against Bourgeois Liberalization: these nationwide campaigns, in autumn 1983, autumn 1986 and spring 1987 respectively, were instigated by left-wingers in the Chinese Politburo and all had similar aims – to restore public morality and rid China of decadent (mainly Western) influences. Each led to a period of tightened control and a clampdown on artistic freedom.

Chakpori: the 'Iron Mountain' which stands opposite the Potala, to the south-west. On the peak, where before 1959 stood the Tibetan Medical College, is now an enormous radio mast among the ruined walls.

Chamba (see **Jampa**): the Future Buddha, or Maitreya.

Chamdo: large town in east Tibet.

Chang: an alcoholic drink brewed from barley grains, usually milky-white in colour, which is often brewed at home continuously, the fermenting liquid being mixed with water to serve to guests. It is sometimes referred to as 'barley beer'.

Chenrezi: the 'patron deity' of Tibet, whose Indian name is Avolokiteshvara, the Bodhisattva of Compassion, The Dalai Lama is recognized as his incarnation.

Chöten (see also **stupa**): literally 'receptacle for offerings', a *chöten* is a masonry structure consisting of five main parts. A square or rectangular base, symbolizing earth, supports a large, roughly hemispherical block representing water, out of which a triangular tongue rises, representing fire (usually divided into thirteen segments, symbolizing the thirteen Bodhisvat heavens). On top of this are usually a crescent moon shape representing air, and the sun.

Chuba: traditional Tibetan jacket or coat, worn rather like a cloak. One of the long sleeves is usually worn off the shoulder, a wide belt being tied around the waist so that a commodious pocket is formed, into which valuables and articles of daily use can be stuffed for safe keeping.

Commune System: system of collective farming operative under Mao Zedong.

Crackdown on Crime: movement launched in the early 1980s to inflict severe penalties (often execution) for crimes, with the aim of halting the rising crime rate.

Criticism-Struggle: group criticism of an individual, who is often publicly humiliated and beaten in the process. Much used in the Cultural Revolution as a means of 'reform'. (Tibetan: *thamzing*).

Cultural Revolution (or **Great Proletarian Cultural Revolution**): launched by Mao Zedong in 1966 to spread 'permanent revolution' throughout the People's Republic. Often referred to in China as the 'ten years turmoil', it caused great suffering in Tibet, in addition to the famine of the late 1950s and the reprisals following the March 1959 uprising when the Dalai Lama fled to India. It is estimated that some 6,000 religious sites were destroyed during the period 1966–76, when the Cultural Revolution finally came to an end with the death of Mao.

Dalai Lama: the spiritual and temporal leader of Tibet, who in 1959 went into exile in India where he still lives. Born in 1935 in Amdo (now part of Qinghai province), he has now spent over half his life away from his homeland. The present Dalai Lama, Tenzin Gyatso, is the fourteenth in a line traced back to a nephew of Tsongkhapa, Gendun Drup, who was recognized to have been an incarnation of Chenrezi.

Damaru drum: a small double hand drum shaped like a child's rattle, with two strikers on strings. When the handle of the drum is rotated or twisted with the wrist, the two strikers swing to hit the two drum skins simultaneously. The drums are sometimes made of two human skulls.

Dharamsala: the hill station in the Himalayan foothills of Himachal Pradesh, which since 1959 has been the home of the Dalai Lama and his 'administration in exile', along with thousands of other Tibetan refugees.

Dharma wheel: golden wheel symbolic of Buddhist teaching.

Dorje: ritual instrument used in religious ceremonies, representing a divine thunderbolt. Held in the right hand, it is used in conjunction with a bell held in the left.

Drepung: large monastery, one of the Three Pillars, situated five miles west of Lhasa. Founded in 1416, its name literally means 'rice heap', which is an apt description of the mass of white buildings seen from the valley below. It used to have over 7,000 monks and was a major centre of power. During the Great Prayer festivals, it was monks from Drepung who were charged with keeping order in Lhasa. During the events of October 1987, it seems to have been Drepung monks who initially demonstrated against the Chinese presence in Tibet.

Drigung: a Kagyu monastery east of Lhasa.

Drölma: patron goddess of Tibet, a female deity symbolizing compassion. She is found in two forms – green Drölma, symbolizing the motherly aspect of compassion, and white Drölma, symbolizing its fertile aspect.

Drölma Lakhang: a small temple at Nyetang, south of Lhasa in the Kyichu valley, dedicated to Drölma. Atisha died here in 1054 and the temple is a shrine to his memory.

Dunbu Chökor: a small Sakya monastery at Chitisho, in the Yarlung Tsangpo valley.

Dzong: a fortress or castle, often found in place-names.

Eight Model Revolutionary Operas: eight operas approved by Jiang Qing (Mao's wife) and permitted to be performed during the Cultural Revolution.

Erhu: a Chinese two-stringed bowed instrument, similar to a violin.

Fen: unit of Chinese currency (100 fen = 1 yuan).

Ganden: a monastery situated some fifty miles east of Lhasa on a high ridge overlooking the Lhasa valley. This monastery was founded in 1416 by the reforming Tsongkhapa, who died here in 1419. A centre for resistance in 1959, the monastery suffered terrible damage throughout the Cultural Revolution and although several buildings have now been rebuilt, the ruins remain a potent symbol of the sufferings Tibet has recently undergone.

Geluk: an order or sect of Tibetan Buddhism, often referred to as 'Yellow Hats' because of the distinctive headgear worn by Gelukpa monks. This 'virtuous order' was founded by Tsongkhapa in the fifteenth century and became the dominant religious group in central Tibet. The Dalai Lama is a Gelukpa, although acting as head of all the other orders.

Gesar: the legendary hero of Tibet, who came from Ling, an old kingdom in eastern Tibet. The Gesar epic is a long tale of heroism and magic, and it is said that Gesar will return to save his country in times of great troubles. His name is almost certainly related to 'Caesar', about whom news would have travelled along the old Silk Route eastwards and then south into Tibet.

Geshe: Tibetan title, roughly equivalent to Doctor of Divinity.

Gompa: a monastery, literally meaning 'solitary place' or 'hermitage'.

Gongar Chöde: a temple south of Lhasa, in Gongar, the airport town.

Guardian kings: four figures to be found at the entrance of all temples, who give protection against evil influences.

Gyume (or the **'Lower Tantric College'**): a Lhasa monastery specializing in tantric practice.

Harrer: Heinrich Harrer, author of *Seven Years in Tibet*.

Hinayana (or **'Lesser Vehicle'**): form of Buddhism in which one is concerned with one's own enlightenment.

Hu Yaobang: until January 1987, General Secretary of the Chinese Communist Party. In 1980 he visited Tibet and apologized for the wrongs inflicted on it over the past few decades. A proponent of religious freedom and a degree of liberalization throughout China, he was to Tibetans a sign of commitment on the part of the Peking government to better treatment of their country. His fall therefore caused some consternation.

Jampa (see **Chamba**, also **Maitreya**): the Future Buddha, or 'Loving One'. The image in the Jokhang of the future Buddha is paraded round the Barkor on the last day of Mönlam, the fifteenth day of the New Year.

Jangtang (Changtang): the vast, desolate, central plateau of Tibet.

Jokhang: the holiest shrine in Tibetan Buddhism, home of the image of Shakyamuni (Tibetan: *Jo*), brought to Tibet in the seventh century by Princess Wen Cheng, the Chinese wife of Songtsen Gampo.

Kadam: order of Buddhism founded by Atisha in the eleventh century.

Kagyu: order of Tibetan Buddhism founded by Marpa, Milarepa and their disciples in the eleventh century.

Kailas: a holy mountain in western Tibet, sacred to Buddhists and
Hindus alike.

Karma Kagyu: the line of incarnate lamas, often called 'Black Hats',
members of the Kagyu order based at Tsurphu, founded in the twelfth
century.

Kashag: the Tibetan Cabinet, composed of monk and lay officials,
governed Tibet until 1959.

Katag: often referred to as 'prayer scarves', these are long scarves of fine
muslin, cotton or, for very special occasions, fine silk. They are bought
to be offered to guests, hosts, at departures and reunions, when they are
white. They are often presented to holy images in temples, when they
may be yellow in colour.

Kham: area of eastern Tibet, home of the Khampas, whose tough
reputation was increased by their fierce resistance to the Chinese in
1950 and 1959.

Khampas: people from Kham, distinctive figures, taller than the average
central Tibetans, with a reputation over the ages for swagger and
bravado, which image they do little to dispel.

Kora: act of circumambulating a holy place.

Kumbum. literally 'one thousand images'. The monastery in Amdo on
the site of Tsongkhapa's birth is called 'Kumbum', as is the huge stupa
at Gyantse.

Kyichu: 'Waters of Pleasure', the Lhasa river.

Lama: often used in English to refer, erroneously, to all monks of
Tibetan Buddhism (or, in older books, 'Lamaism'). 'Lama', strictly
speaking, refers only to a teacher or guide (who may be recognized
as an incarnation of an important religious figure). Only a few monks
are lamas.

Lamp Festival: a festival to mark the anniversary of the death of
Tsongkhapa. Every windowsill around the Barkor is lit with butter-
lamps – a most moving sight.

Langdarma: a ninth-century Tibetan king who persecuted Buddhism,
and was killed by a monk from Yerpa.

Liberation: the People's Republic of China was officially proclaimed on
1st October 1949 in Tian'anmen Square. Within weeks, the People's
Liberation Army had moved towards eastern Tibet, with a view to
freeing the area from feudal oppression. PLA troops arrived in Lhasa
in 1950. 'Liberation' is the Chinese term (*jiefang*) for this revolution,
which effectively brought Communist Party control to all the present-
day area of the Republic.

Lingkor: holy pilgrim circuit around the outskirts of Lhasa, forming the
outer of three holy circuits: one around the interior of the Jokhang, the

second around the Barkor, which encircles the Jokhang, and the third
Lingkor encircling the Holy City.

Longyan: 'dragon's eye' berries, used to make Muslim tea.

Losar: Tibetan New Year. The Tibetan calendar is lunar, like that of
China, but Losar and the 'Spring Festival' do not necessarily coincide.
In 1987, Chinese New Year was at the end of January, while Losar
was at the end of February. In 1988, both fell on the same day, in mid
February. This lay festival immediately precedes Mönlam.

Lukhang: chapel behind the Potala situated on an island in a park.

Mahayana or **'Great Vehicle'**: form of Buddhism adopted in Tibet,
which stresses compassion and lays emphasis on the attainment of
enlightenment.

Maitreya: the Future Buddha (see Jampa).

Mandala: a circular symmetrical design symbolizing a deity, used in
tantric practice.

Mani: the mantra *Om Mani Padme Hum*.

Mani stone: stone on which the mantra is inscribed.

Mantra: prayer formula or chant used as a means of concentrating
the mind.

Mao or **Jiao**: unit of Chinese currency (10 jiao = 1 yuan).

Maotai: white spirit made from grain.

Marpa (1012–1097): founder of the Kagyu order, and Milarepa's teacher.

Marpori (or **'Red Hill'**): the hill on which the Potala Palace is built.

Mentzi Khang: the Tibetan Medical Centre, originally sited on top of
Chakpori, now housed in a modern building at the opposite end of the
main square from the Jokhang temple in central Lhasa.

Milarepa (1040–1123): a celebrated poet–mystic, disciple of Marpa, and
one of the founders of the Kagyu order.

Momo: 'dumplings' of dough stuffed with meat or vegetables, similar
to Chinese *jiaozi*, but in our experience much heavier and much more
filling.

Mönlam or **Mönlam Chenmo**: the 'Great Prayer', a religious festival of
prayers which takes place during the first two weeks of the New Year.

Mindroling: a Nyingma monastery in the Yarlong Tsangpo valley.

Muru Ningbar (see **Nechung Branch temple**).

Nechung: (a) Geluk monastery near Drepung, home of the State Oracle;
(b) Nechung Branch temple: a small temple affiliated to Nechung,
beside the Jokhang.

Nirvana: the state of enlightenment, final release from the cycle of
reincarnation through extinction of all suffering and individuality.

Norbulingka: the 'Jewel Park'. The Summer Palace of the Dalai Lama,
set in a large wooded park about two miles west of the Potala.

Nyingma: oldest order of Tibetan Buddhism, founded at the time of
Padmasambhava. Known as 'Red Hats'.

Om Mani Padme Hum: literally meaning 'Hail the Jewel in the Lotus', a
Tibetan mantra representing enlightened compassion.

Padmasambhava: also called in Tibetan 'Guru Rinpoche', a sage from
India who came to Tibet in the eighth century at the invitation of King
Trisong Detsen in order to help bring Buddhism to the country. He
helped found Samye monastery in the 770s.

Palhalupuk: a small cave temple in the side of Chakpori opposite the
Potala.

Panchen Lama: the head lama of Tashilhunpo monastery in Shigatse,
incarnation of Amitabha Buddha. The first was a disciple of
Tsongkhapa. The present Panchen Lama lives in Peking and is allowed
to visit Tibet only occasionally. While the Dalai Lama fled to India
in 1959, the younger Panchen became a member of the central
government.

Pelden Lhamo: a wrathful deity, patron goddess of Lhasa.

Pinyin: the official standard system for transcribing Chinese in the
Roman alphabet.

Potala: named after Mount Potala, the abode of Avalokiteshvara
(Chenrezi), the palace was originally built by Songtsen Gampo in the
seventh century. Construction of the present building began under the
fifth Dalai Lama in 1645 and was completed in 1694, twelve years after
his death. The Potala is the winter home of the Dalai Lama.

Prayer flag: Tibetan *lung* meaning 'wind horse'. Pieces of cloth printed
with prayers and hung on rooftops, mountain tops, passes, etc, for the
wind to blow through and carry prayers.

Prayer wheel: a large cylinder at the entrance of a temple, or a small
hand-held cylinder mounted on a handle. In both cases, the cylinder is
filled with tightly wrapped prayers printed on a tight spiral of paper,
so that when the wheel is turned clockwise, the prayers are repeated
countless times.

Ramoche: sometimes called 'Little Jokhang', a small temple in the north
of Lhasa.

Red Guards: these young people acted as the vanguard of Mao Zedong's
Cultural Revolution. They were encouraged to travel over the length
and breadth of China, creating revolution. Youthful idealism and hero-
worship of Mao degenerated into violent extremism, and bands of Red
Guards would bring terror, injury and death to people they suspected of
'wrong attitudes'. Inspired by the slogan 'Destroy the Four Olds', they
inflicted terrible damage on monuments and cultural relics throughout
the land.

Renminbi: literally 'people's money': Chinese currency.

Reting: a formerly powerful Geluk monastery north-east of Lhasa.

Richardson: Hugh Richardson, Head of British Mission in Lhasa in the 1940s.

Rinpoche: 'Precious one' – a term of respect for a very high lama.

Riwo Dechen: a ruined temple near Chongye.

Sakya: (a) an order of Tibetan Buddhism; (b) the main monastery of the order, founded in 1073.

Sakya Pandita (1182–1251): title given to a great master of the Sakya order.

Samye: large monastery in the form of a huge mandala, on the north side of the Yarlung Tsangpo river, three or four days' walk south of Ganden. It was founded in the 770s by King Tresong Detsen, when Padmasambhava was in Tibet.

Sera: a monastery two miles to the north of Lhasa at the foot of a mountain. Founded in 1419 by a disciple of Tsongkhapa, it is one of the Three Pillars of the state and has long been a rival to Drepung. Its name means, according to different sources, 'rose fence' and 'merciful hail' (which would fall and destroy the 'rice' of Drepung which means 'rice heap').

Shakyamuni: the most recent Buddha, the historical figure of Gautama Buddha who lived in India between 563 and 483 BC.

Shöl: the village at the southern foot of Marpori, the 'Red Hill', on which the Potala Palace is built. Formerly separated by parks and meadows from Lhasa proper, it is now another part of the built-up area. Formerly, the prison, printing press and various other government buildings were housed here. The old wall is still visible, in places, as are the enormous gateways.

Sho Dun: 'Yoghurt Festival' – a festival of operas and plays during the seventh month. The name originates from a ceremony, the 'Handing out of Sour Milk', which takes place at Drepung at the beginning of the festival.

Sky burial: Tibetan custom of disposing of the dead. In a country where wood is scarce and the ground is often frozen solid or too rocky, cremation and burial are not practicable. Tibetans cut the body up and leave it for the vultures. This is considered an act of compassion, since other beings are nourished by the remains.

Songtsen Gampo (617–649): the first religious king who introduced Buddhism to Tibet, built the Jokhang and unified the country.

Spring Festival: Chinese New Year, celebrated in January or February.

State Oracle: monk with oracular powers resident at Nechung and consulted by the government on matters of national importance.

Stupa (see **chöten**).

Swastika: ancient symbol of *Bön*, where the arms turn anti-clockwise, and of Buddhism, where they turn clockwise.

Tai Ji: Chinese martial art.

Talung: Kagyu monastery north-east of Lhasa.

Tangka: religious painting on cloth, mounted on silk brocade hangings which can be rolled up for easy storage and transportation.

Tantric buddhism (see **Vajrayana**).

Tashi Delek: 'Hello' in Tibetan. Although it is now commonly used as a daily greeting, its original use was as the special New Year's greeting of 'Good Luck'.

Tashilhunpo: the main monastery in Shigatse, the seat of the Panchen Lama.

Thamzing: the Tibetan for Criticism-Struggle session (*q.v.*).

Torma: 'holy food' – a cone-shaped cake of *tsampa* and butter, often coloured red, placed as offerings on altars, etc.

Trisong Detsen (742-797): the second great religious king of Tibet.

Tsampa: the staple food of most Tibetans, 'parched barley flour'. Barley grains are heated over a fire, after which they are milled. This pre-cooked flour can then be mixed with butter tea to form soft balls. Cheese, curd, dried meat, etc can be added.

Tsang: province of old 'west central' Tibet, west of Lhasa, whose capital is Shigatse.

Tsongkhapa (1357–1419): founder of the Geluk or 'reformed' sect of Tibetan Buddhism, he was born in Amdo. A tree grew miraculously from the site of his birth, around which was later built the great monastery of Kumbum (Taersi) now in Qinghai province south of Xining. He died at Ganden, which he founded, east of Lhasa.

Tsurpu: a Karma monastery north-west of Lhasa.

Tukpa: Tibetan noodles.

Tulku: a reincarnated lama.

U: province of old 'east central' Tibet, in which Lhasa is situated.

Vajrayana: also known as the 'Diamond Vehicle' or 'tantrism'. An esoteric form of Buddhism, employing mystic practices as a short cut to enlightenment.

Waiban: Foreign Affairs Bureau, the organization responsible for relations between Chinese and foreigners.

Waiguoren: foreigner.

Waihui: Foreign Exchange Certificates of equivalent value to renminbi, but which can be exchanged for hard currency.

Washing Festival: held in either the seventh or eighth month, when bathing in the river is believed to ensure good health.

Wen Cheng: the Chinese wife of Songtsen Gampo.
Wheel of Life: Buddhist representation of the cycle of birth and death (see pp. 39–40).
Yama: the Lord of Death.
Yamantaka: wrathful deity with a bull's head, the 'Destroyer of Death'.
Yerpa: sacred site for hermits since the seventh century. Desecrated in the Cultural Revolution, the cave-temples are now being restored and monks and nuns are returning to meditate in the caves.
Yoghurt Festival: see *Sho Dun*.
Younghusband: Col. Francis Younghusband, leader of 1904 British expedition to Lhasa.
Yuan: basic unit of Chinese currency (1 yuan = approx 20p).
Yumbulagang: the oldest fortress in Tibet, built in the Yarlung valley, south of Tsetang, reputedly by Songtsen Gampo in the seventh or eighth century. The original was destroyed during the Cultural Revolution and the present building is a replica. It is now a chapel.

Watching the Dragon

Letters from China 1983–85
Charles and Jill Hadfield

Charles and Jill Hadfield spent 2½ years teaching and travelling in China during a period which saw dramatic changes in Chinese society.

They wrote copiously about their experiences and their letters and diaries, put together on their return to the UK, give a fascinating, first-hand account of the effects of these changes on everyday life. **Watching the Dragon** is an honest and revealing record, full of anecdotes and perceptive observations, giving a sense of the rhythm of daily life in China, its pleasures as well as its frustrations.

222 × 141 mm/240 pp
ISBN 0 245–54390–2/Hardback/£8.95

"A delightful set of letters … The letter form makes the book more intimate and appealing than a straight travel account and the Hadfields reveal the idiosyncracies of their well-meaning Chinese hosts in an affectionate and humorous way."

The Bookseller

"Bright and breezy. … fascinating. This is one to pack for light relief on a Chinese holiday."

Daily Telegraph

"Their sympathetic, literate and considered letters to friends are surprisingly enjoyable reading … The travel sections are also clearly and animatedly recounted."

British Book News

Kevin and I in India

Frank Kusy

Frank Kusy and Kevin Bloice first met in a deserted Arab airport lounge on their way to India. It was the beginning of a friendship that was to take them together across the length and breadth of that country, ending up in the foothills of the Himalayas in Nepal.

Kevin and I in India is the unexpurgated, often hilarious diary of their travels. Full of anecdotes, observations and travellers' tales, the book shows above all a land of sharp contrasts — a vast sprawling sub-continent where the two young Englishmen weave a crazy, erratic path through a variety of adventures and misadventures, in constant and comic battle against officialdom, insects, heat, dust, ticket queues and mad traffic.

Here is the real India — stripped of illusion, but adorned with humour and exuberance. Here is a kaleidoscopic pot-pourri of fascinating sights, scenes and people, with each day of the journey more exciting, more packed with incident than the last.

198 × 129mm/224pp
ISBN 0 245–54417–8/Paperback/£4.95

"Frank Kusy remains indefatigably and irrepressibly jocular."
Mail on Sunday

"A very amusing account!"
Radio London